S0-DUW-120

UNDER
THE
CLOUD

Nancy —

May you always

be safe & secure

Under the Cloud —

Jack & Ruth

UNDER

THE

CLOUD

a place of safety and security

in a chaotic world

JACK & RUTH McDONALD

TATE PUBLISHING & *Enterprises*

Under the Cloud
Copyright © 2011 by Jack and Ruth McDonald. All rights reserved.

No part of this publication may be reproduced, stored in a retrieval system or transmitted in any way by any means, electronic, mechanical, photocopy, recording or otherwise without the prior permission of the authors except as provided by USA copyright law.

All scripture quotations, unless otherwise indicated, are taken from the *New King James Version*®. Copyright © 1982 by Thomas Nelson, Inc. Used by permission. All rights reserved.

This book is designed to provide accurate and authoritative information with regard to the subject matter covered. This information is given with the understanding that neither the authors nor Tate Publishing, LLC is engaged in rendering legal, professional advice. Since the details of your situation are fact dependent, you should additionally seek the services of a competent professional.

The opinions expressed by the authors are not necessarily those of Tate Publishing, LLC.

Published by Tate Publishing & Enterprises, LLC
127 E. Trade Center Terrace | Mustang, Oklahoma 73064 USA
1.888.361.9473 | www.tatepublishing.com

Tate Publishing is committed to excellence in the publishing industry. The company reflects the philosophy established by the founders, based on Psalm 68:11,
"The Lord gave the word and great was the company of those who published it."

Book design copyright © 2011 by Tate Publishing, LLC. All rights reserved.
Cover design by Kellie Southerland
Interior design by Chelsea Womble

Published in the United States of America

ISBN: 978-1-61777-286-3
1. Religion, Christian Church, Growth
2. Religion, Devotional
11.08.26

TABLE OF CONTENTS

PART III: SECOND GENERATION

PART IV: HOME AT LAST

PART V: THE CHALLENGE

INTRODUCTION

"Christianity doesn't work!" In a counseling room recently, a former pastor vehemently declared that he and his wife had come to just that conclusion. At least, it wasn't working in his family, and he proceeded, with great detail, to tell me why. Sad to say he is not alone in that declaration. I can confirm, however, that true Biblical Christianity, as it is meant to be experienced, does work. It always has and always will! How did we get so far off track in the age in which we live? Simple! This generation does not even begin to know the Word and, therefore, is just muddling along as best they can. This book is my attempt to alter that thinking, and it comes with a deeply held conviction that it can and will.

You certainly have a right to ask what credentials enable me to make such a bold statement. Neither Ruth nor I have any credentials in the ordinary sense of the word. Furthermore, we are not exactly spring chickens, and this is our first book. What we do have is almost forty years in the trenches, so to speak, teaching small groups. During those years of home Bible studies, we have seen untold numbers of transformed lives, as small groups of sincere people gathered with open Bibles, hungry to know and hear from God. Over the years we have seen marriages mended and teens who thought they had no future discover they had one. We have seen seniors who thought their lives were over discover they weren't, and, yes, we have seen many bound by all sorts of addictions set free. More importantly we have seen people of all ages and from all walks of life begin to believe that worry, fear, and depression need not be a way of life!

I am bold enough to say that if you, dear reader, will study this book with open hearts and minds, the truths contained in these pages will transform your life. How do I know that? Because they have radically changed mine, as well as many, many others, and it is still going on today. The God of the Bible is unchanging and loves unconditionally. Jesus Christ is the same yesterday, today, and forever. No one is more maligned or misrepresented or, in fact, outright lied about.

You will quickly note some repetition; however, any teacher worth his salt knows repetition is often necessary to drive home a truth.

This book is written primarily for Christian brothers and sisters who are tired of the struggle. I was too.

I dedicate it to those in the trenches from a fellow sojourner also living life in the trenches. If you are interested only in doing it *your* way, if you are always trying to persuade family, friends, and God to fit in with *your* plans, do not waste time or money on this book. If, however, you are tired of the struggle, finally facing the fact that the brand of Christianity, highly publicized and taught today, simply does not produce the peace and joy it promises—read on!

PART I: FIRST GENERATION

William Barclay, in his commentary on the gospel of Luke, writes the following account of a Scottish chieftain, perhaps even a distant relative of mine:

> "One of the Macdonalds, a Highland chieftain, was confined in a little cell in Carlisle Castle. In his cell there was one small window. To this day you may see the marks in the sandstone of the feet and hands of the Highlander as he lifted himself up and clung to the window ledge, as day by day he gazed with infinite longing out upon the border hills and valleys that he would never walk again."

BONDAGE

Imprisonment goes against human nature. All prison inmates long for freedom. During their lonely hours of confinement, much time is spent daydreaming of freedom. As the odds of escaping are highly unlikely, most inmates eventually learn to accept their confinement and settle in for years of drudgery and boredom. Similarly, whenever I visit a zoo, it saddens me to see caged animals no longer experiencing the freedom they once enjoyed. At first glance they look impressive, but upon closer examination, you sense they have become despondent, dispirited, and lethargic. You can see it in their eyes. I am told many animals rarely manage to reproduce while in confinement.

All too often today, the Christian experience is similar to that of the prison inmate or the caged animal. No, they are not behind iron bars; nevertheless, they are experiencing a form of confinement. A prison without bars! Their inward struggles take many forms. Some of the most common are worry, fear, depression, anger, financial problems, and marital insecurities. Despite a desire for change, only a small percentage ever experiences any kind of permanent freedom. If you think about it, I am pretty sure you will agree that these emotional struggles are a form of bondage and, left unchecked, over a period of time will cause many physical problems. The medical profession tells us—stress—

which all the above heap on us, continues to be the number one killer.

It has been my observation over the years that many sit in the pews of today's churches with both a calm and peaceful demeanor; internally, however, it is often a different story. They attend church hoping to hear a message from the pulpit that will some-how set them free. Sadly, they almost always leave unchanged. They foolishly return the following week at the same time to the same building expecting a different result. When they examine the lives of others in the congregation, they soon discover they are not alone in their life of boredom, drudgery, and bondage. In time, like the caged prisoner or animal, they become resigned to their way of life. I refer to them as mechanical believers, going through the motions, yet experiencing a substandard brand of Christianity. Over three thousand years ago, the nation of Israel found themselves in just such a state, enslaved in Egypt, surely a form of prison. In their secret thoughts, I expect many wondered,

HOW IN THE WORLD DID I GET IN THIS MESS AND HOW WILL I EVER GET OUT OF IT?

In order to answer the first part of that question, as it applies to Israel, we should briefly recap their history, beginning with Abraham. When God called Abraham out of Ur, he was told he would become the father of a great nation, and that nation would eventually leave Canaan, their homeland, and reside for four hundred years in a foreign country. God also prophesied that while in that foreign country, they would be placed in slavery, and at the end of the four hundred years, He would lead them back home to Canaan (Genesis 15:13-14). That foreign country was Egypt.

Two generations later, that small nation was still residing in Canaan with Jacob as its leader. Because of envy, Jacob's favored son, Joseph, was secretly sold by his brothers into service in an Egyptian home. There came a day when his master's wife falsely accused him of attempted rape. Unfortunately, he still ended up in a hot Egyptian prison. While in prison, two of his fellow inmates, who had been employed by the king, had most puzzling dreams, which Joseph was able to interpret. He told one prisoner (the baker) his dream was not good news, as in three days he would be executed. The other prisoner (the butler) was told his dream was good news, as in three days he would be released and reinstated as the king's butler. Both came true.

Two years later, Pharaoh also had a troubling dream that no one in his inner circle was able to interpret. His butler said, "I know just the guy!" Joseph was summoned. In a nutshell, Joseph's interpretation was that there would be seven years of abundant crops followed by a seven-year famine. He urged the king to put a responsible person in charge of the nation's crops and begin storing grain during the plentiful years. Guess who was given the job? Pharaoh was so impressed with Joseph's wisdom he was put in charge of collecting and storing food for the entire nation. In one day, Joseph went from being a nobody in prison to holding the number two position in the Egyptian government.

True to the prophecy, the seven plentiful years came and were followed by a famine, affecting the entire region—including Canaan. When Jacob, the patriarch, heard of the abundance of food in Egypt, he sent his many sons to purchase grain. When they appeared before Joseph, he recognized his brothers but sought no revenge. Instead he sent them home instructing them to return with the entire nation of Israel, promising to harbor them for the duration of the famine.

Initially, life in Egypt was great. They had an abundance of food, and they were given Goshen, a choice area of land in which to reside. When the seven year famine ended, Israel should have returned to their God given home—Canaan. They did not. They had become entrenched in the Egyptian way of life. I expect the thought of uprooting their lives once again and making the long trek back to Canaan seemed just too much of an effort. After all, they had crops to harvest, newly built homes, kids in school, many new friends, and because of Joseph, they found favor with the Egyptians. Egypt just seemed the place to be. In time, however, a new Pharaoh rose to the throne, one who either was not familiar with or chose to ignore Joseph's previous accomplishments. Over the years Israel's population exploded from the tiny nation of seventy to approximately two million, exceeding the entire population of Egypt, thus causing the new Pharaoh much concern. For instance, what if Israel decided to join forces with a neighboring nation in an attempt to overthrow his throne? Pharaoh's solution was to place Israel in slavery (Exodus 1:7-11). This way he could keep them under his thumb and prevent them from stockpiling weapons.

Many times during their years of slavery, Israel cried out to the Lord to set them free and return them to Canaan, thus fulfilling the prophecy made to Abraham (Exodus 2:23-25). The end of the prophesied four hundred years was approaching, and it would soon be time for the Lord to lead Israel back home. How would this be possible without a unifying leader? And how would Pharaoh ever be persuaded to let his free work force leave? Who would do the menial labor in Egypt? More importantly, finding a Hebrew leader who had access to Pharaoh seemed a total impossibility. Have you discovered that anything is possible when God is on the scene?

> The things which are impossible with men are possible with God.
>
> Luke 18:27

In an attempt to curb Israel's growth, the king took drastic action. He issued a decree stating that every newborn Hebrew son was to be thrown in the river (Exodus 1:22). The wise parents of one son obeyed the letter of the law by placing their newborn son in the river—in a water tight basket (Exodus 2:2-3). Pharaoh's daughter spotted the child, rescued him, and raised him in the palace as her son. That child was Moses!

What a unique upbringing, educated in the palace with total access to the throne, yet a Hebrew by birth. As an adult, at one point, he took the life of an Egyptian, necessitating a sojourn of forty years on the back side of the desert. While there, the Lord appeared telling him of His plan to set Israel free and lead them across the barren desert back to their homeland. Moses was told he was to be their leader (Exodus 3:7-10). His initial response was typical—"Who, me?" (Exodus 3:11). Moses was "I" focused, and knowing Pharaoh well, he was certain there was no possible way to convince him to release Israel. Even if he did, how in the world would Moses get two million people safely across the barren desert to Canaan? God set Moses straight by reminding him that as long as he remained God-focused, His agenda would become a reality. "I will certainly be with you" (Exodus 3:12), music to his ears and the very words Moses needed to hear!

Yes, But...

When told of God's plan, one would think Israel would have been overjoyed with the thought of freedom and returning home. You would expect them to immediately begin packing their bags. After all, the only quality of life they had ever experienced was one filled with stress, fear, anger, and confinement. Anything would be better than existing under such negative circumstances. Despite their poor quality of life, their response to Moses was far from enthusiastic. What was their problem?

Their problem is something that still prevails in many of today's pews—resignation. Lest you misunderstand, resignation is the acceptance of something, often undesirable, but seemingly inevitable. An insidious form of contentment had set in. Over the years, they had learned to not rock the boat and diligently avoided any behavior that might arouse the king's anger. They worried that once Moses confronted Pharaoh concerning their release, he would become annoyed and increase their workload. In fact, the whole idea of freedom sounded like pie in the sky. If, by some miracle, Pharaoh did agree, how would two million people survive crossing the unforgiving desert? How would they find sufficient water and food to meet their needs during such a journey? Even if they somehow survived the trek, how would they deal with the armed squatters who had taken up residence in Canaan? They had built homes and fortified cities, and it seemed unlikely they would willingly pack up and leave when Israel appeared on the scene. Battle stations would be sounded, and with no experience in warfare, Israel would quickly be defeated. Yes, being set free from their bondage and returning home sounded wonderful, *but*...! Israel had become a *yes, but* nation!

I think most will agree that in today's Christian community, many live in various degrees of bondage. Similar to Israel, worry, fear, depression, and anger have become an acceptable way of life. They hear sermons, or read in their Bibles of a different quality of life, but having existed in their negative ruts for many years, they think the freedom Christ promises sounds wonderful, but...! They think the prison bars are so firmly entrenched that God, Himself, is not able to set them free! Worse still, even if He could, they mistakenly think He doesn't seem to care.

If the Son makes you free, you shall be free indeed.

John 8:36

Where the spirit of the Lord is there is liberty.

2 Corinthians 3:17

Motivating Pharaoh

Raised in the palace, Moses always had free access to the throne. Moses met several times with Pharaoh in an attempt to persuade him to release Israel, but the king had his heels dug in. In order to break the king's will, God would have to intervene and alter his thinking. In other words, some heaven-sent motivation seemed to be required.

God's motivation took the form of many well-documented plagues. His purpose was twofold. First, as we shall see, the plagues eventually broke Pharaoh's will, and he reluctantly allowed Israel to leave. Second, Israel desperately needed a faith shot. During their years of slavery, Israel was so preoccupied with day-to-day survival that their relationship with the Lord had grown fuzzy and distant. This current generation had never experienced an intimate relationship with God, as did their forefathers, Abraham, Isaac, Jacob, and Joseph. In their daily drudgery, they had experienced little evidence of God's power. It seems they were always looking down instead of up. "I appeared to Abraham, to Isaac, and to Jacob, as God Almighty, but by My name, Lord, I was not known to them" (Exodus 6:3). God's hope was that when Israel saw His power demonstrated in the plagues, they would then be able to trust Him to set them free from Pharaoh's grasp and escort them safely across the desert to their homeland, Canaan.

Amazingly, the first nine plagues did not fall on the land of Goshen. Each time the Israelites were protected from the devastation. That should have been enough to convince Israel that God was well able to care for them. One would think they would never again doubt their God or His promises.

Following is a quick summary of the first nine plagues as recorded by Moses in the book of Exodus:

1. All waters were turned to blood (vv. 7:17-19, Psalm 78:44). Wouldn't it blow your mind to have fresh water in Goshen, but across an invisible border, the Egyptian wells and rivers were contaminated with blood?

2. Every corner of Egypt was filled with slimy frogs (vv. 8:2-14). Each day the Israelite slaves must have dreaded leaving the protected land of Goshen to work in the frog infested land surrounding them.

3. Lice infested the land of Egypt (vv. 8:16-19). Can you picture the Israelite mothers instructing their children to stay away from those lice infested Egyptian children?

4. With the exception of Goshen, swarms of flies invaded Egypt (vv. 8:21-23, Psalm 78:45). How did the flies know they were not allowed to cross into the land of Goshen? An amazing miracle!

5. The Egyptian animals were all killed (vv. 9:4-7). Israel's animals were spared, as they would be needed for food during their month long exodus to Canaan.

6. The plague of boils must have made life extremely uncomfortable for the Egyptians (vv. 9:8-11).

7. Hail destroyed the Egyptian crops. Israel's crops were spared, as they would also be needed for sustenance during their trek across the desert (vv. 9:23-26).

8. Locusts devoured what was left of Egypt's vegetation and fruit (vv. 10:4-5). Once again, God miraculously prevented the locusts from crossing that same invisible barrier separating Goshen from Egypt.

9. A darkness you could almost feel, or as the saying goes, cut with a knife, came upon Egypt, while Israel basked in sunshine (vv. 10:21-23).

Observing that the plagues did not touch the Israelites, you would expect the Egyptians to immediately turn from their impotent gods to the God of Israel. As we shall see, with the exception of a small number, that was not the case.

Despite the devastating destruction God brought upon Egypt, Pharaoh refused to release his slaves. In anger, he banished Moses from the palace and told him to never darken his door again (Exodus 10:28-29).

> I will bring one more plague on Pharaoh and on Egypt. Afterward he will let you go from here. When he lets you go, he will surely drive you out of here altogether.
>
> Exodus 11:1

One final plague was deemed necessary to break Pharaoh's will.

Questions

- Do you struggle from time to time with worry, fear, depression, anger, anxiety, and/or stress?

- Do you sit in a pew Sunday after Sunday, leaving the building in much the same spiritual condition as you entered—overcome with feelings of resignation and/or apathy?

- If you are anxious to enjoy the freedom Christ promised, perhaps this book is for you. Read on!

UNDER THE BLOOD

The nine previous plagues surely would have placed Egypt on the brink of bankruptcy. Their water supply was polluted. Crops were nonexistent. The stench throughout the land from the decaying animals and fish would have certainly curtailed tourism. Can you imagine living in that heat and not having access to suitable bathing or drinking water? Despite those horrible conditions, Pharaoh dug his heels in and refused to release Israel. To break his will, one final plague would be required. One so devastating the Egyptians would practically boot Israel out the front door. The first born of each family in Egypt would be struck dead (Exodus 11:5). A harsh judgment in order to ensure Israel's release!

Judgment and Provision

Have you noticed that whenever God warns of an ensuing judgment in Scripture, because of His great love for mankind, He always provides a way of escape? For example, in earlier times Noah was told by God that judgment was pending because of the world's sinful state. That judgment would be in the form of a devastating flood (Genesis 6:13-18). For 120 years Noah, not only constructed the ark, he constantly preached of the coming judgment, as well as God's provision for avoiding that judgment. The idea of a flood did not compute with the vast majority as, up to that point in time, it had never rained. The planet was watered by dew and subterranean wells; consequently there were no vast oceans. Large ships were unnecessary. The majority of the population viewed the idea of vast amounts of water falling from the sky and building such a large boat as utter foolishness. Out of millions, a tiny minority of eight heeded God's word and found shelter in the ark.

God's provision for avoiding judgment in Egypt was not an ark. This time each household was instructed to slay a lamb and sprinkle its blood on the doorposts and lintels of their homes (Exodus 12:3-7). Those who were obedient to God's instruction were aware that placing faith in this ritual pictured the true Lamb of God, who would be the ultimate provision for avoiding God's pending judgment upon sin. When John the Baptist saw Jesus approaching, it was no accident he referred to Him as "The Lamb of God who takes away the sin of the world" (John 1:29). John was well aware that Jesus was the fulfillment of this Old Testament Passover ritual.

Those who placed faith in what this ritual pictured still went to the grave in their sins, but clutching a symbolic promissory redemption note that would be satisfied once Christ was slain and resurrected in real time and space. Positionally, those who placed faith in what this Old Testament ritual represented were under the blood of the coming Messiah, which enabled God to announce, "When I see the blood, I will pass over you; and the plague shall not be on you to destroy you when I strike the land of Egypt" (Exodus 12:13). Experientially, the Old Testament saints went to their graves in their sins and remained in that condition until the resurrection of God's slain Lamb.

> If Christ is not risen, your faith is futile; you are still in your sins.
>
> 1 Corinthians 15:17

Being a holy and just God, just as He once judged Lucifer's sin, He is obligated to eventually judge all sin. Unfortunately, just as in the days of Noah, the vast majority of today's population scoff at the idea of pending judgment and still ignore His provision for avoiding that judgment. To most, Jesus remains a religious historical figure who received a bad rap! They fail to view Him as God's only provision for avoiding the coming judgment so clearly recorded in the book of Revelation.

It is worthwhile to note the following similarities between the symbolic lamb slain at the Passover in Egypt and the Lord Jesus Christ:

- Both the Passover lamb and Christ were male (Exodus 12:5).

- The Passover lamb was slain prematurely in its first year (Exodus 12:5). Jesus was executed only three years into his ministry at age thirty-three.

- The sacrificed lamb was to contain no blemishes (Exodus 12:5). Christ certainly had no imperfections (sin), which enabled God to announce to the world, "In Him I am well pleased" (Matthew 3:17).

- The lamb in Egypt was slain and its blood sprinkled (Exodus 12:6-7). Prior to the foundation of this world, it was foreordained that Jesus would come to this world, if necessary, to be an offering for sin. The Lamb of God whose blood would be shed for the sins of the world.

> With the precious blood of Christ, as of a lamb without blemish and without spot, He indeed was foreordained before the foundation of the world, but was manifest in these last times for you.
>
> 1 Peter 1:19-20

To keep Israel focused on the coming Savior, they were instructed to celebrate this ritual annually (Exodus 12:14). For obvious reasons, this ceremony has always been referred to as the Passover Feast.

> Christ our Passover was sacrificed for us.
>
> 1 Corinthians 5:7

God's View of Sin

Before moving on, perhaps we should take a moment to clarify how God views sin. I think you will agree that society places sin in different categories, and it also has different degrees of punishment for those various crimes. For example, a murderer or rapist can expect to be more severely punished than, say, a thief. In today's religious community, it is no different. Such carnal activities as anger, worry, depression, pride, and fear are usually viewed as somewhat acceptable behavior, while murder, drunkenness, or child molesting are viewed as unacceptable. With God, sin is sin! He does not categorize sin, and varying degrees of punishment simply do not exist! In order to clearly understand sin from God's perspective, I think it would be wise to back up in time and examine the origin of sin.

Prior to time (the Creation), Lucifer (Satan) was the top angel in heaven, and at some point he desired equality with God. In other words, he wanted to be a god unto himself. On the surface, this may not appear to be such a big deal, as consciously, or subconsciously, the majority of the world's population has this same desire—viewing themselves as the center of the universe. (This truth can usually be verified when we look at a group photo. Whose picture do we check out first?) Lucifer's ambition introduced sin in heaven and war erupted (Revelation 12:7-9) Since

God cannot dwell in the presence of sin, Lucifer and his cronies (angels who lined up with him) were banished from heaven and earth became their temporal residence.

When Adam and Eve arrived on earth, suddenly there was no longer one kingdom on earth but two—Satan's sin contaminated kingdom and God's righteous kingdom, which initially consisted of two citizens—Adam and Eve. With the arrival of Adam and Eve, Satan began to look for an opportunity to strike back at God, and the battle that originated in heaven was resumed on earth. This warfare continues, even as you read.

When Satan overheard God telling Adam and Eve they could eat the fruit of every tree in the Garden with one exception, that opportunity presented itself (Genesis 2:16-17). If Adam and Eve could be enticed to disobey God's command, they would become contaminated with sin, and in that condition, God's Spirit would be forced to withdraw from their lives. This would obviously change the quality of their lives drastically. No longer would they be citizens in God's kingdom, for their citizenship would be transferred to Satan's fallen kingdom. Adam was created in the image of his Creator—"Let Us make man in Our image"—and in this condition freely displayed the attributes of God (Genesis 1:26). If Adam could be enticed into disobedience, that would no longer be the case. No longer would he be able to turn to God for wisdom and direction. Instead, he would be forced to lean unto his own understanding (Proverbs 3:5-6). No longer would Adam possess his God-given dominion as the legal tenant of this planet (Genesis 1:28). That position would be forfeited and fall into Satan's hands. No longer would he be in the image of God. Once God's Spirit withdrew from Adam, the intimate relationship he once enjoyed would be severed. Adam would find himself naked, no longer possessing the righteousness of his Creator (Genesis 3:7).

If Adam could be motivated to stumble, that act of disobedience would be far reaching and cause a devastating chain reaction throughout our entire history. As the father of mankind, Adam's fallen nature would be passed on to all future generations. Every person who stemmed from Adam's loins would arrive on planet Earth contaminated with his fallen genes. In modern day lingo, every future generation would be tainted with Adam's DNA. They would be born as citizens of Satan's kingdom, without the indwelling Spirit of God and with no other choice but to lean unto their own understanding for direction and wisdom. Poor odds for a successful life! With no indwelling Spirit, man would be left with an inner void, which things of this world would only satisfy temporally. In this state, he would be incapable of displaying the attributes of his Creator, and every action and thought that stemmed from his life would become fleshly based—sin. One and all would be born into a graceless world and under pending judgment. It is clear King David understood this truth, for he wrote, "I was brought forth in iniquity, and in sin my mother conceived me" (Psalm 51:5). David wasn't implying that his mother behaved unseemly, but that he was ushered into this world inheriting Adam's fallen nature.

> Through one man's offense judgment came to all men, resulting in condemnation.
>
> Romans 5:18

Satan started the ball rolling when he enticed Eve to eat the forbidden fruit. The deceiver approached Eve and convinced her God was holding back good things from her. He suggested that eating the fruit would make her equal with and as wise as the God of the universe—therefore being a god unto herself, well able to rule over her own life (Genesis 3:5). The same desire Lucifer had while he was still top angel. He whispered that independence would provide her with a superior quality of life and freedom from God's restrictive control. Man was created to be connected to and, in a sense, dependent upon God for his power source, but He also created man with a free will. God didn't create man as a robot to be programmed to function a certain way. How could He have a personal relationship with a robot? Adam and Eve made a free will decision and, like many today, bought into the lies of the deceiver. The disastrous results of Adam's decision remain with us to this very day. It is interesting to note that the first independent act they performed was prompted by fear (Genesis 3:10).

Fear

Since the fall, fear has dominated mankind. When everything is stripped aside, fear lies at the root of all our worries, anxieties, and even much of our anger. How well I remember being so often overcome with fear. Prior to becoming a believer, I feared financial failure. Sometimes I even feared our marriage might not last. At one stage of my career, I managed a large office for an international investment company and was responsible for training and overseeing a staff of more than eighty. Despite my past successes, I almost always felt I was in over my head, and constantly feared management would replace me with someone more qualified. Each time I returned from vacation, I was always relieved to find that someone else was not sitting in my chair. I was afraid the future would be just like the past—stress filled and boring. It was already pretty clear to me that I would never be able to satisfy my inner emptiness by vacations, new toys, and more success. I felt there must be a purpose for my being on earth that was more fulfilling than the life I was experiencing. I didn't realize it at the time, but looking back, I can clearly see I was living a life similar to the Israelites in Egypt—in a form of prison. On many occasions, in one way or another, I also thought,

"HOW IN THE WORLD DID I GET IN THIS MESS AND HOW WILL I EVER GET OUT OF IT?"

In my search for freedom, and peace, I often examined the lives of others, wondering if they had discovered the secret to life. My search proved futile, as their lives were similar to mine. Occasionally I crossed paths with someone who professed to be a Christian. I always observed their lives very closely, wondering, even hoping they had somehow discovered freedom from the stresses of life. Other than their church affiliation, I soon discovered their lives were similar to mine, and in many cases worse! They had marriage and financial problems, and their faces showed anything but joy and peace. After coming to the conclusion that man did not seem to have the solution to my dilemma, I turned to the world. That search also proved futile, as it didn't take me long to realize the excitement of a new car, an exotic vacation, or a geographical fix was short lived. Once the first car payment arrived and I stopped boring my friends with the details of our last fabulous vacation, the stress soon returned. Over the years, due to business, Ruth and I relocated several times. Initially the new place was exciting, but once the new restaurants and sites were explored, it was back to the same old grind—stress, worry, fear, and discontentment returned!

One day, in a state of deep discouragement, while on my way to work, I parked the car on the side of the road, and for the first time in my life I actually talked to God. It wasn't a lengthy conversation. I simply sent out an SOS. I asked Him to show me if He had a purpose for my life. At the time, I wondered if my words got beyond the car. He was likely far too busy running the universe to be concerned with my problems. However, I have to tell you that in the following few days, unusual things began to take place. First of all, Ruth brought to my attention a newspaper advertisement announcing a musical evening at one of the local churches. Since we both enjoyed gospel music, we decided to attend. As it turned out, the highlight of the service was not so much the music, but the sermon delivered by visiting evangelists who were twins, of all things. During the service, God honored my SOS cry for help in a way I least expected. Sitting there listening intently, I came to the conclusion that the only one in this entire universe who was qualified to successfully manage my life was Jesus Christ. After attending those meetings for several nights, Ruth and I made a life changing decision to invite Christ to be our Lord and Savior. We became Christians! Christ became our new manager in residence!

This change of management took place in 1971, and so far the journey has been anything but dull. Over the years there have been many positive changes in my life and the journey continues even today. It is as if prison bars were removed from many areas of my life, enabling me to experience so much more freedom, and so much less stress! For example, shortly after becoming a Christian, God broke down an invisible wall that I had hidden behind most of my life. Growing up in a split home and experiencing the hurts of that situation as a child, I subconsciously began erecting an invisible, but very effective, protective wall around myself. Why? I suppose because of the fear of rejection. Whenever someone took a verbal shot at me, I just added a few more bricks. I took that wall into our marriage, and you can easily imagine, I am sure, the problems that created. Every time I felt hurt, I would crawl behind my wall, go into silent mode and add a few more bricks. The Lord was aware of the bondage I was living with, and late one night after a long discussion with Ruth and a period of agonizing prayer, He demolished my protective wall. What a relief it was to be finally free of that prison! You see, I had come to realize that the God of the universe loved me unconditionally and would never reject me, and Ruth assured me that neither would she.

Rather early on, another pretty significant change took place in my life. As I mentioned, I managed a branch office for an investment company, and in this position, I was constantly advising people how to manage their finances. However, when it came to managing our personal finances, Ruth was delegated that responsibility. I told myself it was because she had been a banker when I met her. This worked out very well for me, as every time money became tight, I had a scapegoat, someone to blame—Ruth! One evening after a long and rather heated discussion, Ruth plopped our checkbook and a stack of unpaid bills right in the middle in my lap and walked away. That was the day I became responsible for the McDonald family finances, which is just as it should be according to the Word of God. Not only did the Lord remove my protective wall, but He also removed my financial scapegoat. Over the years the Lord has continued to expose negatives in my life, and in each case, it has been another prison bar removed. Yes, in 1971, the Lord definitely heard my SOS plea!

> In my distress I called upon the Lord, and cried out to my God; He heard my voice from His temple, and my cry came before Him, even to His ears.
>
> Psalm 18:6

Independence from God

Just as Satan deceived Eve, he has continued, down through the ages, to deceive people into thinking independence from God is the way to fly. As the saying goes, that is a lie from the pit! A person who is not united with God has no access to spiritual wisdom and is forced to place confidence in his own reasoning powers. Believe me, that is not freedom, but bondage and fear, as it opens the door for many wrong and costly decisions. Unless an adult person has his head in the sand, life should have taught him the odds of making wise decisions when leaning unto his own understanding are poor. Likely in the 50 percent range! No serious gambler would bet on anything with such poor odds.

This idea of independence reminds me of a little kite story I once heard. Despite life being great, the soaring kite began to think if he gained independence from the man holding the chord, he would be truly free. One day the chord did break, and for a brief time, life was wonderful. Eventually, however, the kite tumbled to earth, badly damaged. Worse still, the kite could not repair itself. Seeing the damaged kite, the man picked it up gently, restored its damaged wings and reattached the chord. Once again the kite was able to soar freely in the sky. This time, however, he was constantly comforted knowing that he was safely anchored to his owner, who watched his flight carefully. A wonderful picture of salvation—of being set right!

We see the consequences of man leaning unto his own understanding every time we pick up the newspaper or turn on the television. Despite numerous peace treaties, wars prevail in every corner of the globe. Since September eleventh, we are faced with a new type of war which has introduced additional fears. Our prisons are overcrowded with people who have leaned unto their own understanding, making one bad decision after another. Divorce lawyers thrive on couples who have trusted their own decision making process. Today, every level of society is permeated with the results of people who have trusted in doing what seems right in their own eyes, only to find themselves hooked on alcohol, nicotine, and drugs. Others lean unto their own logic and become involved in "too good to be true" ventures, thus squandering large amounts of time and money. A self-managed life is one destined for mistakes, and an indeterminate amount of stress and sorrow. I once heard it explained this way: leaning unto our own understanding is rather like watching a parade from a very narrow doorway while God watches from the rooftop. How inadequate the decision making process is from that narrow doorway while God, from his vantage point, sees the whole picture.

Yale Key Theory

> He was a murderer from the beginning, and does not stand in the truth, because there is no truth in him. When he speaks a lie, he speak from his own resources, for he is a liar and the father of it.
>
> John 8:44

In the garden, God told Adam if he ate the forbidden fruit he would die (Genesis 2:17). This death would be unusual, as it would involve both physical and spiritual death. When Eve reminded Satan of this warning, the deceiver implied God was lying (Genesis 3:3). By introducing sin into God's righteous kingdom through Adam, both physical and spiritual death would be passed on to all who stemmed from Adam's fallen genes. "By the one man's offense death reigned through the one" (Romans 5:17).

When God created man, His intention was that we would live and reign on earth forever. Physical death was not a part of God's creation, which is one reason we were created with a brain that has the capacity to retain unlimited amounts of knowledge. Medical scientists claim that in our lifetime we utilize less than 5 percent of our brain capacity. Obviously, some of us much less! The 5 percent figure is in direct opposition to evolution where it is said we acquire features as nature demands—the theory of natural selection.

The medical profession remains puzzled as to why our bodies age and eventually die. There is no special disease called old age.

In their little book *Apple Cider Vinegar,* Doctors Paul and Patricia Bragg claim our blood stream is completely renewed every ninety days, that every eleven months we receive a new set of miraculous body cells, and every seven years we have a new set of bones and hard tissues. Physical death was not intended, and it is unnatural, which is why most people fear the event. Despite their flippant attitude, most nonbelievers fear death, as they have no clear understanding of what really lies beyond death's door. On one of his recent television programs, Larry King was discussing fear with his guests. During the course of that conversation, he freely admitted his number one fear was death. One would have to come to the conclusion that all his power, wealth, and celebrity status could not dispel that looming fear.

Have you ever wondered why prior to the flood people lived so long and why the life span of man suddenly dropped drastically after the flood? Adam lived to be 930 and Noah was 850 when he died. After the flood, the life span of man took a huge plunge and throughout history has continued to diminish. Noah's son Shem died at the age of 600, and four generations later, Peleg died at 239. Five generations later, Abraham died at the age of 175, and three generations after that, Joseph lived to be 110. Today, despite the advances in medicine, the average life span of man is, at best, eighty years. There are two reasons for this. The flood is the first. Many are not aware, but the Bible makes it clear that prior to the flood, the earth was surrounded by a canopy of water which filtered the sun's harmful ultra violet rays. This was the origin of much of the flood waters. Scientists tell us that if all the moisture in the clouds fell at one time, it is estimated that a flat earth would only be covered by approximately two inches of water. Certainly not enough depth to require an ark to escape judgment! God surrounded the world with water, and Psalm 148:4 refers to "waters above the heavens." When that wall of water fell, it not only contributed to the flood waters, but also left man exposed to those harmful ultra violet rays. Understandably, this has become a major contributing factor in the reduction of the age of man. The second reason is a result of what I refer to as the Yale key theory.

Whenever I buy a new car, because of the possibility of losing the key, I immediately have a back-up made. I expect you do the same when you purchase a new car or a new home. If, in my stupidity, I lose the original key, I then make a copy of the duplicated key. If this process were to be repeated many times over the years, each new key would become less perfect than the previous and eventually the final duplicated key probably would not even open the door. Adam was created perfectly and for the purposes of this illustration let's say he was the original Yale key. His fallen condition was passed on to each succeeding generation, with each new generation becoming less perfect than the previous. Thus, contributing to the reduction in age.

The Fall not only introduced physical death but also spiritual death. Because of sin, God's Spirit withdrew from Adam and Eve, thus the saying, "They gave up the Ghost," which today has come to mean physical death to us. Unlike physical death, spiritual death took place immediately after their stumble. They no longer had the Holy Spirit to generate spiritual fruit, and for the first time in their lives, they found themselves spiritually dead! Having previously experienced an intimate relationship with God, it's no wonder their first reaction after the fall was fear!

Today, each person born into this world lives with the negative consequences of Adam's disobedience. Just as King David wrote, we all entered this world with an inner void and possessing Adam's negative DNA. Born set wrong and under judgment. A.W. Tozer, in his book *The Best of Tozer*, wrote "Everything is set wrong until God sets it right." Seth was an example of this truth. Adam was created in the image of God, but his son Seth entered this world not in the image of God, but in the image of his fallen father (Genesis 5:3). Like Seth, each of us entered this world set spiritually wrong, and as long as we remain in this condition, God views us in the wrong spiritual condition to spend eternity with Him. To become united with our Creator, we must be set right (righteous).

Getting Set Right

The age old question is: how does a person get set right? What must we do to find God's acceptance? Adam and Eve were the first to be faced with this question. They came up with what they thought was a logical solution to their dilemma by clothing themselves with leaves (Genesis 3:7). The leaves may have made them appear more presentable externally, but the leaves did nothing to alter their inner fallen condition. Despite their noble effort, they remained set wrong and spiritually dead. Those leaves were man's first religious act—attempting to self-justify.

Since the Fall, the vast majority of the world's population has attempted to find God's approval through various good deeds. The Pharisees of Christ's day were a prime example. They attempted to find God's acceptance by fulfilling the law of Moses. Then, as if God's Ten Commandments were not enough of a struggle, over the years they added a long list of their own laws. Their entire lives were devoted to keeping those laws, striving to find God's approval through their own religious efforts. They put on a wonderful external performance, but internally, they remained spiritually dead. Set wrong! Jesus referred to this religious group as "whitewashed tombs"—looking presentable externally, but internally, decayed corpses incapable of displaying any degree of spiritual life (Matthew 23:27). To add insult to injury, Jesus reminded them they were spiritually blind, and in their blindness, were leading their congregations to a lost eternity (Matthew 15:14). When Jesus told this pious religious group they were still in their sins, it is no wonder they began plotting to have

Him removed from the scene. It seems pretty obvious Jesus had never read the book *How to Win Friends and Influence People*.

> By Him everyone who believes is justified from all things from which you could not be justified by the law of Moses.
>
> Acts 13:39

> If righteousness comes through the law, then Christ died in vain.
>
> Galatians 2:21

In today's pews, there are many who sit week after week looking externally presentable, but inwardly they too are spiritually dead. When the apostle Paul wrote to the church in Rome, he obviously suspected there were those within their group who were spiritually blind, for he reminded them it was possible to know *about* God and still have a *darkened heart* (Romans 1:21). A darkened heart is one that has not been illuminated by the Holy Spirit and belongs to a person who is still a citizen of Satan's kingdom. This person can believe such Bible truths as the virgin birth, the crucifixion, and resurrection of Christ and still not be a Christian. Paul tells us that it is possible to "believe in vain" (1 Corinthians 15:2B). We are also told that Satan and the demons believe in Christ, but they certainly are not Christians (James 2:19, Mark 1:24, Matthew 8:29). God's Word makes it pretty clear that He does not look upon man's external religious performance but upon his heart condition.

> The Lord does not see as man sees; for man looks at the outward appearance, but the Lord looks at the heart.
>
> 1 Samuel 16:7

God ignored Adam and Eve's leaves and instead gave them a symbolic picture of His formula for being set right. He clothed them with animal skins (Genesis 3:21). Those skins could not have been acquired without the death and shed blood of an innocent animal. The actual animal skins did not alter their fallen state, but were the first picture in Scripture of The Lamb of God who would one day come to shed His innocent blood on our behalf. They placed faith in what this ritual portrayed, and because of that faith, positionally, God viewed them set right—justified.

The symbolic ritual of clothing Adam and Eve in skins in the Garden of Eden was similar to the ritual performed at the first Passover in Egypt. In both cases the believers looked *ahead* in faith to the coming Lamb of God whose blood would be shed for their sins. Today, believers look *back* in faith to what Christ, our Passover Lamb, accomplished at Calvary. Both the Old and New Testament saints placed faith in the same Passover Lamb—Jesus Christ. How fortunate we are to have lived after the fact. Christ's last words from the cross were, "It is finished." There is no doubt what He meant by that statement. He was the fulfillment of the Old Testament Passover Feast!

God's formula for becoming just was passed forward from generation to generation, which is why we can confidently say the gospel is clearly revealed in the Old Testament. In the passing forward of this ritual, in many cases God's provision for being justified has been either distorted, watered down, or completely ignored. In the fourth chapter of Genesis, we find two of Adam's sons making a sin offering to the Lord. Both Cain and Abel believed in the existence of God and both expected to find God's approval through their offerings. Cain ignored God's pattern for being set right and instead placed faith in his works by offering fruit of the cursed earth (Genesis 3:17-18). There was no death and shed blood of an innocent animal. As a result, God rejected his offering (Genesis 4:5).

Abel also brought of the firstborn of his flock and of their fat. And the Lord respected Abel and his offering.

Genesis 4:4

Abel's offering fit God's pattern. Did you notice the tiny word "fat" in the above verse? Fat could not be obtained without the death and shed blood of the slain lamb. Also, the word "firstborn" speaks of the premature death of God's Lamb. Because of Abel's faith in what the slain lamb pictured, God viewed his offering as righteous, while he viewed Cain's offering as evil (1 John 3:12). Throughout history, for one reason or another, the majority of this world's population have gone the way of Cain—relying on their own efforts to obtain God's approval. No matter how noble the efforts of man, they simply will not cut it with God. "Woe to them! For they have gone in the way of Cain" (Jude 11).

I think it is safe to say that the majority of today's population attempts to find God's acceptance by sewing on various types of leaves, religious or otherwise. Some attempt to find His approval by living a decent and moral life—doing more good than bad. Others, by performing such religious acts as joining a church, undergoing water baptism, fulfilling certain laws, and doing religious deeds. Impressive efforts, but just as with Cain, the Lord does not acknowledge any of these as a way of gaining His acceptance. As long as we place confidence in our efforts for being justified, God views us still in our sins—set wrong.

Throughout history, it has always been a minority that have gone the way of Abel, placing faith in God's provision for being justified. Jesus confirmed this truth when He announced that at any given time, only a few would actually place faith in His provision for being set right, thus receiving the free gift of salvation (Matthew 7:14).

Without the shedding of blood there is no forgiveness of sins.

Hebrews 9:22 (RSV)

For they being ignorant of God's righteousness, and seeking to establish their own righteousness, have not submitted to the righteousness of God.

Romans 10:3

There is no other name under heaven given among men by which we must be saved.

Acts 4:12

For though you wash yourself with lye, and use much soap, yet your iniquity is marked.

Jeremiah 2:22

Two Camps

From God's perspective, there are only two categories of people in this world: Cain's camp and Abel's camp. Cain's camp is composed of those who believe their own accomplishments will gain God's approval, and in Abel's camp are those who place faith in Christ's accomplishments. There are either saints or sinners. Redeemed or unredeemed! Just and unjust!

These two camps were not only pictured in the lives of Cain and Abel, but are also represented by the two criminals crucified alongside Christ (Luke 23:39-43). The unrepentant criminal mocked Jesus and, like most criminals, refused to acknowledge he was a sinner. He stepped into eternity set wrong, following in the footsteps of Cain. The second criminal had an entirely different attitude. He acknowledged his guilt, and believed Jesus had committed no sin. By referring to Him as Lord as well as to His kingdom, it is clear the repentant criminal viewed Jesus as the long awaited Messiah. Prior to drawing his last breath, this sinner experienced a definite foxhole conversion! As he hung there on the cross, Christ assured him that he was paradise bound. In their final moments on earth, both criminals were alongside Jesus, but when they drew their last breath they went their separate ways. The unrepentant sinner stepped into eternity in his sinful condition, while the repentant criminal stepped into eternity possessing the righteousness of Jesus Christ!

Believing and Receiving

> By grace you have been saved through faith, and that not of yourselves; it is the gift of God.
>
> Ephesians 2:8

If our good works could find God's approval, salvation would not be a *gift*, but a *reward* for conduct! As with any gift, salvation is a gift which can only be received. Whenever I am presented with a gift, it does not become mine until I make a personal decision to reach out and receive it from the giver. To become a Christian, we must first believe in what Jesus accomplished at Calvary, and through His resurrection, then personally receive the free gift He provided for a lost world. The key to spending eternity with Christ is receiving what we believe.

> As many as received Him, to them He gave the right to become children of God, to those who believe in His name.
>
> John 1:12

Questions

- If you were to arrive at heaven's gate today, would you arrive set right or set wrong?

- Would you arrive having placed faith in your accomplishments, or having placed faith in Christ's accomplishments?

- Are you still independent from the Lord, running a self-managed life, or have you placed confidence in Christ's ability to manage your life?

- Are you a believer in such truths as the virgin birth, Calvary, and the resurrection of Christ but still seated each week in a pew with a darkened heart because you have never personally received the free gift of salvation? Receiving is the key!

EATING LAMB

Once Israel celebrated the first Passover and placed faith in what it symbolized, the next step was to pack their bags and head for home. To sustain their physical needs during the intended month long desert phase of their journey they were to take with them animals and food preserved during the plagues. God was also very concerned about their spiritual strength. How would they sustain their faith when the journey became difficult and unforeseen problems arose along the way? Would they hold fast to His promise to supply all their needs in the midst of the barren desert ahead? How would they deal with such fortified cities as Jericho when they actually came upon them?

Placing faith in the Passover ritual made them *safe* from pending judgment. However, being under the blood of the Passover lamb did not make them *strong*. That same Passover night each household was instructed to cook and eat the lamb they had just slain (Exodus 12:8-9). Strength for their journey. This is such a beautiful picture of digesting the Word of God. When they placed faith in God's promises to lead them safely to the Promised Land, in a figurative sense they were drawing strength from the digested Lamb. If they were to walk in victory during their exodus, it was imperative Israel remain Word focused.

It is interesting to note what actually happens when food is digested. It begins to be broken down the minute we eat and the process continues as it enters the stomach. Vitamins are then distributed wherever they are needed to enable the body to operate efficiently. Enzymes enhance yet another function. Minerals are sent off in another direction. Potassium, for instance, is needed on a daily basis for the heart to function properly. That is exactly how it should be when we digest God's Word! It should nourish every fiber of our being. The Word and Christ are one and the same. When we neglect the Word, we are in fact, neglecting our relationship with Jesus.

Graduating

During Israel's exodus, we will see that God occasionally placed tests in their path (Deuteronomy 8:2). The purpose was not to make life difficult for Israel, but to reveal their true heart condition. As each test surfaced, instead of displaying fear, worry, and anger, they were to focus on God's power and His promise to escort them safely home. Each time God provided a safe path through the tests, their faith should have been strengthened and, hopefully, by the time they reached Canaan's border, their faith would be rock solid. In Canaan they would be exposed to major challenges, and before they set foot in the land it was imperative that faith in His promises be firmly entrenched in their hearts. Otherwise, they would live a life of defeat in Canaan and would constantly be a negative testimony to the Lord. On the other hand, a display of fear and worry would necessitate an extension until they got it right. In other words, if they flunked a particular test, similar to failing a school exam, God would have them repeat the test. The wilderness phase of their journey would turn out to be their school of hard knocks—it was supposed to have been no more than a month long, with plenty of food and water available, not to mention God's full protection along the entire way.

The formula is much the same today. As a believer the blood of Christ keeps us safe from the pending judgment against sin. However, the blood does not make us strong. Our spiritual strength comes when we make the Word a part of our daily lives. Yes, Christ and the Word are inseparable. One and the same! "The Word (Christ) became flesh and dwelt among us" (John 1:14). "His name (Christ) is called the Word of God" (Revelation 19:13). When we open our Bibles and begin trusting in the promises recorded therein, we are, in fact, digesting Lamb. How we react to the tests, which constantly seem to be in our path, is directly related to the degree of faith we place in His promises. As this story unfolds, we will discover that storing the promises in our minds does not build our faith. Head knowledge will inevitably let us down when the tribulations of life surface. We are told to hide the promises in our hearts. In other words the deepest part of our being. Just as the Israelites physically ate lamb, the Word must become a part of our lives, the motivation behind all that we think and do. "Your law is within my heart" (Psalm 40:8).

In our journey with the Lord, His desire is to bring us to a point where our faith in His promises becomes rock solid. A point where we believe God cannot lie! Only then can we cross into our Canaan, and begin to experience the normal Christian life as it is outlined in our Bibles. I know, I know, you are asking, "Where in the world is our Canaan?" Simply put, it is a place of peace, inner joy, and contentment where we cease from our daily struggle and begin to trust God in all our circumstances. The apostle Paul wrote, "We walk by faith, not by sight" (2 Corinthians 5:7). As we will discover sight walking will not open the door to Canaan!

Many make the mistake of thinking that reading the Word on a regular basis is a rule God made for His benefit when, in actual fact, it is always for *our* benefit. The following are a few of the many positives to be gained from digesting Lamb. Unfortunately, in this fast paced world, the majority of God's children have little appreciation for the Word.

1. (Matthew 22:29, KJV). The Word gives direction and wisdom in our daily walk. Constantly leaning unto our own understanding and ignoring the Word is an invitation to error. There is a vast difference between knowledge and wisdom. Knowledge is knowing the hot stove will burn. Wisdom remembers the blisters! Isn't it funny how quick we are to take directions from a perfect stranger when we are physically lost, yet we are so often reluctant to heed the advice of the God of the Universe as we struggle through life? "Your word is a lamp to my feet" (Psalm 119:105).

2. Obedience brings success and prosperity. I think it is safe to say that is what we all desire. The degree of success and prosperity we enjoy will be directly related to the degree of digested Lamb. When God speaks of success and prosperity, He has in mind every area of our lives—better husbands and wives, better parents, better workers, and responsible money managers.

> This Book of the law shall not depart from your mouth, but you shall meditate in it day and night, that you may observe to do according to all that is written in it. For then you will make your way prosperous and then you will have good success.
>
> Joshua 1:8

When Joshua uses the word "mouth" in the above verse, I think we are meant to get the idea of chewing over and digesting the Word, not just accumulating head knowledge.

3. The Word strengthens our faith. As we will discover later, praying for more faith and peace is basically a waste of time. Pulling ourselves up by our boot straps determined to display faith in the midst of a negative will not cut it either. Instead, we must open our Bibles regularly and begin digesting Lamb, which in turn will produce the necessary

faith and peace for whatever lies ahead. It's that simple! If we neglect the Word, we will find ourselves constantly struggling with fear and worry, and often a great deal more. In addition, our relationship with Christ will undoubtedly be distant and fuzzy. "Faith comes by hearing, and hearing by the Word of God" (Romans 10:17).

4. Digesting Lamb will also cause us to mature. Put another way, it gets us beyond the diaper stage! A lack of Biblical knowledge leaves one with very little discernment, thus making us prime targets for every lie and false doctrine that comes our way.

> You are like babies who can drink only milk, not old enough for solid food. And when a person is still living on milk it shows he isn't very far along in the Christian life, and doesn't know much about the difference between right and wrong. He is still a baby Christian.
>
> Hebrews 5:13-14 (LB)

> Sanctify them by Your truth. Your word is truth.
>
> John 17:17

We can never mature spiritually by attempting to fulfill certain laws, or by accumulating head knowledge, only by digesting Lamb. "How can a young man cleanse his way? By taking heed according to Your word" (Psalm 119:9).

5. Freedom is something everyone desires. We all long for freedom from worry, fear, and depression, to name a few. Many go to great lengths to achieve that freedom, however, few find it on a permanent basis. In fact, despite the vacations and new toys, without a personal relationship with Christ, we will soon find ourselves back in the same old rut, with nothing but more plastic debt to show for it. The amount of freedom we enjoy is directly related to the degree the Word of God abides in our hearts. It is impossible to sidestep this truth! "If you abide in My Word, you are My

disciples indeed. And you shall know the truth and the truth shall make you free" (John 8:31-32).

Potential Danger

Yes, believe it or not, there is a potential danger in reading the Bible! If we read the Word with the intent of accumulating head knowledge, it will definitely do more harm than good. When dark clouds surface, head knowledge will always let us down. We simply must have the Word of God abiding in our hearts well before the dark clouds appear.

Another potential danger with head knowledge is that it tends to puff up—make us proud of our accumulated knowledge. When we fill our minds with Bible verses, there is always the danger of them spewing out in the presence of others, whether appropriate or not. I am reminded of a woman I know who constantly quotes worn out platitudes and Bible verses often at the most inopportune moments. When I hear her working the room, I often wonder if she actually talks like that behind closed doors. For her husband's sake, I hope not! I also recall a man who placed a check mark beside each chapter of the Bible every time he finished reading it. He took great pride in pointing out the accumulated check marks on page after page of his rather well worn Bible.

I cannot go on without mentioning what I perceive to be the most disastrous result of head knowledge, and that is a judgmental attitude. Only when the Word is hidden in our hearts are we understanding, compassionate, and tolerant of the mistakes of others. How clearly the Word teaches that this Christian journey is a personal one. We are instructed not to judge others but to strive to be an encouragement to our fellow travelers.

A person can be totally deceived into thinking he is a Christian because of his head knowledge. He believes in certain Bible truths, and does certain religious works; therefore, he assumes he is a believer. Jesus said many will arrive at heaven's gate, relying on head knowledge and works to get them beyond the gate. "Many will say to Me in that day, Lord, Lord, have we not prophesied in Your name, cast out demons in Your name, and done many wonders in Your name?" To this category of people, Jesus said, "I never knew you; depart from Me, you who practice lawlessness" (Matthew 7:22-23). Frightening words in today's lukewarm church age. Many possess a degree of head knowledge, perform impressive Christian activities, but have never established a personal relationship with Christ. There was never a time when they actually admitted they were sinners in desperate need of a Savior.

> Although they knew God, they did not glorify Him as God, nor were thankful, but became futile in their thoughts, and their foolish hearts were darkened. Professing to be wise, they became fools.
>
> Romans 1:21-22

Watered Down Lamb

Now we come to perhaps one of the most difficult sections of this entire book. When Ruth read the first draft, she wondered if it might be wise to omit the entire section. We had a *long* talk, and after much discussion, she agreed it contained material that needed to be included. With her gift of diplomacy, she has softened much of the original content, and it is my prayer that it is received in the spirit it is intended.

You will remember that prior to their journey, Israel was instructed to prepare a meal from the slain animal. They were told not to boil the lamb, but to roast it, for boiling would remove much of the valuable nourishment (Exodus 12:9). Today, what I refer to as watered down Lamb is being served from many pulpits resulting in undernourished congregations. Each week hungry sheep walk through the doors of today's churches hoping to hear something of substance and value. Sadly, far too many leave in much the same condition as they entered, having heard little or nothing with which to face the onslaught of the coming week. Despite their church involvement, the rest of the week they function similar to their non-believing friends. They worry, have marriage problems, display anger, cheat in business, gossip, live with various addictions—including prescribed drugs, and many of their days are overwhelmed with varying degrees of fear. The real enemy of the church is not Satan, the cults, or the liberal media, but pastors who fail to feed their congregations nourishing spiritual food!

Many of today's pastors are serving mere pablum to their congregations for any one of several reasons. Some because they do not believe the entire Bible to be the inspired Word of God. How can a minister preach solid nourishing sermons with this thinking? He can't! You may shake your head in disbelief at the following statistic: according to a recent survey, approximately 80 percent of those in today's pulpits do not believe the Bible is entirely true. In other words, they think the inspired Word of God is less than inspired! Others preach a watered down version of the Bible simply because they know far too little about the Word themselves. I think it is an established fact that a pastor cannot lead his flock beyond his own spiritual level. Still others preach pablum because they fear alienating the tithers, especially the large ones. They are careful not to step on toes, fearful that members will either leave the church, taking their pocketbooks with them, or worse still, decide it is time for a new face in the pulpit. Charles H. Spurgeon, the great British theologian, once wrote an article entitled, "Are We Feeding Sheep or Amusing Goats?" Unfortunately many of today's pastors are doing just that rather than feeding their flock. Week after week people exit their particular church in the same spiritual condition as they entered, poorly equipped to function in the chaos of the world in which we live.

Lest you think the above in some way lets you, dear reader, off the hook, I want to make it abundantly clear that, in the final analysis, each of us is responsible for our own Christian growth. The Christian journey is a personal one, and if we look to Him, and Him alone, He will see that we are well equipped for whatever the future might hold. How do I know that? Because He has equipped Ruth and me time and time again! We were not always fortunate enough to be under solid teaching. There were many times when we had to make a definite effort to feed ourselves.

It will seem odd to find acknowledgments in the middle of a book. But then we have rarely played by the so called rules. As we look back over our forty-plus years as Christians, there are many men and women who have played a part in equipping us for this exciting journey called Christianity. We will be forever thankful to those listed below and many of them will never know until eternity what an important part they played in our lives:

- Ralph and Lou Sutera
- Pastor Cliff Dietrich
- Dr. M. R. DeHaan
- Henrietta Mears
- Charles Swindoll
- Bill and Gloria Gaither
- Dr. Charles Stanley
- Major Ian Thomas
- Dr. William Barclay
- Bob George
- John Eldredge

- Chuck Missler
- Peter Lord
- Tim LaHaye
- Hal Lindsey
- Dr. David Seamands
- Helen Duff Baugh
- Mary E. Clark

Sorry to say you cannot always count on the church of today to equip you for your journey. Even the enormously successful Willow Creek ministry has acknowledged a degree of failure in this area and rather recently published a book addressing this very issue. Equipping yourselves when you find it necessary will, if nothing else, keep you out of a lot of mischief. If you are at a loss as to where to begin, start with the list above and I assure you the books and/or CDs of these godly men and women will keep you occupied until He comes. Let me hasten to add here that the vast majority of them do not even know we exist. In one way or another, the Lord Himself led us to each of them when their particular ministry was most needed in our lives. You may end up with a vastly different list than ours. Our God will perhaps use different saints to minister to you in your particular need.

Spiritual Malnutrition

Sitting under a pablum ministry invites what I refer to as *spiritual malnutrition*. The sad sight of third world children who are undernourished and suffering from malnutrition has become an all too common sight on our television sets. When malnutrition sets in, the human body has a built-in protective mechanism that causes taste buds to be numbed. When that happens, the child no longer has an appetite for food. A bowl of delicious food can be placed in front of him, and instead of eating, he will just sit and stare with a blank empty look. If the child is to survive, it is imperative he be forced fed in order to stimulate his taste buds.

Similarly, when a Christian sits in a pew week after week deprived of solid spiritual food, it is just a matter of time before he slides into a state of spiritual malnutrition. His spiritual taste buds will become numb, and unless a change takes place, he will lose his desire for solid meat. At this point, if he is exposed to solid teaching, like the starving child, he will sit there with a blank empty stare—constantly glancing at his watch. There will be no digesting, and he will undoubtedly leave the meeting unchanged. Instead, like the Pharisees, he will quickly learn the dos and don'ts of the denomination and make a noble effort to fulfill the rules. Then, once he has learned the denominational drill, he will begin to impose those same rules upon others, evolving into yet another judgmental pew sitter doing more harm than good. He will have a more intimate relationship with his church than he does with Christ. His relationship with Christ will be distant as well as somewhat mechanical. He will be found spending more time reading the newspaper and watching television than studying the Word. He may enter church each week carrying a Bible with worn out covers, but the pages within the book will look much like they did when they came off the press.

This type of Christian presents a problem. A child, in a state of physical malnutrition, can be force fed to have his taste buds stimulated once again. How do you force feed an adult who has no desire to digest spiritual food? You can't! He can be coerced into attending a solid Bible study, but he will soon come up with a zillion excuses for missed meetings. Should he be shamed into regular attendance, he will probably sit in the meeting with a blank look on his face—digesting nothing. Unless he experiences a spiritual change, he will spend the rest of his life living in a state of malnutrition and experiencing a substandard Christian life. There will probably be times when he thinks to himself, "There must be more to the Christian life than what I am experiencing," and there is!

Number One Role of a Pastor

Whenever I ask any group to name the number one role of a pastor, the replies are usually similar. Some say preaching the gospel is his priority. Others say organizing and running the church. Rarely does anyone say, "feeding the flock." Preaching the gospel week after week to a primarily Christian congregation will lull the believers to sleep. They simply tune the preacher out! Certainly a salvation message can be worked into the weekly feeding, but the focus should be on enabling the believers to function as overcomers in their daily lives. Standing spiritually strong in this pressurized world, and being a positive testimony to those who cross our path, requires a regular dose of strong spiritual lamb.

> We are to God the fragrance of Christ among those who are being saved and among those who are perishing.
>
> 2 Corinthians 2:15

When believers are well nourished, they will have a desire to minister both within and beyond the church. In their excitement, they will naturally share their faith with nonbelievers and will also be effective in ministering to troubled Christians. No longer will the pastor carry the entire burden of soul winning, as members of the congregation begin leading people to Christ. In addition, the pastor's calendar will no longer be filled with counseling sessions, allowing sufficient time to prepare solid sermons.

Ezekiel 34:1-15 is a strong warning that should catch the attention of all pastors and Bible teachers. These verses warn that if pastors fail to properly feed their congregations, God will motivate the flock to go elsewhere. Home Bible groups are flourishing these days because many pastors are failing their primary commission—feeding the flock!

Today, it is no longer weak Christians who are the pew hoppers, but the spiritually strong. When the strength in a congregation begins to check out, a downhill spiral takes place. Those remaining in the pews will be either immature believers or seekers. A solid spiritual work cannot be built with either group. When a church position needs to be filled, hoping to find acceptance and recognition, these self-focused members will eagerly volunteer to fill the empty slot. Since the spiritual level of any group cannot rise above the level of the leadership, the organization will begin to experience a downhill slide. Such a slide, once begun, is difficult to stop. The organization may generate a lot of religious activity, but their efforts will produce little lasting fruit. We have in our midst today a long trail of Christian organizations that were once spiritually productive and a bright light for Christ in the community. Lacking solid teaching for many years, however, today they are little more than religious clubs. "Harsh words" you say, but I think, if you are honest, you will be hard pressed to disagree.

We have a beautiful and clear illustration of just such a situation in the Old Testament. Prior to the prophet Samuel coming upon the scene, Israel's spiritual life had declined. During the era of the judges, "Everyone did what was right in his own eyes" (Judges 21:25). Their relationship with God had become distant and mechanical, and worst of all, they were defeated in every battle. Samuel understood the root of their problem. "The Word of the Lord was rare in those days" (1 Samuel 3:1). There was much religious activity in the various temples, but the teaching had become watered down. Solid teaching was rare. Sounds familiar, doesn't it? Samuel began teaching, and the Scripture says, "None of his words fell to the ground" (1 Samuel 3:19). In other words, his teaching did not fall on deaf ears, but took root in the hearts of the hearers. Israel became doers of the Word. Once the people were exposed to solid teaching, revival took place, and once again, Israel began to overcome their enemies and experience the abundant life as promised by God.

If we find ourselves constantly leaving church in the same spiritual condition as we entered, I personally think it is imperative we search out a place where the Word is being solidly taught. By remaining under a watered down version of the Word, it will just be a matter of time before we drift into a state of resignation, or even worse—spiritual malnutrition. There are churches and home Bible groups in almost every area where one can receive proper feeding. If you must, move on!

Good Versus Best

In this fast paced world, it is easy to become involved in good things but miss out on the best. Once you have discovered a place that serves solid spiritual food, make it your priority to be there whenever the door is open. Don't allow watching a football game or taking Fido to the vet interfere with getting fed spiritually. In other words, don't allow the *good* to cause you to miss out on the *best*. The television program can be recorded. Fido's visit can be moved to a different date. Be careful not to allow others to involve you in their good activities and cause you to miss out on the best. Remain in control! As new Christians, Ruth and I would often drive twenty, sometimes fifty or more miles to attend a solid Bible study. Looking back, I can see our efforts were well blessed.

The story of Mary and Martha is a great illustration of doing good and missing the best (Luke 10:38-42). Jesus was visiting the village of Bethany, and his friends Mary and Martha invited Him for a meal. When He arrived, Martha was found busily preparing a meal for their honored guest. Mary chose instead to seat herself at Christ's feet, soaking up His teaching. Martha was certainly occupied with a good thing, but her sister chose the best place— at the feet of Jesus—digesting His Word. When Martha became critical of her sister, Jesus chastised her. He pointed out that Mary had made the best choice, while Martha had missed an opportunity that would never pass her way again. I was teaching this portion of Scripture at one of our studies when a well-intentioned woman became defensive of Martha. She said, "If it weren't for Martha, there would not have been a meal." Not true! The meal certainly could have been prepared before Christ's arrival or after He finished teaching. I can assure you Jesus would not have gone hungry! When you suggest to others that your Bible study time takes priority over their agenda, don't be surprised if they respond as Martha.

Nutritionists tell us, "We are what we eat!" If we are undernourished or consume a poor diet, we eventually become prime targets for illnesses of all sorts. In the spiritual realm, it is much the same. If we neglect the Word for a period of time, or sit under a watered down ministry, we will find ourselves not only spiritually weak, but in danger of attack. Should that be the case in your life, I strongly recommend you search out a place that serves solid spiritual food. Once you have found such a place, make that the *best* place to be whenever the Word is being taught.

Questions

- If your spiritual temperature were taken, would you discover you are undernourished?

- Beyond your church affiliation, does your daily life resemble that of a nonbeliever, plagued with worry, fear, envy, anxiety, and perhaps even a sharp tongue?

- If you have found a place where solid spiritual food is taught, do you view it as your number one priority whenever the door is open—the best place? Or do you allow the world and its residents to distract and manipulate, causing you, all too often, to miss the best?

RED SEA

Egypt was glad when they departed, for the fear of them had
fallen upon them.

Psalm 105:38

The Egyptians urged the people, that they might send them
out of the land in haste. For they said, we shall all be dead.

Exodus 12:33

After the final devastating plague, Pharaoh reluctantly agreed to
allow Israel to depart for Canaan. Prior to leaving, God instructed
the Israelites to ask the Egyptians for gold, silver, and even clothing. So relieved to see them on their way, the Egyptians gladly
satisfied Israel's every request (Exodus 12:35-36). Personally, I
view this as compensation for the many years Israel toiled as non-
salaried employees. The bottom line is Israel departed with great
possessions, which indeed fulfilled a prophecy given to Abraham
approximately six hundred years earlier. I hope you are beginning to get the idea that, in His time, every promise God makes
becomes a reality.

The nation whom they serve I will judge; afterward they shall
come out with great possessions.

Genesis 15:14

Under the Cloud

The Lord went before them by day in a pillar of cloud to lead
the way, and by night in a pillar of fire to give them light.

Exodus 13:21

Crossing a vast desert can be a dangerous venture. If Israel were
to arrive safely in Canaan, it was imperative they have a reliable
guide. Like most people, whenever I plan a car trip through unfa-
miliar territory, I always put an up-to-date road map in the car.
In Israel's day, there were no road maps, no compasses or road
signs every few miles pointing the way to Canaan. Without a
reliable means of guidance, I suppose Israel would have wandered
in circles and eventually perished in the hot barren desert.

As always, God was one step ahead. He provided them with
an unusual, but infinitely reliable compass—His cloud. To remain
on track, all they had to do was occasionally look up! Simply put,
when the cloud moved, they moved, and when the cloud stopped,
they pitched their tents. Prior to leaving Egypt, God promised
to supply their needs, defeat their enemies, and lead them safely
home. To experience those promises, all Israel had to do was
remain *under the cloud*, and in approximately a month's time, they
would have arrived safely on Canaan's doorstep. In their journey
across the barren wilderness, there would be no need for worry
or fear, for as long as they remained *under the cloud*, life would be
sweet.

The cloud served two purposes: it not only provided Israel
with guidance, it also served as the world's first air conditioning
system. The cloud hovered over the entire Israelite camp provid-
ing relief from the scorching desert sun (Psalm 105:39). I wonder,
has it ever occurred to you that in our exodus with Christ, we
also have a reliable road map to keep us on track—the Word of
God—His cloud? If we are committed to reading and studying

on a regular basis, the Word will give us direction in our daily journey and prevent us from making costly mistakes (Matthew 22:29). As long as our desire is to be obedient to the Word, our lives will remain on course. To put it another way, as long as we remain *under the cloud,* there will be no need to sweat life as our needs will be met. In our journey with Christ, in His time, He will defeat each and every enemy we encounter. Our journey will be a walk of freedom—one no longer crippled by worry, fear, anxiety, and anger. Instead of the world and its residents manipulating our emotions and time, *under the cloud* we will have dominion. Being cloud focused is the only way to fly! "Your word is a lamp to my feet" (Psalm 119:105).

When our Bibles remain on dusty shelves, it is as if we have made a decision to step out from *under the cloud.* Without God's Word as a guide, we will be forced to lean unto our own understanding for direction, which greatly increases the odds of making wrong and costly mistakes. Since the Word and Christ are one and the same, a dusty Bible is an indication of a distant and fuzzy relationship with Him. Do you realize we can sit in a pew and still not be *under the cloud?* If our only exposure to the Word is the few minutes we spend in church each week, we are, in fact, not *under the cloud.* If we hear or read the Word and are challenged to make changes in our lives, and refuse to do so, we are definitely not *under the cloud.* In this condition, we may occupy our church pew religiously each week, but our Christianity will become mechanical, and we will find ourselves leaving, week after week, in the same spiritual condition as we entered. Sad to say, that kind of person will eventually become a clock watcher, looking forward to the highlight of the day—lunch! If we are to enjoy the Christian life as it is defined in our Bibles, it is vital that we constantly dwell *under the cloud!*

Boxed In

The Red Sea proved to be a time of testing for Israel. When they arrived at the western shore, they certainly must have been shocked; never had they seen such a vast body of water. Their first thought must have been, "How will we ever get to the other side?" As slaves, there probably had never been an opportunity to learn to swim. No vast fleet of ships was waiting to transport them to the eastern shore. Think about it! Even if there were boats that could accommodate one thousand passengers each, two thousand boats would have been required to transport two million Israelites to the other side. In addition, numerous large barges would have been required to transport their animals and food. When they saw the Red Sea, I expect many began to think, "Is God a reliable guide? Can we really trust Him to be the guiding force in our lives?" Have you ever entertained that thought? If I am honest, especially as a young Christian, I have to admit those very thoughts crossed my mind more than once.

This huge body of water in front of them was not their only problem. Pharaoh apparently had a change of heart, as he dispatched his army to drag the Israelites back to the slave camps (Exodus 14:9). Israel found themselves boxed in. Picture the scene. There were rugged mountains both to their right and left. The sea prevented them from moving forward, and Pharaoh's army was closing in from the rear. Being boxed in is always a scary situation, and Israel surely must have thought,

HOW IN THE WORLD DID WE GET IN THIS MESS AND HOW WILL WE EVER GET OUT OF IT?

As always with God, there was a way out. All they had to do was remind themselves of His promise to protect and guide them, then look up to make sure they were *under the cloud!* Rather than being *promise* focused, they became *problem* focused. Self-preservation surfaced, and instead of having a victory party in their hearts on the western shore, they were filled with fear (Exodus 14:10). Instead of walking by faith and trusting in God's promises, they walked by sight and allowed the negatives of life to rob them of their peace. Rather than whining and bellyaching, they would have been wiser to remember the miracles they had seen God perform back in Egypt. If He did it before, surely He would do it again! Once again, it was time to *look up* and begin to visualize themselves camped safely on the opposite shore. Had you been in their shoes, how would you have reacted? "We walk by faith, not by sight" (2 Corinthians 5:7).

Since becoming a Christian, have you ever felt boxed in? In my early Christian days I remember a specific time when I felt completely boxed in. Ruth and I were shoveling snow off the roof of our house in Prince George, British Columbia, Canada, for the third time that particular winter. Leaning on her shovel, Ruth asked, "What in the world are we doing living here anyway? We love warm weather, sunshine, and the ocean!" That was the day we began to pray. Within the year, Heather, our oldest, would have to leave for college. I was doing very well in my job. In fact that year I was the top producer internationally for my company and was to be feted at a large gathering of my peers in Hawaii. You know the usual convention routine. Yet, perhaps it was time to make a change.

Longing for those warm ocean breezes and days filled with sunshine, we jumped on a plane headed south, winding up in Daytona Beach, Florida. Through a series of circumstances, we met the local manager of a large national insurance company. Ruth's mother was living with us at that time, and we knew one of the first things we had to do was inquire about health insurance for her, as she had a pre-existing medical condition. I met for lunch with that manager, and I noticed he quietly prayed over his food. I asked if he were a Christian, which he was. Surprise, surprise! We quickly settled my insurance questions, and then he asked about my background. By the time lunch ended, he had offered me a job. Next day we were off to Jacksonville to meet the regional manager who also turned out to be a Christian. That was the only time I ever gave my entire testimony on a job interview! He confirmed the offer of a job and assured me their lawyers would take care of all the immigration details concerning our international move.

We flew back to Prince George, called our real estate agent, and she sold our house that very weekend before the for sale sign was ever staked out on our lawn. And to buyers who had cash in hand! God was definitely in the details. We felt assured of that. The move was on! With much excitement, we made our plans and set out for Florida.

It was scarcely a year later when the first letter arrived from the Jacksonville Immigration Office informing us that our temporary visa was about to expire and that we must leave the country. How could this be? Both girls were in school, we had purchased a home and had already begun the lengthy citizenship application procedure. Soon after that, a second letter arrived from the Miami Immigration Office telling us not to leave the country until our citizenship application had been finalized. Boxed in, you better believe it! I hastily made several telephone calls with zero results, which is so often the case with government bureaucracy. Finally, we were able to secure an appointment with the Immigration Department in Jacksonville. When the day came, Ruth and I quietly slipped out of town, discussing the situation neither with my employer nor our family. It had seemed so clear that this move was God's will for our entire family, and He doesn't make mistakes. So what was this all about?

Soon we were seated at the desk of the least bureaucratic government official I have ever met. We showed him both letters. He opened our file and immediately spotted the problem. We had been brought into the United States on the wrong visa designation. It was one that should have been issued to a visiting professor or doctor who would do his thing for a year, then return to his home country at the end of that time. That certainly was not our situation. We told him our girls were in school, we had purchased a home and so on. He assured us he would not send us back. Then he said, "It's just too bad you don't have any family who are American citizens." At that point, Ruth spoke up. Her older brother had recently decided to become a naturalized U.S. citizen after living in the country for more than ten years. He slapped his desk and said, "That will do nicely!" There were a myriad of new forms to fill out, and he couldn't have been more helpful. When it came time to leave his office, he told us to go home, resume our normal lives, and eventually our papers would come through. He did tell us not to hold our breath, as it was during the influx of the Vietnamese boat people who took priority. We would be placed at the bottom of a very long list, as there were literally hundreds being processed in the Jacksonville office alone—amazing when we were the ones with a job, a bank account, a home, and even spoke the language. Several years passed before we finally stood in the Court House in Deland, Florida, the county seat, to be sworn in as citizens. Were we filled with worry and fear during that long wait? No, we were not! We carried on as normal as we had seen God's hand at every turn. It was a wonderful growing experience for our entire family, and one we will remember all the days of our lives!

Three-Step Program

Whenever we find ourselves faced with a Red Sea (boxed in) situation, we need to put in motion what I have come to call the "Three-Step Program."

When Bill Wilson founded Alcoholics Anonymous, he devised a twelve-step program designed to help alcoholics find freedom from addiction. I think you will agree that any form of addiction boxes one in. Members of Alcoholics Anonymous have always referred to themselves as "Friends of Bill." My Three Step Program enables "Friends of Jesus" to break free from such crippling addictions as worry, fear, anger, and depression. You may not have thought of these behaviors as addictions, but in a very real sense, they are. They rob us of the same things the other obvious addictions do. How much peace and joy does an alcoholic have? What joy is there in the life of a worrier? My little Three Step Program enables Christians to have victory in their hearts in the midst of any crisis situation. The next time you are faced with a problem, just give it a try. It works!

> Step 1: We do what we can to rectify the problem. The Lord created us with a brain and expects us to use it. For example, when my car has a flat tire, even with my limited mechanical knowledge, I can solve that problem. However, there are times when a problem is beyond my ability to solve. That is when Step 2 comes into play.

> Step 2: Having exhausted our resources, we then turn the problem over to the Problem Solver, trusting in His ability to defuse the problem and get us to the other side, so to speak. The Bible instructs us to do exactly that when it encourages us to cast all our cares upon Christ (1 Peter 5:7). Having made Step 2 a reality in our hearts, Step 3 is a natural progression.

> Step 3: Walk on in peace. Once the problem has been placed in Christ's capable hands, by faith we must then visualize ourselves standing on the other side. It may take an hour, a day, or perhaps a year or more for the Lord to deal with the negative, but in His time, He will make a path through the problem. In the meantime, we can feel secure *under the cloud,* moving on with peace and joy in our hearts.

Moses was faced with the exact same problem as his followers; however, his reaction was entirely different. Instead of whining and complaining, he chose to believe God did not lie, and therefore, would fulfill His promise to lead Israel safely to Canaan. Instead of believing what he *saw*, he chose to see what he *believed*. Now you have to think about that one for a minute! There is an old expression that says, "Seeing is believing." There is absolutely no faith involved in that one, but believing what is yet to come, now that takes faith! Moses held tightly to God's promise and visualized the nation of Israel camped safely on the eastern shore. I believe that is exactly how the Lord expects His kids to function when confronted with a Red Sea situation!

Without even knowing it existed, Moses put into motion my little Three Step Program. He did what he could to rectify the problem, which in this situation was nothing except to believe in God's promises and to look up to ensure he was *under the cloud*. Then it was a matter of waiting until he received specific instructions and walking on in obedience. What a unique thrill it must have been to see the sea roll back and confidently lead over two million people down into the dry river bed, between two walls of water, safely to the other side. I firmly believe we miss many totally unique experiences in our lives simply because we do not hold onto our faith.

Desert Pete

It is impossible for God to lie.

Hebrews 6:18

Let's get to where the rubber meets the road. Do we really trust the promises of Christ that are recorded in the Bible? When confronted with a Red Sea, as a Christian, do we respond like the sight-walking two million majority, or as the faithful minority of one—Moses? When confronted with a dark cloud, do we find fear and anxiety surfacing, or does faith automatically prevail? Are our lives here on earth stress filled, hoping that it will all be better in the sweet by and by? The degree of faith we experience on earth is directly related to our being *under the cloud* and the amount of faith we are able to place in the promises of Christ—truly believing Jesus cannot and will not lie! A very wise Christian once said, "We can never break the Lord's promises by leaning on them!" I think we have pretty well established that, if God has promised it, we can take that promise to the bank. In fact, the only other thing we can do is break ourselves upon His promises. How sad!

A story is told about a man driving across a barren desert. Half way across his car broke down, leaving him stranded and without water. After a couple of days wandering, he came across a deserted property with a well that had one of those old fashioned hand pumps. In his desperation, he began pumping, but no water came. He soon realized the problem. The pump's sucker needed to be moistened. For that very purpose, a small bottle of water had been placed at the base of the well. Attached to the bottle was a note which read, "There is plenty of fresh water in the well, but you must use the water in this bottle to moisten the sucker. Once the water begins to flow, kindly refill the bottle for the next person. Have faith. Don't drink this water before priming the pump." The note was signed—Desert Pete!

Had we found ourselves in that situation, how would we have responded? Would self-preservation have surfaced, causing us to ignore the instruction and immediately drink the very small bottle of water? A quick fix, yes, but missing out on the promise of an abundance of water once the pump was primed. When challenging situations surface, do we take matters into our hands and go for the quick fix, or do we place faith in the promise contained in the Lord's note—His Word? We attempt to do many noble things with the intent of pleasing the Lord, but the Bible says, the only thing that truly pleases Him is our display of faith in His promises. "Without faith it is impossible to please Him" (Hebrews 11:6).

The question that arises in almost every heart that reads the above verse is, "If faith pleases God, does the lack of faith make him mad?" I am quick to assure you, no, it does not! However, it saddens and grieves Him when He sees us settle again and again for a small bottle of water when faith and obedience would give us access to the entire well!

Here's a thought that can revolutionize the way we think and act as a Christian: Instead of viewing the tribulations of life as negative, view each problem as an *opportunity* to display faith in the promises of Christ. For many Christians, that is a revolutionary way of functioning! To live this brand of Christianity, we must believe Jesus cannot lie! Viewing the dark clouds of life as negatives immediately causes worry, anxiety, and fear to surface, while this way of thinking allows the Holy Spirit to generate His fruit through our lives—peace, joy, unconditional love, etc. Two million Israelites viewed the Red Sea test as a negative, while one person viewed it as an opportunity to display faith in the promises of God.

> Do not be afraid. Stand still, and see the salvation of the Lord, which He will accomplish for you today. For the Egyptians whom you see today, you shall see no more forever. The Lord will fight for you, and you shall hold onto your peace.
>
> Exodus 14:13-14

Don't you love the instruction Moses gave to Israel? In today's lingo, he basically told them to, "Shut up, look up, and hold onto your peace!"

Until we begin placing faith in Christ's promises, and acting upon them, our days will continue to be consumed by anger, fear, depression, and, at best, small bottles of water. This fallen world, and its residents, will be constantly manipulating our emotions—jerking our chain! Instead of soaring like eagles, we will find ourselves flopping around like decapitated turkeys, kicking up a lot of dust, but going nowhere fast. Instead of experiencing an exciting and multi-faceted Christian journey, our lives will, all too often, resemble that of the trained drill soldier who on cue automatically performs as expected. That is the best we can ever expect from a life dictated by religion and rules.

> In Me you may have peace. In the world you will have tribulation, but be of good cheer, I have overcome the world.
>
> John 16:33

Two promises are contained in the above verse. First, Jesus promised we *will* have tribulation in this world. A promise with which we can all identify. A promise we can take to the bank. Second, He promised that in the midst of tribulation, we *may* have peace. May is a conditional word. May only becomes a reality in our hearts when we have turned the management of our lives over to Christ and chosen to place faith in His promises. We often deceive ourselves when we say, "Christ is the Lord of our lives." It is easy to acknowledge Christ as Lord verbally, but making Him Lord in our hearts is a whole different ball game. The "Lord, Lord" gang in the seventh chapter of Matthew confirms this truth. They addressed Jesus as Lord and reminded Him of the many wonderful works they had performed in His name, yet Jesus said, "I never knew you; depart from Me, you who practice lawlessness!"

If a survey were conducted and people in the pews asked if Christ was their Lord and Savior, I expect close to 100 percent would reply, "Certainly." Some might even become indignant when asked such a question. If professing Christians claim Jesus to be their Lord, why are worry, fear, and depression a way of life for so many? How can a believer claim Jesus as the Lord of his life and then be regularly overcome by such sins? Isn't that a contradiction? The normal Christian life can only be experienced when we have made a heart decision to invite Christ to be both our Savior and Lord. Anything apart from Acts 2:36 is abnormal Christianity!

I was teaching about breaking free from fear and worry when a woman in the group asked, "Isn't it natural to worry and be fearful when tribulations surface?" My response was, "Yes, fear and worry are pretty normal, but not for a Christian who has made Christ the manager of his life." In today's church circles, many think exactly like that woman. They consider worry and fear normal behavior—acceptable conduct for a Christian. Many pastors are of the same thinking, consequently never actually calling such behavior sin. Is it any wonder the Bible refers to this last age as the lukewarm church?

> Whatever is not from faith is sin.
>
> Romans 14:23

> Faith is the substance of things hoped for, the evidence of things not seen.
>
> Hebrews 11:1

Problem Solved

The same God who performed miracle after miracle in Egypt, once again, demonstrated His power at the Red Sea. Not only did He part the waters, He made the seabed bone-dry, enabling Israel to cross in ease (Exodus 14:16, 22). I think it is safe to say that the path through the sea was somewhat wider than the Disney Land replica. If two million Israelites, plus their animals, walked through the sea two abreast, it is estimated it would have taken them a month to make the crossing. Had that been the case,

Pharaoh's army surely would have overtaken them and dragged them back to the slave camps in Egypt. In order to make the crossing in one night, it is estimated the path must have been at least three miles wide.

When Pharaoh's army arrived at the western shore and saw Israel passing through the sea, the general of the army made a serious blunder. Today we would say, "He wasn't the sharpest knife in the drawer." First of all, he should have realized the power that parted the sea could also close the sea at any given moment. With full steam ahead, he went down into the seabed in hot pursuit. *All* the chariot wheels fell off at once. This should have been his second clue that something entirely supernatural was taking place. Seems to me almost anyone would have immediately high-tailed it back to shore (Exodus 14:25). Instead, the fool continued on, obviously with much difficulty. Once Israel reached the eastern shore, God closed the sea, leaving Egypt without an army, drowning every last one of them.

Having seen the sea parted and the Egyptian army destroyed, one would think Israel would never again doubt God's promises. Every time I teach this portion of Scripture, someone in the group says, "If I had witnessed such miracles, I'd never again have a problem with faith." Oh, that that would be the case! How quickly we forget. As soon as a new problem arises, it becomes our entire focus. We immediately forget all the good things that have gone before.

Once the sea closed, Israel could never return to Egypt. One of many, many beautiful pictures contained in the Scripture of the eternal security of believers. As we will see in more detail in future chapters, once we leave the kingdom of Satan behind, there is no going back. Once we abide in Christ, we possess a new citizenship, and that citizenship will never be revoked because of our bad conduct. In our stupidity, we may decide to live like the world, but once in the kingdom of Christ, always in the kingdom. Not only was the bondage of worldly Egypt behind them, the negative quality of life they experienced there was also meant to be left in the past. Now set free from their imprisonment, and *under the cloud,* the worry, fear, anger, and stress experienced in Egypt should have been history. In the same way, once we become a Christian, we are not only set free from the *penalty* of sin, but God also means for us to be set free from the *bondage* of sin. Through the indwelling power of the Holy Spirit, as believers, we have the built-in capacity to enjoy a brand new and vastly superior quality of life (Galatians 5:22-23).

Over the years, there have been many attempts to discredit the parting of the Red Sea. Historians agree with the Biblical account of the crossing and also that Israel eventually did set up camp in Canaan. Several historians bear out the fact that Israelites such as Joshua, David, and Solomon actually lived in the land of Canaan, which we know to be modern day Israel. What the skeptics dispute is *how* Israel crossed the sea. The critics claim the depth of the water was a scant few inches at the crossing point, enabling them to easily wade to the eastern shore. Like all criticism of Bible truths, this theory is full of holes. If two million Israelites waded across in shallow water, surely the Egyptian army could have done the same and forced Israel back to the slave camps. Either method of crossing speaks of a miracle. Parting of the sea was a miracle and drowning the Egyptian army in a few inches of water certainly would also have to be considered a miracle.

More Than Conquerors

When Israel reached the eastern shore and saw Egypt's army had been destroyed, they immediately threw a victory party (Exodus chapter 15). No longer boxed in, now standing on solid ground, suddenly their faith blossomed. Or did it? They were conquerors! In ancient days, when a conquering king returned home, it was customary for him to throw a party to celebrate the victory—a party after the fact. This is exactly how Israel behaved on the eastern shore—conquerors who walked by sight and celebrated after the fact. As we shall soon see, despite their victory party, faith-wise nothing had changed.

> In all these things we are more than conquerors through Him who loved us.
>
> Romans 8:37

In the above verse, the apostle Paul talks about a Christian being "more than a conqueror." It seems to me one who is more than a conqueror is so sure of victory that he is confidently able to celebrate before the fact. Of the two million people standing on the western shore, Moses was the only one who had been more than a conqueror. He experienced victory in his heart before seeing the sea parted and before Pharaoh's advancing army was defeated. Moses believed it was impossible for God to lie, and by faith, visualized Israel camped safely on the other shore.

Most Christians walk by sight. Their mood is dictated entirely by what they see. When life is going smoothly, peace prevails. However, when negatives surface, peace is replaced by the, oh so familiar: worry; fear; and anxiety. Once the negative is removed, they feel like conquerors and usually share their victory with everyone in sight, bragging about their peace until the next rough spot in the road appears.

A spiritual Christian functions differently. Like Moses, while still boxed in, by faith, he sees himself standing victoriously on the other side of the problem. He is able to hold his victory party before the fact—before he sees daylight at the end of the tunnel.

Perhaps you will agree that many in today's denominations are what one might call "yes, but…" Christians. In their minds, they know many Bible promises, which they are quick to quote to others. However, they rarely, if ever, put them in practice in their own lives. On a regular basis, I hear professing Christians say, "Yes, I know what the Bible says, but, if you had my problem…" Or "Yes, but, if you had my boss, my spouse, my parents," yadda, yadda, yadda. They make the mistake of thinking the world and troublesome people are the cause of their not having peace and joy. This thinking is a lie from the pit! If our peace is based upon people and circumstances lining up with our desires, we can expect to experience very little, if any, peace and joy. My heart's desire, and my goal in writing this book, is that Christians would grab on to this truth! I sincerely believe the Bible teaches we can be more than conquerors right here, right now, in the twenty-first century, in the midst of our tribulations! If that is your desire, please keep reading.

Had Israel shown faith in God's ability to get them across the Red Sea when they were standing on the eastern shore, it is entirely possible He would have led them directly to Canaan!

Rigged Fights

In Old Testament times, when nations were about to go to battle, occasionally each army would select their top warrior and send them to do battle with each other. The winner determined which nation was the victor. This way there would be only one life lost rather than hundreds, or perhaps even thousands, and the battle would be over in a single day, thus eliminating the need for spending huge amounts to support a long drawn out war. I know what this custom triggers in your mind! You're likely thinking this is what the United States should have done in the Middle

East. We should have sent Rambo to do battle against Saddam, saving many military lives and billions of dollars.

One of the most famous rigged fights in all Scripture was during the time Israel was challenged to do battle against the Philistines. Goliath was the Philistine's Rambo. He was ten feet tall and his coat of mail weighed 125 pounds! His spearhead weighed an amazing 15 pounds! When Goliath began to taunt Israel's army, every Israelite soldier must certainly have cowered in fear saying, "Not me, no way."

A shepherd lad by the name of David arrived on the scene and made a very bold announcement. He told King Saul that he could defeat the giant. Little David viewed the battle with Goliath as a rigged fight. Was David just being a cocky teenager? Or did he have an ace up his sleeve? He had an ace! If you remember the story, earlier on God promised David he would eventually be king of Israel, and young David was not yet seated on the throne. With that promise safely hidden in his heart, David knew it was impossible for him to be defeated in the battle with Goliath. He had also experienced God's protection in his previous battles both with a bear and a lion. The weapon David used on the battlefield was incidental, as he could have spit on Goliath and God would have been obligated to drown him. David's best weapon was not his sling, but his faith in God's promise. David is often portrayed in Sunday school departments as "Brave Little David," but a more appropriate title would be "Faithful Little David!"

As Christians, we should be able to view our Red Sea and Goliath challenges as rigged fights. As believers, our weapon of mass destruction is not our sharp tongue or our cunningness, but our belief in and acting upon the promises contained in the Word. As long as we remain *under the cloud* we can definitely view any battles that come our way as rigged fights. Instead of holding our victory parties after the fact, we should experience peace in our hearts continually, knowing that God is well able to overcome no matter what the problem. The most powerful force in the world is not a nuclear bomb or some mighty army, but the Word of God. Many Christians have this ready arsenal in their homes and at their disposal, but rarely, if ever, make use of it. Yet we wonder why we are so easily defeated, most days struggling and striving from morning to night.

Marah Test

Celebrating after the fact is never an indication a person's faith has been strengthened. Three short days after their victory party on the eastern shore, Israel was faced with another test. This test also involved water. This time there wasn't too much water; instead the water was undrinkable (Exodus 15:22-25). Self-preservation quickly surfaced, and once again, Israel was consumed with fear and anger. God solved the problem by sweetening the water. Israel breathed a sigh of relief and behaved like conquerors—once again celebrating after the fact!

Most Christians have no problem placing faith in Bible promises that pertain to future events. For example, they faithfully look forward to the Rapture, and the Millennium Reign where they expect Jesus to reign as their king. In fact, they look forward to having King Jesus rule over their lives for all eternity. They have no problem with that. The problem is trusting Him with their lives for the brief period of time they have here on planet earth. It seems very strange to me that most believers have faith to trust the Lord to manage their lives throughout eternity, yet cannot trust Him to manage their lives for mere nano seconds here on earth.

At a recent meeting, I asked people to raise their hands if they believed the following Bible promises. Their response was interesting:

Question: "Do you believe Christ is the only way to the Father?"

Response: All hands were raised!

Question: "Do you believe in the coming Rapture and the Millennial reign of Christ?"

Response: All hands shot up!

Question: "Do you believe you can trust the Lord to manage your life throughout eternity?"

Response: All hands were raised!

Question: "Do you believe in Christ's promise that we will experience tribulation while we are in this world?"

Response: A few amens were uttered, as all hands were raised!

Question: "Do you believe that right here and now, in the midst of your tribulations, you may experience peace and be more than a conqueror—viewing your battles as rigged fights?"

Response: Half the hands were slowly raised!

Question: "Do you believe Christ is the most capable person in the universe to manage your life?"

Response: Surprisingly, all hands went up!

Question: Naturally the final question was, "Then why won't you let Him do it?"

Response: Dead silence!

Stationary Cloud

Israel left Egypt with enough food to sustain them for the brief one month period it should have taken to reach Canaan. Because of their disobedience and lack of faith in His promises, God was forced to keep extending their time in the wilderness. Had God taken them directly to Canaan in such a weak spiritual condition, He knew they would have constantly been defeated by the challenges facing them in the Promised Land. Furthermore, they would have been a very negative testimony to any and all onlookers. As we will see in later chapters, time after time, their lack of faith held back good things from them! Because of disobedience, they wandered around the barren desert like spiritual paupers, living in sand infested tents, while their inheritance awaited them in the land of rest. In a sense, their lack of faith caused them to rob from themselves.

> Little by little I will drive them out from before you (the illegal squatters), until you have increased, and you inherit the land.
>
> Exodus 23:30

During the long wilderness phase of their journey, the cloud would occasionally remain stationary. Sometimes for a few days, a month, or even a year (Numbers 9:22-23). Human nature being what it is, during long layovers I can visualize some being reluctant to make the effort to pack up and move on when the cloud, once again, began to move. In the wilderness, their daily needs were supplied. The cloud provided shade during the daylight hours, the pillar of fire cast a warm glow over the entire camp during the chilly nights, and each morning their daily supply of manna miraculously appeared. During a long layover, dad may have added an addition to the tent or planted crops. Moving on not only required effort, but because of weight they may have accumulated, it would have meant leaving behind newly acquired possessions. Rather than moving forward, it is logical to assume some dug their heels in and chose to remain behind.

Once that decision was made, life would suddenly have become stressful. No longer *under the cloud*, they would be exposed to the scorching desert sun. Beyond that, finding food and water would require constant effort. With the departure of their road map, they would find themselves floundering like a rudderless boat in a sea of sand. In time, some may have thought, "Why did God abandon me, and why is life suddenly so stressful?" Surely the question should have been, "How could I have been so stupid?"

> He instructed them from the pillar of cloud; they observed His injunctions.
>
> Psalm 99:7 (MLB)

Moving On with the Lord

Moving on with the Lord demands change and often means leaving behind unnecessary weights. The book of Hebrews tells us to "Lay aside *every* weight" (Hebrews 12:1). Even in today's world, there is great freedom in traveling light. Ruth and I found this out the hard way a few years ago. We had set off on a year of extended travel across England and several others European countries. We began our journey with five suitcases of varying sizes, not all that much for a full year's travel. One day we were traveling by train in England from Penzance to Bath. When we settled into what we thought was our car, we heard an announcement saying the train would soon be splitting, with half the cars going to London and the other half to Bath. We discovered we were in the section going to London and our proper seats were five car lengths away. It was summer holiday time and school kids had the aisles crammed with various sorts of baggage, making it difficult to haul five heavy suitcases five cars forward. I came up with a great idea. Ruth would go forward to the proper car and secure our seats, while I'd remain with the suitcases. At the next stop I'd throw the baggage on the platform and haul them forward to our designated car. At the time, the idea seemed brilliant!

When the train stopped, I got off the train, only to discover it had begun raining. In England, trains don't stop for long and when I finally arrived at our car, soaking wet, the door had already closed. The train was about to move on. After pounding on the door for what seemed an eternity, someone saw this drenched fool on the platform with five suitcases and opened the door. Ruth's immediate question at my drenched condition was, "What happened to you?" I replied, "You're not going to believe it!" Had the train left me standing on the platform, Ruth would have continued the journey with no train ticket, neither did she have the name or address of the bed and breakfast we had reserved in Bath. Both were in my pocket. To add to the confusion, Ruth probably would have searched the train for me and likely come to the conclusion I had been raptured, along with all five suitcases! That was the very day we decided to unload a lot of unnecessary baggage. We continued our travels with one suitcase each. Traveling from that point on became a piece of cake!

It is the same in the spiritual world. Have you heard the expression, "He brings with him a lot of baggage?" We all began our journey with Christ carrying excess baggage accumulated in the old kingdom. I think it is safe to say a lot of that baggage is unseen. Doctor David Seamands, a Christian psychologist and writer, very aptly refers to these negatives as *damaged emotions*. In his epistles, Paul doesn't spend much time writing about the rather obvious sins—drunkenness, smoking, murder, cursing, etc. Instead, he devoted most of his writing to addressing the harmful more subtle sins—anger, imaginations, fear, worry, anxiety, and envy to name a few. Unfortunately, in many of today's church circles these weights are not even called sin but almost seem to be acceptable Christian behavior. When was the last time you heard a sermon labeling murder, spousal abuse, rape, smoking, drug addiction, or perhaps even drinking and dancing as sin? My guess would be—recently. On the other hand, when was the last time you heard a stirring sermon calling worry, fear, pride, and envy sin? Perhaps never. Once we truly believe all fleshly activity is not only sin but bondage and physically harmful, we should be more inclined to discard these harmful weights and position ourselves *under the cloud* of God's protection and direction. Only then can we begin to experience the freedom Jesus promised (John 8:32).

A habit learned can be unlearned!

If I agreed to run a race against the fastest runner in the world, who would you expect to win? It is doubtful the Las Vegas bookies would give me very good odds. However, if my opponent agreed to strap a 200-pound weight on his back, the odds would immediately shift in my favor. The apostle Paul compares our Christian journey to running a race. If we are to run a good race, and not become sidetracked or bogged down, we must discard many weights along the way, some of them observable, others deeply lodged within. We would be fools not to, don't you agree?

> Make straight paths for your feet, so that what is lame may not be dislocated, but rather be healed.
>
> Hebrews 12:13

Remaining *under the cloud* demands action on our part. It may mean discarding such fleshly activity as anger, envy, and a loose tongue. It will mean no longer viewing ourselves as the center of the universe. Remaining cloud-focused may mean walking away from a pablum ministry and searching for a place where solid spiritual food is taught. Clouds move; therefore, we must constantly guard against getting too comfortable at any point along our way. Rather than being a conqueror, and holding our victory party after the fact, we are meant to be more than conquerors—experiencing victory in our hearts even when boxed in. Remaining *under the cloud* is a life of excitement and freedom.

Shortly after becoming a believer, I mentioned to a woman in our church how excited I was about being a Christian. Initially, her response puzzled me, but now I understand where she was coming from. She said, "Enjoy it while you can, the bloom will soon fade and you will end up like the rest of us!" Somewhere along the way, her spiritual progress stalled. For whatever reason, she made a conscious decision to stop following the cloud. She had learned the church drill and performed to the congregation's expectations. However, her personal relationship with Christ was now both mechanical and unexciting. Instead, her relationship was with the programs and activity that took place within the religious building. The saddest thing of all is that she seemed to believe that was normal Christianity.

The Bible, thanks be to God, teaches something quite different! Christ's desire is to set us free from the ways of the old satanic kingdom—the world. This is an ongoing process which Scripture calls sanctification. Simply put, there should never be a time when we become complacent or peak out anywhere along the way. For a Christian who has invited Christ to manage his life, there are always new and exciting challenges around the bend. Most of us love to travel and experience new places, and the Christian life is meant to be just that—an exciting adventurous journey. The key word being journey! If we think and function the same today as we did a year ago, I can guarantee you, we have been dragging our feet and are no longer *under the cloud!*

> Since a promise remains of entering His rest, let us fear lest any of you seem to have come short of it... Since therefore it remains that some must enter it.
>
> Hebrews 4:1, 6

I think we all believe there will be a life of rest in heaven. However, the above verse speaks of a life of *rest* that is meant to be experienced right here on planet earth. Don't misunderstand. This rest the Bible speaks of is not necessarily a life of bliss and ease, but a rest that can be experienced in the midst of any and all storms and difficulties that come our way. It is a natural byproduct of living a Christ-centered life, sitting under solid Bible teaching and being obedient to what is taught. In other words—*doers* as James so clearly teaches.

Questions

- When faced with a Red Sea experience, do you hold your victory party before or after the fact?

- Do you view the negatives of life as opportunities to exercise faith in the promises contained in the Bible? Or do you walk by sight, displaying fear, anger, worry, and so on, at every negative turn in the road or whenever you feel boxed in?

- Do you respond like the majority when faced with a Red Sea situation? Or do you respond like the minority (Moses), visualizing yourself camped on the other side of the problem, more than a conqueror?

- Do you function as David did, visualizing life's battles as rigged fights?

- Do you think Jesus tells lies *or* do you place 100 percent faith in His promises?

- Do you find yourself living *under the cloud*, anticipating the next exciting event in your exodus with Christ, or have you slid into a somewhat comfortable rut?

CHRIST'S WILL

Little by little I will drive them out from before you, until you
have increased, and you inherit the land.

Exodus 23:30

God's intention was to set Israel free from their life of bondage. They were to spend approximately one month in the desert strengthening their faith. Once they learned to totally trust
in Him for deliverance and guidance, His plan was to then lead
them into Canaan where they were meant to claim their promised inheritance. Simply put, His desire was to get them *out* so
He could get them *in!*

Jesus also has a purpose for each Christian's life (Romans
8:28). His desire for believers today remains the same as in the
days of Moses. Once we place faith in what Christ accomplished
at Calvary and through His resurrection, His purpose for us is
to begin distancing ourselves from the ways of the old kingdom,
leaving behind that old life filled with worry, anger, fear, and
stress. Then, through a brief wilderness phase, build up our faith
to the point where we begin placing confidence in Christ's promises and view Him as the most qualified person in the universe to
manage our lives. Having reached that level of maturity, we are
then in the right spiritual condition to enter the land of rest—our
Canaan! In other words, His purpose is to get us *out* of bondage,

so He can then lead us *into* a life of freedom. Once we make that step of faith, we then, and only then, have full access to our inheritance. Anything short of making Christ Lord of our lives means experiencing an abnormal brand of Christianity. We can't have it both ways. We cannot live a self-managed life and then expect to experience the Christian life as it is described in our Bibles. When the Word describes the normal Christian life, it is with the assumption that we acknowledge Christ as both Savior and Lord (Acts 2:36). If we are not experiencing *rest* in our pilgrimage with Christ, our unrest is a result of living a self-focused rather than a Christ-focused life.

> There remains therefore a rest for the people of God.
>
> Hebrews 4:9

Wealthiest Person in the World

> In Him (Christ) we have obtained an inheritance.
>
> Ephesians 1:11

> Though He was rich, yet for your sakes He became poor, that you through His poverty might become rich.
>
> 2 Corinthians 8:9

I once asked a group who they thought was the wealthiest person in the world. Immediately, names such as Bill Gates and Warren Buffet were mentioned. When everything is stripped aside, I truly believe the wealthiest person in the world is the person who has received Christ as his Savior, and has learned to trust Him to manage his daily life while here on planet earth. Once that becomes a reality, we have legal access to a vast inheritance, a rest in the midst of our negatives, and freedom from the traps and snares of the old kingdom. If it were possible to package the

Christian life as it is defined in our Bibles, and place it for sale on store shelves, we'd become zillionaires overnight. Non-Christians spend large amounts of money, time, and effort searching for inner peace and contentment. Despite sincere efforts, their daily lives remain filled with various degrees of stress and anxiety. When they are being open and honest, they all agree the joy and peace gained from the world is temporal! With their focus on the "Three Ps"—position, power, and popularity—many nonbelievers give the impression they are experiencing a fulfilling life. Internally, it is a different story. Without knowing them personally, how can I say that? Because I was once in that camp! I was once one of them! Like the citizens of the world, I looked like I had it made but, internally, it was a different story.

Here's a hard pill for Christians to swallow: With the exception of their church affiliation, far too many Christians function similarly to nonbelievers. Suffering from a lack of solid Bible teaching and not being obedient to the little bits of the Word they do know, many find themselves struggling through their days, which are pretty much stress filled and unsatisfying. The pressures of the world and the daily stress of life dictate their moods. They behave as Israel did on the eastern shore of the Red Sea, experiencing peace and joy only when the negative is behind them, and continue to struggle with anger and fear, each time their flesh is challenged. Jesus promised we would be exposed to varying degrees of tribulation on a regular basis. If our peace and joy are conditional on pleasant happenings, they will be fleeting—temporal. Unless we have made Christ Lord of our lives, totally trusting in His promises, we may appear to have our act together in church, but in the real world we will function much as nonbelievers do—struggling endlessly with almost everything that comes down the pike.

Where there is a testament (will) there must also of necessity be the death of the testator. For a testament is in force after men are dead, since it has no power at all while the testator lives.

Hebrews 9:16-17

Many Christians are not aware that Jesus prepared a will, and as members of His family, we are the legal beneficiaries of that will. The New Testament is Christ's last Will and testament! I expect that is why it is called the New Testament!

Here's how a will actually works. A testator is one who owns the estate, prepares the will and names the beneficiaries. As long as the testator is alive, a will is of no use to the beneficiaries. It only becomes of value once the testator dies. Exciting news! Jesus is the testator of His Will, and approximately two thousand years ago He died, which means His Will is now in force. As legal members of His family, we Christians are free to spend our inheritance. How would we react if a lawyer called to inform us that a very wealthy relative had just died and left us a sizable inheritance? I expect, the first words out of our mouths would be, "When and where is the will being read?"

Except for a few isolated verses scattered throughout the New Testament, the majority of believers have not taken the time to read Christ's Will. As a result, they live like spiritual paupers, not aware they have access to a vast inheritance. Before moving on with Israel's exodus, let's pause and review some of the benefits of being a beneficiary of Christ's Will. Following are some of those benefits, perhaps you can add to the list:

His Power

Without Me you can do nothing.

John 15:5B

When a person becomes a Christian, the Holy Spirit takes up residence within his life. By drawing on this inner power, we can begin to experience the normal Christian life as it is defined in the Will (Galatians 5:22-23). Without this power, the best we can do is counterfeit the fruit of the Spirit, through the energy of our flesh. The problem is, when the pressures of life surface, the phony fruit will not remain. Instead of experiencing the promised peace and joy, we will find worry, fear, depression, and/or anger surfacing. Counterfeit fruit is of little benefit; it is undependable, never there when we need it.

Having our lives in the right spiritual condition, thus allowing the Holy Spirit to generate His fruit through us, is relatively simple. First, we must lay a solid spiritual foundation with a genuine salvation experience. Then, we must be exposed to solid Bible teaching regularly, and respond in obedience to the Word taught. In that condition, regardless of external pressures, spiritual fruit will flow from our lives and we will begin to enjoy the rest and freedom Jesus promised.

It is the Spirit that gives life; the flesh profits nothing.

John 6:63

His Word

The written Word is also a part of our inheritance. Until the author of the Word (the Holy Spirit) takes up residence in our lives, the Bible remains an uninspiring dead book. Prior to becoming a Christian, I made several attempts to read the Bible, but after a few chapters, I soon became bored and set it aside. After becoming a believer, the Bible suddenly came alive to me and, as Ezekiel puts it, the Word became honey to my lips (Ezekiel 3:3B). I began to discover the degree of peace, rest, and freedom

I experienced was directly related to the amount of time spent reading and digesting the Word. It is unfortunate that the only exposure many have to the Word is the few minutes of watered down teaching they receive each week from pablum preaching pulpits. The sad result (of this lack of feeding) soon becomes evident. Once they leave their place of worship and enter the real world, they find themselves functioning similarly to the citizens of the other kingdom, experiencing stress, a lack of freedom, and enjoying little or nothing of their spiritual inheritance.

> Give attention to my words; incline your ear to my sayings. Do not let them depart from your eyes; keep them in the midst of your heart; for they are life to those who find them, and health to all their flesh.
>
> Proverbs 4:20-22

The Word of Christ is the most powerful force in the world. For example, our vast universe was not formed by some Big Bang accident, but by the spoken Word of Christ. "He spoke and it was done" (Psalm 33:6, 9). Jesus visualized planet earth and spoke it into existence. Man does not have the ability to create. We can only invent from things previously created by Jesus. The elements of electricity were always there. Man simply harnessed them. Yes, man invented the wheel, but the basic elements had been previously created. The Word had the power to boot Satan, along with one-third of the angels, out of heaven. As we will see in a later chapter, it was Christ's Word that brought the walls of Jericho down and its inhabitants to their knees. If we truly understood the power of the Word, we'd likely be inclined to spend more time reading our success manual. Yes, Jesus and the Word are one and the same. If we neglect the Word, we are neglecting our relationship with Him. Show me a person who neglects the

Word and I'll show you a person whose relationship with Christ is impersonal and mechanical.

> The Word became flesh and dwelt among us.
>
> John 1:14

His Name

Another aspect of our inheritance is His name! In the early New Testament church age, because the disciple's daily walk resembled the *way* Christ walked, they were initially referred to as, "The Way." Later on, a more appropriate name was coined, and the followers of Christ became known as Christians (Acts 11:26). The *ian* at the end of the name means a follower of the name that precedes the suffix. For example, a disciple of Herod would be called an Herod*ian*. When we say we are a Christ*ian*, we are making a public statement that we are a disciple of Christ, and that the desire of our heart is to walk the talk. "I will declare Your name to My brethren" (Hebrews 2:12).

Today, the name Christian is a title that is loosely tossed about. A street survey was conducted to see what percentage of people viewed themselves as Christians and the results were amazing! Can you believe over 80 percent of those interviewed claimed to be Christian? Jesus disagrees with that percentage, as He said only a few would become believers at any point in history (Matthew 7:13-14). I don't know what percentage a few is, but it certainly suggests a figure much lower than 80 percent!

People profess Christianity for various reasons. Since they are not a Muslim, a Hindu, or a member of some cult, they assume they must be Christians. Others claim they are Christians because they were born in a Christian country, or raised in a church-going family. Many think they are Christians because they walk into a religious building on a regular basis and perform certain denominational rituals within that building. One day I noticed a new couple in our church and asked one of the elders if they were Christians. He replied, "Certainly." When I asked him how he had come to that conclusion, he said, "Well, for the past three Sundays they have been attending church—carrying a Bible." I was immediately reminded of the slightly worn saying, "Spending time in a garage doesn't make one a car!"

How many times do you think the word Christian appears in the Bible? One would think the title would appear on every page of the New Testament, but that is not the case. The name only appears three times in the entire Bible, and it is interesting that each time it is associated with witnessing. The author of the Bible does not casually toss about the word *Christian*, as does today's society.

His Wedding

Another aspect of our inheritance is a reserved seat at the number one wedding in the entire universe—the marriage supper of the Lamb. Several years back, Ruth and I were given reserved seats for the Super Bowl. Having grown up in Canada, we are not dyed-in-the-wool football fans. However, since the tickets were free, we decided to attend the game. As you can imagine, many of our friends, who were avid football fans, envied our reserved seats. As Christians, we have seats reserved at a far more impressive function than the Super Bowl—the Wedding Feast of the Lamb. I can tell you that we are far more excited to possess those reserved seats. That guest list is made up of all whose names have been preserved (sealed) in the Lamb's Book of Life.

When we attend an earthly wedding we are usually expected to arrive in our finest attire. The acceptable dress code at the heavenly wedding will not be *our* finest, but the finest attire in the universe, the *righteousness* of Jesus Christ. Jimmy Buffett recorded a song called, "There is a Party at the End of the World." There truly is going to be a party at the end of this church age, quite different from the one Jimmy sings about, however. As Christians, we have a reserved seat. Our names have been preserved in the heavenly guest list!

> The marriage of the Lamb has come, and His wife has made herself ready... Blessed are those who are called to the marriage supper of the Lamb.
>
> Revelation 19:7, 9

In the twenty-fifth chapter of Matthew, as He so often does, Jesus used a parable to illustrate the requirements for attending the heavenly wedding feast. In Christ's day, the customs at Jewish weddings were quite different. When the groom made the announcement of his plans to marry, he did not state the exact day or hour the wedding would take place. Part of the custom was to hold the wedding feast at night. When the wedding hour approached, trumpeters would precede the groom into the darkened streets calling the guests to the wedding. Prior to the wedding day, certain maidens were chosen to be lamp bearers. When the trumpets sounded, it was their responsibility to enter the street with lighted lamps to illuminate the way to the groom's home. Since the maidens did not know the exact day the wedding took place, it was vital they have their lamps filled with oil in advance—fully prepared for the sound of the trumpet. Those who joined the procession unprepared, with no oil in their lamps, were not allowed to attend the wedding feast.

In this parable, ten maidens were selected to be lamp bearers. Five were wise, for their lamps were filled and they eagerly awaited the sound of the trumpets. The other five were very unwise! Out of neglect, procrastination, or just plain stubbornness, they failed to fill their lamps, arriving at the groom's home with empty lamps, only to be left standing outside the gate.

> The Lord Himself will descend from heaven with a shout, with the voice of an archangel, and with the trumpet of God. And the dead in Christ will rise first. Then we who are alive and remain shall be caught up together with them in the clouds to meet the Lord in the air. And thus we shall always be with the Lord.
>
> 1 Thessalonians 4:16-17

The spiritual lesson to be gained from this wedding parable is obvious. In Scripture, oil is always symbolic of the Holy Spirit. When the trump of God is sounded, the church age will come to a close, and all believers will unite with Christ in the air. Then, the church (the bride) will be escorted by Jesus to the heavenly wedding feast. This calling out of the church is commonly referred to as the Rapture! The qualification for attending the marriage supper of the Lamb is arriving at the pearly gates in the proper spiritual condition—Oil in our vessels. If one arrives unprepared, as did the five foolish maidens, he or she will be barred from attending. How sad to be standing at heaven's gate with a heart that hasn't been previously illuminated by the Holy Spirit. Paul wrote that it is possible to believe in God, yet have a spiritually darkened heart (Romans 1:21).

This parable raises an obvious question. Has your heart been illuminated by the Spirit of God, or is the Holy Spirit still a force outside your life? If you arrived at heaven's gate today, would you be invited in with open arms, or barred from the wedding? Only you can answer that question. My heart's desire for you, dear reader, is that your answer is a resounding "Yes."

> Do you not know that you are the temple of God and that the Spirit of God dwells in you.
>
> 1 Corinthians 3:16

His Image

He made Him who knew no sin to be sin for us, that we might become the righteousness of God in Him.

2 Corinthians 5:21

He is our profit, that we may be partakers of His holiness.

Hebrews 12:10

As Christians, we are meant to take on Christ's image. Christ arrived on earth in the image of God (Colossians 1:15). The word image stems from the Greek word *elkon*. Our English word "portrait" comes from the same root word. Jesus reminded us of this truth when He said, "He who has seen Me has seen the Father" (John 14:9). Jesus was the *elkon* of God. As someone once said, "Jesus was the best photograph God ever had taken."

In his epistle to the Corinthians, Paul referred to Christ as the "last Adam" (1 Corinthians 15:45). To label Jesus as the second Adam would have implied there would be other Adams. Jesus was definitely the last Adam! In the Garden of Eden, prior to the Fall, Adam was the first to arrive on earth bearing the "image of God" (Genesis 1:27), and Christ was the second and last to arrive on earth bearing that image. While the first Adam was the originator of *physical* life (the father of mankind), the last Adam is the originator of *spiritual* life.

When Adam stumbled, his image was severely tarnished. Because of sin, the Spirit of God withdrew His presence and Adam was forced to lean unto his own understanding for direction and wisdom. In other words, his life became fleshly generated, rather than God directed. The results of his fall were far reaching, for his fallen condition was passed on to all future generations. Instead of being born in the image of God, all who stemmed from Adam were born in his image—possessing his fallen genes (1 Corinthians 15:49a). This is how King David perceived it: "I was brought forth in iniquity, and in sin my mother conceived me" (Psalm 51:5).

In His mercy and love, God provided a way for fallen man to be rescued from this condition. When we place faith in Christ's sacrifice at Calvary, and His resurrection, we are not only translated from the dark kingdom to the kingdom of Christ, but in God's eyes we are viewed as holy and blameless—possessing the image of the last Adam (Colossians 1:22).

The purpose of what is termed "the sanctification process," is to lead us back to the pre-Fall quality of life, where we are able to display dominion, freedom, and spiritual fruit. As Christians, we call the shot. We determine the degree of that spiritual life we experience. Unfortunately, many of God's children function as if they were still abiding in fallen Adam, struggling daily with fear, worry, anxiety, anger, and depression.

Big Swap

The Lord loves justice, and does not forsake His saints; they are preserved forever.

Psalm 37:28

Another benefit of our Christian inheritance is that we have been preserved. The word *preserve* brings back memories of the days when my grandmother preserved fruit. Believe it or not, there was actually a time before cans! In order to remove all impurities from the jars she would sterilize them. Once the fruit was placed in sterilized jars, she would seal the jars to ensure the fruit remained safe from outside impurities. When she sent me to the basement, instead of telling me to get some peaches or strawberries, she would actually say, "Jackie, go get a jar of preserves."

I love to point out what I call the "Big Swap" verse, which takes place the instant we make a conscious decision to become a Christian. Our impurities (sins) are imputed to Christ's account, and His righteousness is imputed to our account (2 Corinthians 5.21). Once that exchange takes place, our status in Christ remains sealed; we can never again be contaminated with sin. We remain forever preserved in the kingdom of Christ. From Christ's perspective, we have been 100 percent sterilized—clothed in His righteousness and fit for the wedding feast! Hallelujah!

> In Him you also trusted after you heard the word of truth, the gospel of your salvation; in whom also, having believed, you were sealed with the Holy Spirit of promise, who is the guarantee of our inheritance until the redemption of the purchased possession.
>
> Ephesians 1:13-14

"Until" is a temporal word. As Christians, our name remains permanently sealed in the Lamb's Book of Life until... *Until* becomes a reality when the fifth chapter of Revelation takes place shortly after the Rapture. At that time, Christ will rise from His current seated position in heaven, step forward, and break the seals on the Lamb's Book. At that precise moment, the Book will be opened, and the names of the redeemed will be confirmed. The Lamb's Book is not only God's census book, listing His citizens, it is also the guest list for the wedding feast. Until this event takes place, similar to grandmother's preserved fruit, our names, not only remain sealed, but we are preserved from outside contamination. Once saved, always saved! I think another wonderfully appropriate name for believers would be *the preserved!*

Do you know that Jesus even used the occasion of the Last Supper to teach a lesson on eternal security? In Christ's day it was customary for Jews to drink wine to toast special occasions, the wedding at Cana being an example of this custom. At the Last

Supper, Jesus drank wine to toast a special event that would soon be taking place—Calvary. He then announced, "I will not drink of this fruit of the vine from now on until that day when I drink it new with you in my Father's kingdom" (Matthew 26:29).

This is one of those verses that is easily passed over, missing entirely the importance of what is actually promised here. I hope by now you are seeing that the Bible contains many exciting promises. This particular promise, it seems to me, has to be very near the top of the list. It seems clear that Jesus was saying He would not drink wine with them again *until* it was time to toast another special occasion, which would be at the heavenly wedding feast, when He toasted His bride. I don't know if the disciples picked up on what Jesus was actually saying, but that announcement should have made their hearts leap for joy. Reading between the lines, Jesus was saying, regardless of their future earthly conduct, each of the eleven disciples would be attending the wedding feast. I find it very interesting that Jesus made this promise knowing Peter was about to stumble big time! For those who believe a big sin can nullify one's salvation, Peter's denying and cursing the Lord to His face, would seem to fit that bill, certainly a major sin by anybody's earthly standard. When Jesus made this promise, He was making it pretty clear a believer's earthly conduct could never cause them to lose their seat at the wedding feast. Yet another way of saying, once saved, always saved! Once preserved, always preserved! Once in the kingdom, always in the kingdom! When Peter stumbled, he certainly experienced a temporal loss of fellowship with Christ, but his stumble did not terminate his position in Christ's kingdom. Had Peter died the instant he denied and cursed Christ, his name would still remain preserved in the Lamb's Book.

The righteous will never be removed.

Proverbs 10:30

Regardless of a believer's conduct, his name will never be blotted out of the Lamb's Book of Life. On the other hand, when we see people who profess to be Christians committing sin habitually, I think it is very likely that they are what I call "head knowledge believers," still possessing a spiritually darkened heart!

> Those who trust in the Lord are like Mount Zion, which cannot be moved, but abides forever.
>
> Psalm 125:1

White Stone

> I will give him a white stone, and on the stone a new name written which no one knows except him who receives it.
>
> Revelation 2:17

There is yet another aspect of our inheritance—one that is not so well known. When we become Christians, Biblically speaking, we are seen as one who possesses a white stone. To understand the symbolism behind this term, we must know how the court system functioned in the days of the apostle John, the writer of the book of Revelation. When a person was accused of a crime, and found guilty, the judge declared his guilt by presenting him with a black stone. If the accused was found innocent, the judge presented him with a white stone. Just as it is today, there was no double jeopardy in the court system of John's day. Once the accused was declared innocent of a particular crime, and presented with a white stone, he could never again be charged for that same offense. The judge could never retract his stone and replace it with a black one.

Here we have yet another illustration of a truth so many Christian's still struggle with today. Possessing that white stone is another way of saying we are eternally secure in the kingdom of Christ. Here is how it works. When we become a Christian, our offenses against God are imputed (charged) to Christ's account, and our heavenly judge confirms our innocence by presenting us with a symbolic white stone. In God's courtroom there is also no double jeopardy. Since we are no longer under the judgmental law, it is impossible for God to remove the righteousness inherited from Christ and replace it with Adam's fallen nature. Once presented with a white stone, always possessing a white stone. Once under the redeeming blood of Christ, always under the blood! Once free of condemnation, always free! Good news? You bet!

> There is therefore now no condemnation to those who are in Christ Jesus.
>
> Romans 8:1

> Sin is not imputed when there is no law.
>
> Romans 5:13B

> The law is not made for a righteous person (Christian), but for the lawless and insubordinate, for the ungodly and for sinners…
>
> 1 Timothy 1:9

Lamb's Book of Life

A major part of our inheritance as a believer is knowing, with assurance, that our name is permanently etched in the Lamb's Book of Life. Contrary to what many believe, a person's name is not recorded in the heavenly census when he becomes a believer. If God knows our every hair, He obviously would not usher us into this planet without having first made a detailed record of our existence—some means of identification. That record is the Lamb's Book. Before Adam set foot on planet earth, the names of every person who would be born into this world were inscribed in that heavenly ledger (Revelation 17:8).

As the familiar old hymn states, there will come a time when "the roll is called up yonder." If a person arrives at heaven's gate having rejected God's provision for salvation (no oil in his lamp), he will discover a blank space where his name was once recorded. It will be as if the delete key on the heavenly computer had been hit, erasing the entire record of his existence. What a shock it would be to arrive at heaven's gate, only to find a blank space where one's name had once been recorded! As a person's name is blotted out of God's census ledger, his name will be transferred, I believe, to another permanent census ledger—Satan's!

> He who overcomes shall be clothed in white garments and I will not blot out his name from the Book of Life.
>
> Revelation 3:5

> There shall by no means enter it (heaven) anything that defiles, or causes an abomination or a lie, but only those who are written in the Lamb's Book of Life.
>
> Revelation 21:27

This blotting out is not a New Testament truth. The Old Testament saints were also aware that there would come a time when the names of nonbelievers would be blotted out of the Lamb's Book.

> Let them be blotted out of the book of life, and not be recorded with the righteous.
>
> Psalm 69:28 (MLB)

You have destroyed the wicked. You have blotted out their
name forever and ever.

Psalm 9:5

At that great day of reckoning, we will find ourselves in one of
two permanent categories. Either our name will have been blotted
out of the Lamb's Book of Life, or our sins will have been blotted
out by the blood of Christ. There will be no middle ground! The
decision we make on earth concerning God's provision for our sin
determines in which camp we will spend eternity. If we discover a
blank space where our name was once recorded, there will be no
room for appeals or retrials. Our arrival condition remains *fixed*
for a very long time. Eternity is a long time! The key to spending
eternity with our Creator is to exit this earth in the right spiritual condition, with Oil in our lamp and in possession of a white
stone! You may prefer another method, but I am here to tell you
that this is the only way to the Father, and the Bible is filled with
a multitude of Scriptures testifying to this all important truth.
After all, He is God and He can choose any method He wishes.
His is the choice and we are called to comply. This may sound
a little harsh, which, of course, our God is not, still in a sense it
is His way or the highway! Perhaps, in this case a better phrase
would be the low way.

New Covenant

Still another wonderful part of our Christian inheritance is the
fact that we are no longer trapped under the law based Old
Testament covenant. We have been set free under the grace based
New Testament covenant.

Today, the word covenant is not a familiar term. It has pretty
much been replaced by either the word contract or agreement.

A covenant is simply a legal contract between two parties. For instance, a marriage certificate or mortgage contract is a covenant. Under the rules of a covenant, if one of the parties dishonors the contract, the other party is entitled to take negative action. Those who have been involved in a divorce have likely experienced the negative consequences of violating their marriage covenant. When several months go by without paying a mortgage or car payment, the door has been opened for negative action from the other party.

In the Old Testament, God made a covenant that involved two parties—Himself and Israel. As long as Israel was obedient to His Word, the blessings from heaven flowed. The Old Testament covenant had a built-in flaw. It was law-based which constantly exposed Israel's sin. In other words, the covenant was based on Israel's performance. Because of the weakness of the Old Testament covenant, God promised there would come a time when the old covenant would be replaced by a new and superior covenant. One that would not be based upon man's conduct, but upon the conduct of two heavenly parties—God and Christ.

> The days are coming, says the Lord, when I will make a new covenant with the house of Israel and with the house of Judah—not according to the covenant that I made with their fathers in the day that I took them by the hand to lead them out of the land of Egypt. My covenant which they broke, though I was a husband to them, says the Lord. But this is the covenant that I will make with the house of Israel after those days, says the Lord: I will put My law in their minds, and write it on their hearts... For I will forgive their iniquity, and their sin I will remember no more.
>
> Jeremiah 31:31-34

The new covenant is not law-based, but blood-based. Since God and Jesus are the two parties involved in the new covenant, based upon the authority of the Word, I can assure you, neither party will mar or dishonor the new covenant. During His earthly ministry, Jesus fulfilled the law of Moses and He will continue to do the same throughout eternity. As believers, we are no longer under the Old Testament law-based covenant, but under the New Testament grace-based covenant. Since a Christian is no longer under the judgmental law, his earthly conduct can never negate the new covenant. In other words, once presented with a white stone, always possessing a white stone! A believer's conduct can never cause his white stone to turn black. Once in the club, we are always in the club, for our membership fee has been paid up throughout eternity by the blood of the Lord Jesus Christ.

Today, both the old and new covenant remain in force. Nonbelievers are under the Old Testament law-based covenant, which leaves their sins exposed and places them under judgment. The purpose of the law of Moses was simply to expose a sinner's status and hopefully steer him to the Passover lamb sacrifice which, of course, pointed to the true Lamb of God, the Lord Jesus Christ. Those who placed faith in God's provision for their sins had their sin status imputed to Christ's account and come under the New Testament blood-based covenant.

Isn't it comforting to know we cannot lose our position in the kingdom of Christ because of bad behavior? If our negative conduct could alter our spiritual status, I think all would agree, none of us would make it to glory, as each day we all sin to some degree—either in thought or in deed. It is vitally important to understand how God views sin, which by the way, is completely different from the way the world views sin. With Him, the degree of sin is not the issue. From His perspective, there are not big sinners and little sinners. Just sinners!

> Whoever shall keep the whole law, and yet stumble in one point, he is guilty of all.
>
> James 2:10

A person who lands at the pearly gate with just a tiny lie recorded on his rap sheet will be judged as if he were in the same fallen condition as a murderer (Revelation 21:8, 21:27). Both will be labeled sinners. Both will find their names blotted out of the Lamb's Book. Both will spend eternity in the sinner's camp. For you see, God views sin as a condition not as an individual act. We humans are the ones who have categorized sin, or perhaps it was our adversary the devil! I can offer no proof, but I can't help but wonder if this is where the old expression, "We are all tarred with the same brush," comes from. The Scripture puts it another way. "A little leaven leavens the whole lump" (1 Corinthians 5:6b).

Here is a valid question. If a Christian is no longer under the law of Moses, how does he know how to function? What is his guideline? Doesn't a believer need a set of rules to tell him how to live? Over the years I've had people say, "Being no longer under the law sounds great, but doesn't that thinking give a Christian the license to sin big time?" This may be true in the case of a self-centered carnal Christian, but a spiritual believer will not function that way. The indwelling Holy Spirit has several ministries, and one of His ministries is to write His desires upon the hearts of believers.

> I will put My laws in their mind and write them on their hearts.
>
> Hebrews 8:10b

> Your law is within my heart.
>
> Psalm 40:8b

A sincerely committed Christian does not need rules etched on tablets of stone to tell him how to function. The Holy Spirit will dictate His desires to the fleshly tablets of his heart. He will find himself beginning to satisfy the law of Moses, but not in a strug-

gling and legalistic manner. Because of his intimate relationship with Christ, he will find his desire is actually to do what
is right. Prior to becoming a Christian, I lied, swore, and slan-
dered, among other things. Shocked? I bet, if you are willing to
be honest, you did too. Such activity was simply a way of life. As
I embarked on this new journey called Christianity, I soon found
my life style began to change. For instance, when I was about to
tell a lie or about to take the Lord's name in vain, an inner voice
seemed to be saying, "Improper conduct for a Christian." No, I
have never heard an audible voice, but somehow there are those
very strong instincts that lead in a new and better direction. If
you are a believer, surely you have heard that same inner voice.
No doubt about it, that is the voice of the Holy Spirit who wants
to guide us into all things new and better, *not*, I hasten to add, for
His benefit but for *ours*.

> Do we then make void the law through faith? Certainly not!
> On the contrary, we establish the law.
>
> Romans 3:31

Being set free of the law, yet satisfying the law, is confusing to
a legalist. His daily walk is dictated either by adhering to a list
of rules or attempting to satisfy the desires of others. As long
as a believer remains law-focused, his spiritual maturing will be
restricted. Mostly what happens is that he becomes judgmental
of those who fail to abide by his list of dos and don'ts. He may
attend a church where he learns the denominational rules, but his
relationship to Christ will be mechanical and distant. I guarantee
you he lives with a lot of self-imposed guilt and frustration, as he
will constantly find himself falling short of his own self-imposed
rules. It is for these very reasons the apostle Paul pleads with
Christians to break free of the bondage of the Old Testament
law-based covenant.

> Stand fast therefore in the liberty by which Christ has made
> us free, and do not be entangled again with a yoke of bondage.
>
> Galatians 5:1

In our early days as Christians, Ruth and I attended a church that had a long list of dos and don'ts. I searched for the actual list, but could never find it. Yet the list was definitely in force. For instance, the don't list frowned on women wearing pants to church on Sunday, but it was okay to wear pants to Wednesday night prayer meeting. In other words, the rule said God approved of pants, but only on certain days of the week! Puzzling! The same imaginary list frowned on dancing, but roller skating together to music at church-sponsored functions was definitely okay. More puzzling! Women wearing lipstick and heavy makeup, especially those in the choir, was on the don't list. Going to a movie was also on the don't list, but somehow it seemed permissible to watch the same movie at home on television. Still more puzzling! Furthermore, worry, fear, anger, envy, pride, slandering, gossiping, being judgmental, and depression were not on anyone's list. Such conduct seemed to be widely accepted and viewed as rather normal behavior.

I have listed above a few of the many positive benefits available to a beneficiary of Christ's will. In order to keep focused on our legal rights, it is imperative we read His Will on a regular basis. Rather than living like Cheese and Cracker Christians, we should to be enjoying our full inheritance!

Cheese and Cracker Christians

There was an Irishman who always dreamed of moving to America. After scrimping for many years, he finally saved enough money for the boat fare. After purchasing his ticket, he only had a few dollars left. Realizing he was facing a five-day voyage, he spent his remaining money on a supply of cheese and crackers. For the next four days at sea, he ate his meals in his cabin, existing on his boring diet of cheese and crackers. On the final day of the voyage, he saw a steward carrying a delicious tray of food and asked him what that tray of food would cost? The steward replied, "Nothing, all meals are included in the price of the ticket!" How sad to have missed out on what had been previously paid for and rightfully his.

I fear that today's pews are overflowing with cheese and cracker Christians. Week after week they sit looking externally presentable, but internally, they are in a state of spiritual poverty. It's as if they had a million dollars in the local bank, at the same time continuing to live as paupers. They hear or read about a different quality of spiritual life, but for various reasons, much of that Christian life remains beyond their reach. Jesus paid a huge price to redeem us and to provide us with a limitless inheritance, and it is His desire that we spend it!

It was God's desire to get Israel *out of* Egypt, build their faith during the brief wilderness trek, and then lead them *into* the land of promise where they could begin to enjoy their inheritance. Christ's desire remains the same for each of His children today.

Questions

- If you were to arrive at heaven's gate today, which covenant would you be under—the old or the new?

- Would you arrive having your sins blotted out, or your name blotted out of the Lamb's Book of Life?

- If the Rapture of the saints took place today, would you be in the right spiritual condition to attend the wedding feast, or would you arrive at heaven's gate without Oil in your lamp?

THE ROCK

In the Red Sea chapter, we left Israel standing safely on the eastern shore of the Red Sea, waiting to begin their trek across the desert to Canaan. In this chapter, we find them in the early days of that journey.

In Exodus chapter seventeen, Israel's faith was once again tested by water. This time, it wasn't that there was too much water, or that the water was bitter, there simply was no water. Self-preservation resurfaced, and once again, we find Israel going around the same lack of faith mountain. In their anger, an emergency board meeting was held, and Israel decided the first thing to do was get rid of Moses (v. 17:1-4). They began to think they probably never should have left Egypt. In Egypt they were never confronted with such difficult hardships. Life there was limited, certainly, but also very predictable and uncomplicated. When they were told to jump they were expected to respond, "How high, sir?" Do you see a pattern surfacing? God promised to lead them safely to the Promised Land, but he did not promise the journey would be without difficulties. He simply said, "Remain faithful and *under the cloud,* and you will arrive safely in Canaan." Sadly, Israel continued in their disobedience and lack of faith, thus prolonging their time in the barren wilderness. Until they shifted from sight walking to faith walking, they continued to rob themselves of the freedom, rest, and inheritance that awaited them in Canaan. Cheese and cracker believers!

In this lukewarm church age, many of God's children are functioning in much the same manner. Every time a dark cloud approaches, self-preservation surfaces along with fear, worry, and anxiety. Israel constantly failed to put into motion my Three-Step Program. In this lack of water situation, Israel could bypass Step 1, as there was nothing they could do to rectify the problem. Finding sufficient water in the desert to satisfy the needs of two million people was humanly impossible. Instead of whining and complaining, they should have implemented Step 2 by ensuring they were *under the cloud* and trusting in the Lord's ability to deal with this particular problem as well. Only then would Step 3 have become a reality in their hearts.

God instructed Moses to strike a nearby rock with his staff, out of which flowed more than enough water to quench the thirst of the entire nation, as well as their animals. When I first read this story, somehow I visualized a trickle of water flowing from the rock, but this surely was not the case. A trickle would not have quenched the thirst of two million Israelites!

> He opened the rock, and water gushed out; It ran in the dry places like a river.
>
> Psalm 105:41

> They drank of that spiritual Rock that followed them, and that Rock was Christ.
>
> 1 Corinthians 10:4

What an unusual statement! What could it mean? How could that rock be Jesus? Just as the communion wine is symbolic of the shed blood of Christ, the striking of the rock pictured the blow Jesus would receive at Calvary. The bruising of His heel, which took place at the cross (Genesis 3:15). The blow to Christ's heel was painful, but not fatal, as three days later He fully recovered. Out of that sacrifice flowed life. Life available to all those who would believe.

> Looking unto Jesus, the author and finisher of our faith, who for the joy that was set before Him endured the cross, despising the shame.
>
> Hebrews 12:2

This verse does not say Jesus counted it joy to endure the *pain* of Calvary, but the *shame*. Crucifixion is an excruciating way to die, but the physical agony Christ experienced paled in comparison to the spiritual shame and separation He experienced. We know God cannot abide in the presence of sin. When the sins of the entire world were imputed to Christ's account, for a three-day period, God was forced to turn His back on His beloved Son. During that time, because of the sins He bore, He remained separated from the other two members of the Trinity. After Christ was resurrected, and His blood sprinkled on the heavenly mercy seat, the Trinity was once again united. With our human understanding, it is difficult to comprehend all that transpired at that time, as well as the shame Jesus experienced when He was separated from the Father. The best insight we get is when we read His lonely cry from Golgotha—"My God, My God, why have You forsaken Me?" (Mark 15:34).

> He has borne our griefs and carried our sorrows; yet we esteemed Him stricken, smitten by God and afflicted. But He was wounded for our transgressions. He was bruised for our iniquities... He was led as a lamb to the slaughter... He bore the sin of many, and made intercession for the transgressors.
>
> Isaiah 53:4-5, 7, 12

Spiritual Thirst

The water that flowed from the rock was also symbolic. It pictured the life of Christ that flowed from Calvary—His blood. Just as the flow of water from the wilderness Rock was sufficient to quench the physical thirst of all Israel, the shed blood from Calvary is sufficient to quench the spiritual thirst of every resident of this planet. As foolish as it may sound, there was a requirement necessary for Israel to drink from that desert rock. They had to have a physical thirst! Because of the desert heat, it would be logical to assume every Israelite immediately headed for the stream that flowed from the Rock. There is also a requirement to have one's spiritual thirst quenched. There must be an inner thirst. A longing for a different quality of life. When it comes to the world having their inner thirst quenched, that is not the case. Jesus said that at any time in history only a *few* would come to Him (Matthew 7:14). Just as the rock's water kept Israel physically alive, the shed blood of Christ provides us with spiritual life. "In Him was life..." (John 1:4).

> If anyone thirsts, let him come to Me and drink.
>
> John 7:37B

Today, the vast majority, in various ways, looks to the world to have their inner thirst quenched. Many rely on expensive toys and assets to satisfy their inner emptiness. Others attempt to satisfy their unrest by taking an exotic vacation or by relocating to another part of the world—a geographical fix. Ruth and I recently spent ten years living in Mexico. During our time there, we saw many northerners relocate to Mexico for that very reason. For a period of time, they found their Mexican surroundings exciting and stimulating, but soon the novelty wore off and the discontentment they had experienced on the other side of the border returned. Others turn to religion and cults searching for inner peace, but eventually their unrest and emptiness returns as well. Many attempt to keep themselves distracted by keeping their calendars filled—rushing from one event to the next—never allowing time to reflect on the discontent in their lives. I know of Christians who are also caught in this same trap.

After bunting my head against this stress filled world for thirty-three years, I finally came to the conclusion that the toys, vacations, and relocations only provide temporal relief from the drudgery and stress of this world. Once the new toy became a few months old, and the vacation pictures were put away, discontent returned. When I first heard the gospel clearly presented, I was quick to make the most important decision of my life. Once I believed Christ was the most qualified person in the universe to manage my life, I had no hesitation in making the decision to invite Him into my life, as well as, offering Him the management position. As I began to grow, and mature spiritually, the stress and anxiety I had been experiencing began to subside, and despite external negative happenings, an inner peace and joy began to flow from my life. When I became a Christian, I made the only geographical fix that makes sense. Not a physical move, but a spiritual move. I was immediately translated from Satan's kingdom to the kingdom of Christ. From the kingdom of darkness to the kingdom of Light.

> He has delivered us from the power of darkness and conveyed us into the kingdom of the Son of His love.
>
> Colossians 1:13

> He who believes in Me, as the Scripture has said, out of his heart will flow rivers of living water.
>
> John 7:38

When Jesus saw the Samaritan woman approaching the well, He knew her story. He was aware that behind her external mask was a troubled and empty person who had been living a life of stress, drudgery, and guilt. Having been married five times, she no doubt carried a lot of negative baggage, and now that she was living common-law, she was filled with guilt (John 4:18). In order to avoid the snide remarks of the village women, it seems she chose to visit the well at the hottest hour of day (John 4:6).

The woman wasn't dumb. When Jesus told her the well water would only provide her with temporary relief, she understood He was using the well water as an object lesson. The phrase "living water" would have made a definite statement to her, as living water meant a flowing stream or river (John 4:10). In that region of Samaria, there were no streams or rivers, and the only source of water was that very well. Because of His insight into her past, and the love He radiated, she became convinced she was standing eye to eye with the long awaited Messiah. Face to face with Christ she became a believer, receiving the living water He was offering (John 4:15). In her excitement she did a very natural thing. She returned to her village eager to tell others of her encounter with Jesus. Because of her testimony many of the villagers also became believers (John 4:39), thus becoming the first New Testament missionary in Samaria.

Our Position as Kings

You have redeemed us to God by Your blood. Out of every tribe and tongue and people and nation, and have made us kings and priests to our God.

Revelation 5:9B-10

Paul clearly taught that Christians have a purpose for being on earth (Romans 8:28). Have you ever wondered what your purpose is—why you were born? Prior to becoming a Christian, I often pondered that thought. God's first desire for our lives is to have us defect from Satan's kingdom and become a citizen in His kingdom. Only then does spiritual life begin. Only then does the fruit of the Spirit begin to flow outwardly from our inner being, like a river. Once we are citizens in the kingdom of Christ, God has another purpose for our lives. He assigns us two new occupations, and it is God's desire that we fully inhabit these new positions. We are to fulfill our role as kings and priests.

As kings, we are not assigned or are we to actually sit on a throne, but in our daily journey with Christ, we are encouraged to exercise authority and dominion in this stress-filled world. Not in a brash arrogant way, but in a quiet authoritative manner. As kings, instead of having the world, and its residents, manipulate our emotions and time, we should remain in control. We should be calling the shots!

> Your descendants shall possess the gate of their enemies.
>
> Genesis 22:17B

In Abraham's day, the city hall was located at the main gate of a city, and that was where the city officials sat and exercised authority and dominion. You may remember that Boaz went to the main gate to legalize the transaction to redeem property. As believers, through the indwelling power of the Holy Spirit, we have the capacity to display dominion at our gate, which in our case, is wherever our daily pilgrimage with Christ leads us.

> A highway shall be there, and a road, and it shall be called the Highway of Holiness. The unclean (nonbelievers) shall not pass over it... But the redeemed (believers) shall walk there.
>
> Isaiah 35:8, 9

What a powerful verse! As Christians, we walk on a holy high-way. Satan, the prince of this spiritually darkened kingdom, has absolutely no authority to trod upon this path. As the above verse states, it is for believers only! Satan is relegated to the dark side-lines of the Holy Highway! Oh, that we would not only get this straight in our heads but also deep in our hearts! This truly is excit-ing news for a believer. Since Satan does not have the authority to step on this holy path, there is no way he can force a Christian to sin. Flip Wilson may have been a great comedian, but his doctrine was all wrong when he said, "The devil made me do it." Not so! When Flip sinned, like you and I, he made a conscious decision to do so! We need to recognize the deceiver for what he is—a bait tosser! All Satan can do is toss tempting bait in our path, hoping we will pick it up. Every day we are faced with various degrees of temptation, and when we spot the temptation, our *will* is then challenged to make a conscious decision. Do we pick up the bait and become hooked? Or do we ignore the temptation and walk on in victory? Do we exercise our position as kings? Or does the bait tosser become an influential force in our lives? The choice is always ours to make! This is a truth many Christians are reluctant to face. They mistakenly blame the negatives of the world and obnoxious people for causing them to display such sins as anger, worry, and fear. Not so! A spiritual Christian always sins knowingly.

Allow me to cite a couple of examples that illustrate this truth. Satan didn't have the authority to shove the forbidden fruit in Eve's mouth. The deceiver simply tossed the tempting bait her way. There was a definite point when Eve made a conscious deci-sion to disobey the Word of God and succumb to Satan's deceitful suggestion. The world is still reaping the negative consequences of that choice. Neither did Satan force Bathsheba into David's bed. Both David and Bathsheba made conscious decisions to sin. Satan cannot force harmful substances into a Christian's body. The individual makes a conscious decision to drink too much booze, inhale nicotine, eat more calories then his body requires, or pop way too many drugs, prescription or otherwise. The deceiver cannot force a believer to worry, to be overcome with fear, to be filled with self-pity, or consumed by anger. All Satan can do is create situations that encourage a person's flesh to respond in such a manner. Once we make the decision to pick up the tempting bait, we have given Satan the dominating position in our lives, rather than maintaining control of our gateway.

We need to understand a Biblical truth about picking up bait. The law of the harvest continues to prevail, and we will eventually reap what we sow, to some extent, at least. Adam learned about negative reaping the hard way, as did King David! When we respond in anger to someone who takes a verbal shot at us, it is then his turn to strike back. Now we have entered into a prolonged game of ping-pong—negative reaping. The teenager who begins experimenting with booze, nicotine, and/or harmful drugs may find himself reaping much more than he ever expected. If he continually picks up the bait, one day he may find himself hooked! When we constantly make decisions to display anger and stress, in time we may become like the drug addict—hooked. Yes, such fleshly traits as worry, fear, anger, and depression can become addictions. It is readily observable in today's society that, for far too many, stress has become a way of life. Stress will eventually catch up, and many will find themselves aging prematurely, with health related problems surfacing way too soon.

The period of time between viewing the bait and actually making a decision to pick it up can take seconds, days, or much longer. For example, a Christian man can spend weeks thinking about having an affair with the office cutie. Once he steps across the line, he has made a conscious decision to violate his wedding vows. In time, negative consequences will follow his action—perhaps even a costly long drawn out divorce. A Christian alcoholic may spend hours, days, or perhaps months thinking about returning to the bottle before he makes the willful decision to take a drink. Many decisions of the will are not spread over long periods of time, but are immediate. For example, when someone takes a verbal shot at us, our will then makes a conscious decision. We either decide to ignore the bait and walk on in victory or pick it up. There is a wonderful illustration of this truth in the little story of the young lad who returned home from school one day with a black eye. When asked by his father if he struck back, the boy, with all his little boy wisdom, responded, "No. Then it would have been his turn again!"

When a spiritual Christian is considering picking up the tempting bait, a tiny voice in the recesses of his heart says, "Inappropriate behavior." Then his will either responds to the voice of the Holy Spirit or ignores it and carries on. Have you heard this voice? A carnal Christian is more prone to habitual sin, and may be insensitive to the voice. If he has been a carnal believer for several years, worry, fear, anger, and depression have become a way of life—addictions—and he has become more or less accustomed to the life style.

> They shall eat the fruit of their own way.
>
> Proverbs 1:31

> Whatever a man sows, that he will also reap.
>
> Galatians 6:7B

If we could look around the corner and see the negative consequences of responding to Satan's temptations, I expect we would be more inclined to respond to the messages the Holy Spirit dictates to our hearts. One day I was walking in the park with one of our children and we came across a freshly painted bench. On the bench was a sign, "Don't Touch—Wet Paint!" She just needed to know if it really was wet, and it really was! She soon discovered getting rid of the stain took much longer than getting it! We have used that simple little object lesson time and time again in our girls' lives, and in the lives of many others who have crossed our paths over the years. When we ignore life's wet paint signs, we may find ourselves living with the stain for a long time.

I recall talking with a Christian man, in a counseling room, who admitted having a heated argument with his brother forty years earlier and still bore the stain of that dispute. Every time his brother came to mind, the scab was picked and anger surfaced once again. Even though his brother lived hundreds of miles away, and he hadn't spoken to him in all those years, the mere mention of the incident still jerked this Christian's chain—controlling his emotions. Those who have hurt us in the past cannot continue to hurt us, unless we choose to hold onto the pain, through anger and resentment. Surely you must see that it is imperative that we learn to exercise our position as kings, otherwise we are vulnerable at every turn in the road.

Anger is one letter removed from danger!

Our Position as Priests

Perhaps in your travels you have heard someone use the phrase, the priesthood of believers. As believers, we are all in the ministry. We may not have graduated from a seminary, or minister on some distant missionary field, but we all have a ministry. The Holy Spirit is the power behind our ministry, and we are simply His hands and mouth—displaying that power.

> The Spirit and the bride (believers) say, "Come!" And let him who hears say, "Come!" And let him who thirsts come. "Whoever desires, let him take the water of life freely."
>
> Revelation 22:17

During His time on earth, Jesus was somewhat limited in His ministry; in His human body, He could only be in one place at a time. After Christ's ascension, the Holy Spirit moved His headquarters from heaven to earth, taking up residence in the hearts of believers. Today, there are Christians in every corner of the globe, who are empowered by the Holy Spirit, enabling them to fulfill their role as priests. This is done primarily in two ways. The first is to invite nonbelievers to *come* into the fold. The second is accomplished whenever we encourage troubled Christians to move to a new level of freedom. The word priest stems from the same Latin word as bridge-builder. A bridge-builder enables a person to move from one place to another, and in that sense, Christians are called to function as bridge-builders.

> You shall receive power when the Holy Spirit has come upon you; and you shall be witnesses to me.
>
> Acts 1:8

In this verse, there is a tiny key word that is often overlooked. That word is *be*. We can exercise our position as priests in two different ways. The wrong way is to *go*, attempting to fulfill our role as priests under our own power. *Going* draws upon our strength. This verse calls upon us to *be* witnesses. When we have our lives in the right spiritual condition, without any effort on our part, Christ will begin to set up spiritual appointments for us. Once at the appointment, we work in unison with the Holy Spirit. He uses our mouth and feet and we draw from His power. When Jesus said, "I say to you, he who believes in Me, the works that I do he will do also; and greater works than these he will do, because I go to My Father," this is what He had in mind (John 14:12).

There is a major difference in the results of these two methods of witnessing. A survey was taken asking people how they became Christians. The results were most amazing!

- Through a TV and radio ministry
  - less than 1 percent

- Through the efforts of a church and pastor
  - less than 10 percent

- Through a friend, or relative
  - over 80 percent!

I find it interesting that the method requiring the most effort and expense produced the least results. A leader in the world of business would soon be hanging out a bankruptcy sign if his efforts produced such poor results. It is also interesting that the most productive method required basically no expense or effort, other than time and love.

The stats clearly indicate which method of witnessing is the most productive. *Going* to witness is often a result of a church sponsored outreach program, where the intent is honorable, but in most cases, the results bear little lasting fruit. Employing this method, the participants often become discouraged with the poor results for the time and effort involved and eventually most programs are canceled. Then several months later, the pastor resurrects the witnessing program and the majority in the pews, thinks, "Here we go again!"

In our first church, I was made the director of evangelism and, with much enthusiasm, launched a city-wide outreach program. I divided the city into sections and assigned people to various areas. Within a couple of months, because of discouraging results, I decided to abandon the entire program. I can now look back and see the problem. We were *going* to witness, rather than *being* witnesses.

By far the most effective method of witnessing is to work in unison with the Holy Spirit to *be* a witness. It requires the least amount of effort on our part, and as the above survey indicates, produces the most encouraging results. Being a witness is rather like the football player who gets himself suited up and in tip top condition. He then sits, expectantly, on the bench waiting for the coach to call him into the game. When the time is right, he will be called to fulfill a vital role, one he has been well prepared to execute.

When we are spiritually suited up, our coach will call us into the witnessing game when just the right opportunity arises. The Lord will bring us in contact with people He thinks we can minister to effectively. Often the appointment is made without any conscious effort on our part—a divine appointment. When the appointment is with a nonbeliever, the first few meetings may be devoted to developing a friendship. Until a relationship is established, it is unlikely that person will let his guard down and open up about any of the real concerns in life. Some of those appointments may be in the strangest places. Remember, Jesus was accused of being a "friend of sinners."

Let's face facts! If we are struggling with worry, fear, anger, and depression ourselves, we will not be in the right spiritual condition to comfort and/or encourage others. I defy anyone to share Christ effectively when his life is filled with such foolish behavior. When a nonbeliever sees such a negative lifestyle displayed, it is unlikely he will be impressed, nor will he have any desire whatsoever to become a Christian. Once the following points become a reality in our lives, we will find ourselves experiencing a productive priesthood. We will *be* an effective light for Christ!

- Solid salvation experience

- Lordship of Christ

- Sitting under solid Bible teaching

- Being obedient to the taught Word

As we begin to experience the normal Christian life, our roles as priests will unfold. When Jesus sets up the appointment, the encounter will not be a sweaty palm uncomfortable experience, and the person will leave the meeting feeling encouraged and hopefully with something to chew over.

The number one thing to be discarded, if we are to ever be effective witnesses, is a judgmental attitude! The world can smell it a mile away and it really turns them off, while genuine love and concern attracts them like flies to honey. A productive priest is a good listener. Rather than trying to impress others with our Bible knowledge and boring them to death by quoting worn out Christian platitudes, we must learn to guide the conversation to their concerns, asking lots of questions. We should sit there with an open ear, and for most part, a closed mouth! Such a problem for most Christians! It is difficult to learn how a person thinks and feels when our lips are the only ones moving. Be sensitive to the leading of the Holy Spirit, and you will know when to speak and what to say. Everything will flow naturally, and most times the door will be left open for a follow up meeting. By the way, it is perfectly okay to say, "You know I don't actually know the answer to that question, but give me a few days and I will do some research and get back to you." Now you have a ready made reason for that follow up meeting.

> The Holy Spirit will teach you in that very hour what you ought to say.

> Luke 12:12

There are various ways to share Christ, but one of the most effective ways is to follow the example of the woman at the well. She never graduated from a seminary, never attended a witnessing class, yet she was extremely effective by telling her personal conversion story. "Many of the Samaritans of the city believed in

Him because of the word of the woman who testified" (John 4:39). We each have a personal story to tell, and that story will have more influence on the hearer than all the preaching in the world. The survey stats support this fact. Our personal testimony should be tailored to the particular hearer's circumstances and should cover the following points:

- What life was like before becoming a Christian

- How and why we came to the conclusion that Christ is the only way

- How life has changed since making that decision

Abide in Me, and I in you. As the branch cannot bear fruit of itself, unless it abides in the vine, neither can you, unless you abide in Me... for without Me you can do nothing.

John 15:4-5

The wonderful thing about living the normal Christian life is that it requires so little conscious effort on our part. We simply get in the right spiritual shape and life will flow like a river (John 7:38). The spiritual fruit will be seasonal. When we need patience and peace, they will be there. When we need to show unconditional love towards some obnoxious person, that love will flow naturally. When we find ourselves boxed in, peace will prevail. The most exciting thing is that we can stop trying to improve our acting ability allowing, instead, the Holy Spirit to generate *His* fruit through our lives. That's freedom! The quality of life we display will be the same whether we are at church, at our place of employment, or at home behind closed doors. It is good to keep in mind that God must do a work *in* us before He can do a work *through* us!

In today's church circles, there appears to be a lot of flesh polishing—Christians attempting to counterfeit spiritual fruit.

Polishing and educating our flesh is similar to attempting to generate a breeze by turning a fan blade with our finger. Despite much desire and effort, the breeze created will be unimpressive, and it will just be a matter of time before we tire of the fruitless effort. A better way of generating an enjoyable breeze is to plug the fan into a power source. Power is an interesting word. The word originates from the Greek word *dunamis*, from which the English word "dynamite" originates. Dynamite explodes outwardly, which is exactly how normal Christianity is meant to work. The Holy Spirit's desire is to explode His power (fruit) outwardly through our lives. We simply need to be cleansed and available to display that power. Fit for the Master's use!

Why is it that so many professing Christians choose to play Holy Spirit by attempting to self-generate spiritual fruit? The reasons vary. Some pick up on the church drill and then constantly struggle to put on an impressive performance, by acting as expected. Mechanical Christianity. Counterfeit fruit is short lived. Upon leaving church, they quickly revert to the ways of the world, ensnared once again by worry, fear, and depression. Oh, they may hear a stirring sermon one Sunday about loving their neighbor as themselves and return home determined to display that quality of life. Everything goes well until someone takes a verbal shot. Another sermon is preached about anger and worry being sin, and they leave for home vowing never to fall in that trap again. We all know how long that is apt to last.

Pearl of Great Price

> The kingdom of heaven is like a merchant seeking beautiful pearls, who, when he had found one pearl of great price, went and sold all that he had and bought it.
>
> Matthew 13:45-46

The normal Christian life is well pictured in the parable of the pearl of great price. It is intriguing how a pearl is formed. A grain of sand becomes imbedded in an oyster causing pain. To eliminate the annoyance, the oyster produces a protective fluid that surrounds the grain of sand. Eventually the fluid solidifies and a pearl is formed. Without the fluid covering, the grain of sand remains unimpressive. Once covered, however, that same little grain of sand is transformed into an item of beauty and value. In order to attract customers, the merchant places the pearl in a prominent place in his shop window, and when people view the pearl, they cannot see the grain of sand, admiring instead the end product.

Prior to becoming a Christian, from God's perspective, we were like that grain of sand—possessing no spiritual beauty and of no eternal value. Citizens of the *set wrong* kingdom! When we become a believer, we are clothed in the righteousness of Christ—*set right!* In this condition, just as the merchant did with the pearl, it is Christ's desire to put us on display in this spiritually darkened world, in order to demonstrate what He can do with a useless grain of sand. He is able to take a nobody like me, for instance, from the darkened kingdom, and through the power of the Holy Spirit, transforms me into a somebody in His kingdom. "The apple of His eye" (Psalm 17:8).

Abraham was a nobody in Ur, and the Lord raised him up to become the father of a mighty nation—a somebody. God took a sheepherder from the backside of the desert and molded him into a somebody. That man was Moses! A former slave in Egypt by the name of Joshua was raised up to become a somebody—a ruler over all Israel. God took an insignificant shepherd lad by the name of David and made him a somebody—a king. Christ took an uneducated fisherman, Peter, and made him a somebody in the early church. Paul was a religious zealot who delighted in persecuting Christians, and in so many words Jesus said, "I'll take him." God transformed him into a somebody by commissioning him to be the apostle to the Gentiles, and the writer of almost half the New Testament. Christ took a nobody by the name of John Bunyan, sitting in a damp old prison cell, and anointed him to write *Pilgrim's Progress—From This World to That Which Is to Come*. Jesus took a Bible college dropout by the name of Billy Graham and used him to preach the gospel to more people than anyone in history. As Christians, we must view ourselves from God's perspective—a somebody in His kingdom. Remember, we possess the righteousness of Christ! What higher level could there be? As Christians, it should be our constant desire to walk our position as kings and priests!

God's Letters

> You are our epistle written in our hearts, known and read by all men.
>
> 2 Corinthians 3:2

As Christians, we are Christ's epistles and meant to be read by the world. When we tell people we are a Christian, like it or not, they begin to read our lives. The world is not impressed by the position we hold in our church, how much we tithe, or by the Scripture verses we can quote. Have you ever wondered why so many are reluctant to attend today's churches? The number one reason given is the negative behavior of the epistles. When they hear about church board disputes, the slandering that takes place between church members, and observe the church crowd out in the community with absolutely no joy in their lives, they think, "Who needs that?" When they hear about church couples consulting divorce lawyers, they think, "Well, their religion doesn't seem to be much help to them." When they hear about the scandalous behavior of some of our prominent Christian leaders, the word that quickly come to mind is hypocrite. Way too many Christians walk the streets of our communities with their faces looking as if they had been baptized in vinegar. From the world's perspective, instead of wasting time joining a religious club, they are pretty sure they will find more enjoyment and less infighting at their country club. Too often they are right! How do I know how nonbelievers think? I used to be one! For years I watched the lives of professing Christians, and until I crossed paths in British Columbia with Ralph and Lou Sutera, I was unimpressed with the quality of life displayed by the professing Christians I had met. We must get it clear in our heads that once we label ourselves as a Christian, we become an epistle to the world—either a positive or negative one.

The world is looking for a different quality of life than what they see displayed in the lives of the majority of the church crowd. They are looking for Christians who have solid marriages, well mannered children, who are reliable workers and, despite the trials of life, have some measure of peace and joy in their daily lives. Until the world sees a different quality of life displayed by the Christian community, it is unlikely they will be anxious to fill today's church pews.

I am reminded of an elder who looked down his judgmental nose at members of the congregation who smoked. One day, during a conversation with one of his golfing buddies, he referred to that elder as a hypocrite. When I asked, "Why that label," he said he was aware his golfing friend criticized the church folks who smoked, but once on the golf course, out came the cigar. A common dictionary definition of a hypocrite is, "A person who pretends to have moral or religious beliefs he does not actually possess." The word hypocrite has a long history. It was coined during the days of the early Greek theater. In those days, one actor often performed several roles, simply changing hand-held masks as he changed characters. The actor was referred to as a hypocrite! This pious church elder lived two different lives—one around the church gang and another in the world. Unfortunately, that is the case with many professing Christians.

Nonbelievers are also quick to pick up on the slandering that takes place within the Christian community. An acid tongue can cause a lot of damage, not only in our communities in general, but also within the Christian community itself. Once we publicly slander someone, the venom has gone beyond our lips, and it is difficult to undo the harm that has been created.

> Keep your tongue from evil, and your lips from speaking deceit.
>
> Psalm 34:13

> I will guard my ways, lest I sin with my tongue; I will restrain my mouth with a muzzle.
>
> Psalm 39:1

There is a story told of a man who was quick to spread gossip concerning a fellow church member, only to find out a few days later that it was untrue. Suffering with guilt, he went to his pastor for advice. He was told to take a bag of feathers and place a feather on the doorstep of each home in his neighborhood. The man was puzzled by this strange instruction, nevertheless, he obeyed his pastor's advice. Two days later he returned to the pastor and said he had finished the task. The pastor then told him to return to each home and retrieve the feathers. His response was, "That's an impossibility, the wind will have scattered the feathers all over town." As Christians, we must closely monitor each and every word that comes out of our mouth, as once the gossiping and slandering becomes public, it is virtually impossible to undo the harm. Don't be one of those people who say, "I probably shouldn't be telling you this, but…," or "I don't mean to be gossiping, but…"

Walk in wisdom toward those who are outside, redeeming the time. Let your speech always be with grace, seasoned with salt.

Colossians 4:5-6

Those spoken of in the above verse as outsiders are nonbelievers. Our conversation should be seasoned with salt in the community as well as in the church. Hypocrisy and gossip will also cause problems within our homes. Children are quick to spot parents who live two lives. When little Johnny sees dad acting piously and holy in church, but displaying an abusive temper at home, he is apt to secretly label dad a hypocrite. When mom displays a somewhat pious demeanor at church, but at home is filled with self-pity, worry, and is a constant nag, little Susie may view mom as a hypocrite. When children hear their parents slandering fellow Christians around the dinner table, it is unlikely they will be impressed with dad and mom's brand of Christianity. Then, when the children leave home and begin drifting from the Lord, those same parents generally blame the world for leading them astray!

Questions

- Do you find yourself having a thirst for spiritual things? Or are you still attempting to quench your inner thirst by things of this world and a flurry of religious activity?

- Are you exercising your designated position as king? Or does the world, and its residents, still manipulate your emotions and function as the dominating force in your life?

- As a priest, have you found an avenue of ministry in your daily exodus with Christ? Or is one hour in the pew on Sunday the extent of your spiritual activity?

- Have you come to view yourself as a pearl of great price? Or do you still see yourself as a nobody?

- Are you a positive or negative epistle for Christ? Are others touched by the quality of Christian life you display, or are they indifferent?

ONCE IS ENOUGH

Losing One's Salvation—Fact or Fiction?

In the twentieth chapter of Numbers, we find Israel once again complaining about a lack of water. This time around instead of striking the rock, God instructed Moses to speak to the rock. Thoroughly frustrated with the whining Israelites, in a fit of temper, Moses struck the rock. Because of that act of disobedience, he was not allowed to enter the Promised Land (vv. 8-12). Harsh punishment for what appears on the surface to be a rather trivial mistake. Why would God banish this great man of faith from Canaan? After all, Moses was the Lord's chosen vessel to persuade Pharaoh to allow Israel to leave Egypt. It was Moses who was given the Commandments and the pattern of the tabernacle on the mount. Moses was chosen to record the first five books of the Bible. Yet, because of this particular disobedience, he would never set foot in Canaan, until approximately fourteen hundred years later, when he met with the Lord on the Mount of Transfiguration. What terrible thing could Moses have done to cause God to keep him out of Canaan? If anger and frustration were the reasons, not a single Israelite would ever have set foot in the Promised Land, for they constantly displayed such fleshly traits. However, the consequences of his disobedience were far reaching, for you see Moses marred a beautiful picture.

The first time Moses struck the rock was symbolic of Christ being bruised on the cross on our behalf. When he struck the rock a second time, he marred that beautiful picture suggesting the coming Messiah would need to be struck down (crucified) more than one time for sins committed by a believer. In other words, he muddied what we refer to today as the doctrine of eternal security. Today, in certain Christian circles we have an open door to that dreadful doctrine, which causes those who buy into this false belief to live with a lot of unnecessary guilt and fear. To believe the death of the Lord Jesus Christ on Calvary's cross was not sufficient to pay the redemption price for our past, present, and future sins is not only foolish, but it is a belief not supported by Scripture. In my opinion, believing a Christian can lose his salvation as a result of committing a big sin is the most troublesome false doctrine that prevails in Christianity today. The Bible says this belief heaps *shame* upon Christ. Even that wonderful old gospel song says it correctly, "Jesus paid it all."

Today, because Scripture is misinterpreted, there are many who believe they will lose their salvation if they commit a big enough sin. They must visualize some sort of record keeping secretary sitting at the great computer in the sky. And when a big sin is recorded, a screen pops up saying, "Big sin! Sorry! Your name has just been deleted from the Lamb's Book of Life!" Then when the biggie is confessed, they must visualize another screen appearing saying, "Good news! Your name has been reentered. You have just been born again, again…"

> In Him you also trusted, after you heard the word of truth, the gospel of your salvation; in whom also, having believed, you were sealed with the Holy Spirit of promise.
>
> Ephesians 1:13

Paul assures us in the above Scripture that once we become Christians, our names are permanently sealed in the Lamb's Book of Life. "You have destroyed the wicked. You have blotted out their name forever and ever" (Psalm 9:5). This blotting out will take place at some future time—when the fifth chapter of Revelation becomes a reality. The individual sins of a believer do not have the power to break those seals—only Christ has that authority!

When Jesus announced from the cross, "It is finished," He was making it clear it would never again be necessary to repeat that horrific act to deal with sin in any or all its forms.

> Such a High Priest (Christ) was fitting for us, who is holy, harmless, undefiled, separate from sinners, and has become higher than the heavens; who does not need daily, as those high priest, to offer up sacrifices (daily offerings), first for His own sins and then for the people's, for this He did once for all when He offered up Himself.
>
> Hebrews 7:26-27

> There shall by no means enter it (heaven) anything that defiles, or causes an abomination or a lie, but only those who are written in the Lamb's Book of Life.
>
> Revelation 21:27

If the sins of a Christian could be recorded (charged to our account), no one would make it to heaven as, on a daily basis, we all sin to some degree—either in *deed* or in *thought*. Daily we commit such sins as worry, anger, envy, slandering, fear, and lying. Only a fool would say otherwise. "As he thinks in his heart, so is he" (Proverbs 23:7). If we think anger, we have sinned. The above verse clearly states if we arrive at heaven's gate with a little white lie recorded on our rap sheet, we will be labeled a sinner and denied entrance. Have you noticed how often the Bible lists murder and lying in the same verse (Revelation 21:8)? If a liar and a murderer arrived at heaven's gate with exposed sin, both will be viewed as sinners. Not a little and big sinner—just sinners.

> Whoever shall keep the whole law, and yet stumble in one point, he is guilty of all.
>
> James 2:10

This truth creates a problem for a Christian who believes he can lose his salvation by committing a big sin. What would happen if a believer became angry, or told a little white lie, and departed from this world with his sin not confessed? Where would he spend eternity? Would he be found acceptable to spend eternity with Christ? I assure you that because of God's fool-proof redemption plan, he would be welcomed with open arms. The redemption plan not only deals with our past sins, it also encompasses any and all future sin committed by a Christian—regardless of the magnitude. If you believe you can commit a sin, which would nullify your family membership, my advice is to never get off your knees. Remain in constant prayer, confessing all sins committed in both deed and thought.

Here's the deal! God has only one means of judging sin and that is the law of Moses. "I would not have known sin except through the law" (Romans 7:7b). In order to avoid judgment, we must get free of the judgmental law. That freedom becomes ours the moment we are saved. From that point on, we are no longer under the judgmental law, we are now under the redemptive blood of our Savior. "The law is not made for a righteous person (Christian), but for the lawless and insubordinate, for the ungodly and for sinners" (1 Timothy 1:9). The very moment we become a believer, we are no longer under the Old Testament judgmental covenant, but under the blood-based New Testament covenant. Thankfully, this covenant is not based upon our conduct, but on the conduct of the two New Testament covenant parties—God and the Lord Jesus Christ. If we are no longer under the law, it is impossible for God to judge and revoke our membership in His family. We must never, never forget that God said, "When I see the blood I will pass over you."

> There is no one who can deliver out of My hand; I work, and who will reverse it?
>
> Isaiah 43:13B

If a believer could lose his salvation because of a particular sin, wouldn't you think there would be verses on every page on the New Testament saying, "Beware of committing these sins"? I feel sure that if it were possible for a Christian to lose his membership in the kingdom, Jesus would have prayed differently in John 17:15. Instead of asking the Father to leave believers on earth for a period of time, He would have asked to have them removed the instant they were converted—before they committed a whopper sin, like Peter, for instance.

When Moses disobeyed and struck the rock a second time, he forever marred a beautiful picture and in a sense cast *open shame* upon what Christ would eventually accomplish at Calvary (Hebrews 6:6). It seems to me this has to be the reason Moses was prevented from entering the Promised Land. In addition, without realizing it, he gave Satan an unbelievably powerful weapon with which to defeat Christians all down through the ages, even to this very day.

The Bible says it is impossible for a believer to *repent* after he has stumbled (Hebrews 6:4, 6). As I have studied the Bible, it has become clear to me that repentance is a one-time event which takes place at conversion. The Bible says repentance can only be experienced by a nonbeliever. "I have not come to call the righteous, but sinners, to repentance" (Luke 5:32). There is no need for a believer to repent/confess because he is no longer under the judgmental law, but under the prevailing blood of Christ. His past, present, and future sins are not recorded against him! "Sin is not imputed when there is no law" (Romans 5:13B).

> There will be more joy in heaven over one sinner who repents than over ninety-nine just persons who need no repentance.
>
> Luke 15:7

> The righteous will never be removed.
>
> Proverbs 10:30

Question: Removed from what?

Answer: The Lamb's Book of Life.

Once our sins are blotted out, our name can never be blotted out of the Lamb's Book. As believers we are sealed in the Book, and the only one who has the authority to break the seals is the Kinsman Redeemer—Christ (Ephesians 1:13). Fortunately, our sins do not have that power.

> I am He who blots out your transgressions for My own sake; and I will not remember your sins.
>
> Isaiah 43:25

> I have blotted out, like a thick cloud, your transgressions, and like a cloud, your sins.
>
> Isaiah 44:22

If we are to mature and experience freedom in our Christian journey, it is imperative we understand our sins cannot somehow cause the seals on the Lamb's Book to be broken and our name to be removed. King David realized his (*big*) sin affected his relationship with God, but didn't alter his status in the kingdom. When Bathsheba became pregnant, in order to cover his adultery, David placed her husband, Uriah, on the front lines of the battlefield—in harms way. If it were possible to categorize sin, David's adultery and premeditated murder would certainly be labeled "big." His carnal conduct, tarnished his relationship with his Lord for a period of time, and he certainly reaped negative results, but his sin did not alter his position in God's kingdom. Bathsheba bore David a son who died shortly after birth. When David's servants asked him why he wasn't in mourning over the loss of the child, David said, "I shall go to him, but he shall not return to me" (2 Samuel 12:23B). David knew, that despite his sin, he would eventually join his son in heaven.

Again, if it were possible to categorize sin, Peter publicly denying and cursing Christ (to His face) would be considered a *biggie.* Because of his stumble, for a period of time he experienced a loss of fellowship with Christ, but his position in the kingdom remained rock solid. Peter did not have to be born again, again! He could only repent as a sinner once! When a Christian stumbles, his relationship with the Lord suffers until he gets back on track, and there is also bound to be some degree of negative reaping. Nevertheless, his position in the kingdom of Christ remains like Mount Zion—fixed!

> The Lord loves justice, and does not forsake His saints; they are preserved (in the Lamb's Book) forever.
>
> Psalm 37:28

> Those who trust in the Lord are like Mount Zion, which cannot be moved, but abides forever.
>
> Psalm 125:1

Repentance and Confession

In the Old Testament, the words repent and confess appear many times, because those saints were under the law-based covenant, which constantly exposed their sins. Until the resurrection of Christ, Old Testament believers remained in that condition. "If Christ is not risen, your faith is futile, you are still in your sins" (1 Corinthians 15:17).

You would think the word "confess" would appear on every page of the New Testament, but that is not the case. In the entire New Testament, the word is only recorded seventeen times, and not once does it refer to a Christian confessing his sins. Fifteen times the word is associated with witnessing—confessing Christ before men. One time is about Christians confessing their faults one to another, and the other is found in a salvation chapter, instructing a sinner to confess his sins (1 John 1:9).

Picture repentance as a turning point. Once a sinner repents of his sins, that's it! From that point forward, he is no longer under the judgmental law, which means there are no sins recorded on his rap sheet. There is nothing to confess. Like David and Peter, from time to time, we all stumble. When we do, we are meant to pick ourselves up, learn from our stupidity, and continue moving forward.

A righteous man may fall seven times and rise again.

Proverbs 24:16

The trap of constant confession keeps us sin-focused, instead of blood-focused. Satan has worked down through the ages, in many and various ways, to keep Christians focused on their failures and shortcomings, which, all too often, instill feelings of worthlessness and guilt. Confession has been his primary tool. In times past, Protestants have scoffed at Catholics for confessing their sins only to return the following week to confess basically the same set of sins. Today, that is exactly what most evangelical Christians are doing. Week after week, they find themselves going around the same confession mountain, saying, "Lord, I am sorry, I did it again, please forgive me." Spiritually speaking, going nowhere fast. The byproduct of constant confession is that there is little forward movement or freedom from our fleshly bondage. Confession keeps us focused on our (often poor) performance rather than on Christ's perfect performance on our behalf. It keeps us in a constant state of guilt and unworthiness. Jesus has promised us a life of freedom. Living today under the Old Testament law-based covenant never produces freedom—only bondage.

> Stand fast therefore in the liberty by which Christ has made us free, and do not be entangled again with a yoke of bondage (law).
>
> Galatians 5:1

When the Bible speaks of eternal life, for believers, it means exactly that (John 3:15, 5:39, 6:54, Romans 5:21, 1 John 2:25). Regardless of our earthly conduct, eternal life is a status that remains with us for a long time—forever! Jesus made that pretty clear when He said, "Neither shall anyone snatch them (Christians) out of My hand" (John 10:28). When Paul wrote about our being "Sealed with the Holy Spirit," he clearly understood this same truth—once saved always saved! When David wrote about believers being "preserved forever," he wasn't just coining a catchy phrase. To say we can lose our salvation is to cast "shame" upon what Christ accomplished at Calvary, which is what Moses did by striking the rock a second time.

> It is impossible for those who were once enlightened (Christians), and have tasted the heavenly gift (salvation), and have become partakers of the Holy Spirit (believers), and have tasted the good word of God (Christians), and the powers of the age to come, if they fall away (sin), to renew them again to repentance, since they crucify again for themselves the Son of God (strike the Rock again), and put Him to an open shame.
>
> Hebrews 6:4-6

Whenever I teach that Christians have no recorded sins to confess, a law-focused person panics, saying, "Doesn't this teaching give Christians a license to sin?" A spiritual Christian would never ask such a question, for he understands he has come full circle. The apostle Paul addresses this truth. First, he tells Christians they have been set free of the law—"The law is not made for a righteous person [a believer]" (1 Timothy 1:9). Then, in the next stroke of his pen, he says, "We establish the law" (Romans 3:31). Confusing thinking to a legalist! A spiritual believer does not require laws etched in stone to dictate his daily walk, as he knows the Holy Spirit writes His desires on the fleshly tablets of his heart (Hebrews 8:10). Being obedient to this inner voice, he begins to naturally fulfill the very laws from which he has been set free. Clearly, King David also understood this truth—"Your law is within my heart" (Psalm 40:8). Instead of "forgive me" praying and walking away until the next time, how much better to pray, "I agree my behavior was stupid. Show me why I behaved that way? What is at the root of it"? When we understand the reason for our fleshly conduct, we will then know the source of our problem. I guarantee you this kind of praying will get results. Remember, in so many words, Jesus said to the woman caught in the very act of adultery, "I condemn you not, simply quit doing it!" So, what am I saying? Most have been taught to ask for forgiveness whenever we stumble. Suggesting that if we do not ask we are not forgiven. How can that be? Is there a great secretary in the sky constantly pushing buttons as we confess? I don't think so! None of this will make a lot of sense until we come to the conclusion deep in our hearts that obedience is for our benefit, not God's. He is unchangeable. It is we who must change if we are to enjoy our walk through this fallen world as we are meant to. There is an old expression that says, "Put your money where your mouth is." "Not very godly" you say. Think about it! What does that expression mean? I think it means "Back up your words with action." That is what I am trying so desperately to convey here. If we simply talk and talk and talk some more about our failures and shortcomings, we will never get anywhere in our walk. Action is what is desperately needed. We repented (turned around) at our salvation, from that day on it is simply a matter of continuing to walk away from the old lifestyle and walk toward the new as the God of the Universe, by His Holy Spirit, points the way.

> The righteous requirement of the law might be fulfilled in us who do not walk according to the flesh but according to the Spirit.

> Romans 8:4

The Bible speaks of two types of Christians—carnal and spiritual. The carnal Christian has a more intimate relationship with his rules, his religion, and his church than he does with his Savior. Instead of Jesus being the focal point, the denominational dos and don'ts become the focal point. He mistakenly believes the more he adheres to the rules, the more God, and others, will approve of him. Instead of having an intimate relationship with Christ, his experience is mechanical and somewhat distant.

The spiritual man enjoys a much different brand of Christianity. Because of his deeply personal relationship with Christ, without any conscious effort, he will have a desire to satisfy the very laws from which he has been set free. In his Christian journey he will experience more freedom and less guilt. His relationship with Christ will be far more intimate and satisfying.

A carnal and spiritual man can be seated side-by-side in a pew, both displaying a similar external quality of life. The carnal man's relationship with Christ is a result of a law-based do and don't relationship—mechanical. The spiritual man's performance is a natural and spontaneous result of his love relationship with

Christ. Which man's heart and daily experience is filled with the peace and joy promised as our birthright?

Three Acts of Imputing

> Blessed are those whose lawless deeds are forgiven, and whose sins are covered; Blessed is the man whom the Lord shall not impute sin.
>
> Romans 4:7-8

The word *impute* means to credit something to the account of another. The Bible records three acts of imputing. The first was when Adam's fallen status was imputed to each successive generation.

> By the one man's offense death reigned through the one... Therefore, as through one man's offense judgment came to all men, resulting in condemnation... For as by one man's disobedience many were made sinners.
>
> Romans 5:17-19

David also understood this truth, which he recorded in the Psalms—"Behold, I was brought forth in iniquity, and in sin my mother conceived me" (Psalm 51:5).

The second act of imputing takes place when a person becomes a Christian. The moment we are saved, our sin status is imputed to Christ's account. "He made Him who knew no sin to be sin for us" (2 Corinthians 5:21A).

The third act of imputing also takes place at our conversion, and that is when Christ's righteousness is imputed to our account (2 Corinthians 5:21b). Obtaining Christ's status is the only ticket to glory! Anything short of that lands us permanently in the wrong camp! Once His righteousness is imputed to our account, our symbolic white stone can never be painted black.

When we exit this world, we arrive at heaven's gate in one of two conditions. With Adam's fallen genes imputed to our account, or with Christ's righteousness imputed to our account. We arrive either set wrong, or set right! Either under the judgmental law, or under the redeeming blood of Christ. Under the Old Testament judgmental covenant, or under the New Testament blood-based covenant.

> The Lord Himself will descend from heaven... And the dead in Christ will rise first. Then we who are alive and remain shall be caught up together with them in the clouds to meet the Lord in the air.
>
> 1 Thessalonians 4:16-17

There will come a time when believers will depart from this planet. We will meet Christ in the air, and He will personally escort His sheep to heaven. I'm told sheep are fairly dumb animals. Perhaps the reason Jesus plans to personally escort us to heaven is that he fears we might get lost in such a vast universe. Just a thought! During our ten year stay in Ajijic, Mexico, there seemed to be a constant supply of new Gringos arriving on the scene (one of the reasons we finally left). One of their first questions was how to locate Walmart or Costco in Guadalajara. Our first response was to tell them the way. That usually led to much frustration and their getting lost. We knew several couples who never did venture into the city a second time because of such bad traffic experiences. We finally decided a better way was to say, "We are driving into the city next Monday, why don't you follow us?" Apparently Jesus feels the same way, for His recorded plan is to meet us in the air.

Have you ever wondered what life will be like in heaven? The Bible provides us with little information about eternity. The apostle Paul was given a vision of heaven, but found the place beyond words and could never put into print all he saw. However, the Bible does provide us with clues of what life will be like. The apostle John was also given a vision of heaven, and he saw a "pure river of water of life, clear as crystal, proceeding from the throne of God" (Revelation 22:1). In the Bible, a river of flowing water always speaks of the fruit of the Spirit flowing from the heart of a believer (John 7:38-39). Because of the Holy Spirit's presence in heaven, only such spiritual fruit as peace, joy, and love will flow from the throne. Throughout eternity, there will be no such fleshly activity as anger, fear, or worry. The Bible tells us that we will be in a position of authority in eternity—"They shall reign forever and ever" (Revelation 22:5B). As kings and priests, we will be in some sort of a ruling and ministering position. How and where, I do not know, but it will be exciting to find out. Will our position as kings and priests be determined by the on-the-job-training we experience here on planet earth? Seems logical!

The Bible also provides little information concerning the quality of life in Satan's eternal camp. However, we can speculate with some degree of accuracy. Since the Holy Spirit will not be present, the quality of life will be totally fleshly generated activity. Can you imagine spending eternity surrounded by self-centered people constantly displaying anger, hatred, envy, fear, and stress? Furthermore, can you imagine living under such conditions knowing life will never improve? Sounds to me like a *hell* of a way to spend eternity!

> Behold, the tabernacle of God (Christ) is with men, and He will dwell with them, and they shall be His people. God Himself will be with them and be their God. And God will

wipe away every tear from their eyes; there shall be no more death, nor sorrow, nor crying. There shall be no more pain, for the former things have passed away.

Revelation 21:3-4

Note

There are two things I want to say before closing out this chapter. First of all, I realize this will be the most controversial chapter in the book. However, I ask you to pray before you reject the truth contained herein, for I believe it is God-given.

Secondly, I think we are meant to look at the fact that Moses was not allowed to finally lead his people into the Promised Land not so much as a punishment but a consequence of his disobedience. After all, skipping Canaan and going directly on to be with the Father is not exactly punishment! What a joy and blessing it would have been, however, to have completed the journey with his people! To be with them as they crossed over Jordan and see them finally settled in the land of milk and honey, sadly, was not to be. This seems to be one of those cases where Jeremiah 5:25B comes into play. "Your sins have withheld good things from you." Knowing what he now knows, do you not think Moses would take back that fit of anger and disobedience if he could? There is another verse that comes to mind here which basically says, "These things are recorded for your example, learn from them" (1 Corinthians 10:11).

Questions

- Do you agree with God that sin is sin, or do you still think God categorizes sin?

- Do you believe it is possible to lose your salvation by committing certain sins? In other words, are you still striking the rock?

- Do you accept the fact that the righteousness of Christ is permanently imputed to your account and that this status cannot be altered because of misbehaving?

PART II: TABERNACLE

LAW AND TABERNACLE

What's That?

After wandering in the desert for three months, Israel found themselves at the foot of Mount Sinai. By now, they should have been residing in Canaan for approximately two months, enjoying the abundant life and the rich inheritance God had promised. Instead, they were living a substandard quality of life in the barren desert. Today, struggling with self-managed lives, many Christians find themselves in much the same condition—beyond their Sunday routine, living a quality of life basically no different from the world in general. They keep hoping for a more vibrant and less stressful way of life, instead, year after year, they find themselves going around the same mountain—struggling with the same set of sins. They yearn for a more intimate relationship with Christ, but much of their Christian routine remains mechanical and boring. Stuck in this rut, many spend their entire lives never effectively sharing Christ with another single person. To them, Revelation 22:17 is one of those interesting sounding verses that bears no reality in their daily lives. The topics of the day are sports, fixing up the house, the big sale at Macy's, planning the next vacation, their 401-ks, and their favorite television program. Nothing terribly wrong with any of those things, but if

Christ is not at least occasionally included in our conversation, something is drastically wrong spiritually.

As slaves in Egypt, their lives were filled with drudgery and boredom. Going to the slave pits day after day, there was nothing exciting to look forward to—just more of the same. Bondage was a way of life. Daily, the world of the Egyptians led them around by the nose. Like many believers today, they viewed God as someone who resided in some remote corner of the universe, and they experienced little or nothing of His power as Lord in their lives. "By My name, Lord, I was not known to them" (Exodus 6:3). Now it was time for God to reveal Himself to Israel in a more intimate way. He did that by inviting Moses to a meeting at the top of Mount Sinai. There He presented him with two significant articles. Two items that changed the course of the world. One, with which Christians are very familiar, the other they most definitely are not!

Whenever I ask a group what Moses carried off the mount, with few exceptions, the response is always the same—the law! A 50 percent grade! The famous director of the Ten Commandments also receives a 50 percent mark for his movie depicted Moses coming down the mount carrying the tablets containing the law. The movie should have also shown Charlton Heston descending with the pattern for the tabernacle neatly rolled up and tucked under his arm. (Exodus 25:9).

Some years ago while teaching at a church in Florida, when asked by a senior elder what I would be teaching next, I replied, "I am considering a series on the tabernacle." His response was shocking. In a puzzled tone he asked, "What's that?"

It is interesting to note that the Ten Commandments occupy seventeen short verses in Scripture (Exodus 20:1-17), while the details of the tabernacle are spread over forty chapters. More space in the Bible is devoted to the tabernacle than any other topic! I find it utterly amazing that we constantly hear sermons on every aspect of the law, but hear so little teaching on the tabernacle. Think about it! When was the last time you heard a sermon on some aspect of the Commandments? Likely, recently. When was the last time you heard a series of teachings on the tabernacle? The odds are never! Otherwise, why would a senior church leader in a mega church be asking, "What's that?"

Satan Loves the Law

By Him everyone who believes is justified from all things from which you could not be justified by the law of Moses.

Acts 13:39

Satan loves to promote the law for two obvious reasons. First, he knows if he can keep people trusting in the law as a means of finding God's approval, they will step into eternity unjustified, and as permanent citizens of his kingdom. Secondly, if he can keep a believer law-focused, that person will not only experience little freedom in his daily life, he will also be a very poor witness to those around him, as he flaunts his list of dos and don'ts. Have you discovered that a judgmental Christian can be spotted a mile away, and the world, in general, will go to great lengths to avoid having any close contact with him? For obvious reasons, Satan loves the law of Moses, and goes overboard to promote it, while the apostle Paul, for instance, warns believers to stay clear of it (Galatians 5:1).

Let's park here for a few moments and discuss Christians who go through life with a judgmental attitude. Is there ever a time when we can judge others? It may surprise you to know that the answer to that question is "yes!" The Bible says once we have removed *all* the beams from our eyes, we then have the right to judge the specks in the eyes of others (Matthew 7:3-5). (I sometimes like to ask trick questions. I find it gets a person's attention). However, this license to judge presents an obvious problem. As the sanctification process is ongoing in the life of a Christian, we will always be dealing with a beam of one size or another. Instead of playing Holy Spirit, and attempting to clean up the world for Jesus, it seems to me we have a full time job dealing with the beams in our own lives, one that will keep us fully occupied until the trumpet sounds. Jesus is often referred to as the Great Fisherman; why not allow Him to clean His own fish? As Christians, we are not called to judge, but to love one another. A judgmental attitude steers people away from Christ, while love draws them to the Savior like flies to honey. Even the most obnoxious person eventually responds to genuine unconditional love.

The Pharisees were probably the most law-focused and judgmental group ever to set foot on the planet. Forever attempting to gain God's approval, their entire lives were devoted to keeping the law of Moses. As if the Ten Commandments were not enough of a challenge, over the years they beefed up God's list of ten by adding volumes more of their own invention. They taught that a person could self-justify by keeping laws, which kept, not only themselves, but their flock in a state of spiritual blindness and uneasiness. Jesus was not very complimentary when he spoke of the legalistic Pharisees. In so many words, He said they were spiritually blind and keeping their congregations in the same state (Matthew 15:14). Paul emphasizes that striving to keep the law cannot alter our status in the eyes of God—"You have become estranged from Christ, you who attempt to be justified by the law" (Galatians 5:4).

> Though you wash yourself with lye and use much soap, yet your iniquity is marked.
>
> Jeremiah 2:22

> Woe to you, scribes and Pharisees, hypocrites! For you are like whitewashed tombs which indeed appear beautiful outwardly, but inside are full of dead men's bones and all uncleanness.
>
> Matthew 23:27

When Jesus told the Pharisees they were like whitewashed tombs, He was being anything but complimentary. In His opinion, those pious religious leaders put on an impressive external performance, but internally they were like "dead men's bones." Is it any wonder they began plotting to get rid of Him? Sometimes I wonder what Jesus would have to say about the leadership of so many of today's churches? I guess we have the answer to that question when I think about it. Revelation 3:16 says the last church age, the Laodicean Church, which most seminaries and Bible scholars teach we are living in today, actually makes Him sick to his stomach. I kid you not. Look it up!

> Can the blind lead the blind? Will they not both fall into the ditch?
>
> Luke 6:39

There was a factory worker whose responsibility it was to blow the whistle at the end of each shift. A man asked him how he knew the right time to sound the whistle. He replied, "I go by the clock at the front gate." The man then went to the front gate and asked the gatekeeper how he knew the time to set his clock. The gatekeeper said, "I set my clock by the factory whistle!" Need I say more about the blind leading the blind?

Purpose of the Law

> I would not have known sin except through the law.
>
> Romans 7:7B

Whenever I ask a group "What is the purpose of the law?" I usually receive a variety of answers. However, the vast majority think the law of Moses is to instruct believers how to live the Christian life. Perhaps it will surprise you to learn that is not the case. The law has always had one purpose, and one purpose only. It is to make us aware that we have fallen short of God's requirement for justification (salvation). The apostle Paul tells us the law acts as our schoolmaster, informing us we have all broken God's commandments to some degree. It is the yardstick by which we are all measured. Having come to this understanding, hopefully, the law then steers us to the tabernacle—the only place where we can be set right—justified. God's formula for being set right is clearly pictured in the tabernacle. As we study the tabernacle in detail in the chapters that follow, you will begin to clearly see that every station of worship in that structure speaks of our Savior, the Lord Jesus Christ.

> The law was our tutor to bring us to Christ, that we might be justified by faith. But after faith has come, we are no longer under the tutor.
>
> Galatians 3:24-25

> Therefore by the deeds of the law no flesh will be justified in His sight, for by the law is the knowledge of sin.
>
> Romans 3:20

When Moses first read the Commandments to Israel, their initial response was, "We will obey them all" (Exodus 24:3, LB). How foolish they were to think they could satisfy the laws every second of every day—both in *deed* and *thought*. Their response should have been, "That's an impossibility. There must be a better way." And there was! The tabernacle!

The tabernacle and its stations of worship picture how a person becomes a believer (justification) as well as how he is able to mature spiritually (sanctification). Today's denominations, however, often have their own versions of each.

Since the tabernacle reveals God's formula for both justification and sanctification, is it any wonder Satan has been working overtime down through the ages, attempting to water down tabernacle teaching? It is obvious the Deceiver has been very successful in his endeavor when one hears a church elder reply, "What's that?" The next time you are in a Bible bookstore, ask the clerk where you can find books discussing how to live the Christian life. You will be shown a section with an abundance of material, 99 percent of which are law based. Then ask the clerk to direct you to the section where books on the tabernacle can be found. Don't be surprised if the clerk replies, "What's that?" Today, tabernacle teaching has pretty much disappeared from our churches and Sunday schools.

Under the law with its tenfold lash,
Learning, alas, how true,
That the more I tried, the sooner I died,
While the law cried, YOU, YOU, YOU.

Hopelessly still did the battle rage,
O, wretched man, my cry.
And deliverance I sought, by some penance bought,
While my heart cried, I, I, I.

Then came a day when my struggling ceased,
And trembling in every limb,
At the foot of the Tree, where One died for me,
My heart cried, HIM, HIM, HIM.

Author unknown

Satan Hates the Tabernacle

If you believed Moses, you would believe Me; for he wrote
about Me.

John 5:46

How was it possible for Moses to write about Christ when Moses
was born many hundreds of years before Jesus arrived on earth? If
Moses wrote about Christ in the Old Testament, why doesn't the
name Jesus or Christ appear in the five books Moses recorded?
When Moses recorded the details of the tabernacle he was actually writing about the One to come, The Messiah, yes, the Lord
Jesus Christ. Each of the six worship stations we will study in the
tabernacle pictures a different attribute and ministry of Christ.
There are many teachings in the Bible that Satan despises, but
the portion of Scripture that is at the top of his hate list has to
be those verses dealing with the tabernacle. Do you not find it
interesting that the deceiver has never made any attempt to water
down the law? In fact, he actually promotes the law! On the other
hand, Satan has gone to great lengths to have anything to do with
the teaching of the tabernacle watered down—to the point that
it is nearly extinct.

From childhood you have known the Holy Scriptures, which
are able to make you wise for salvation through faith which is
in Christ Jesus.

2 Timothy 3:15

For I delivered to you first of all that which I also received: that
Christ died for our sins according to the Scriptures, and that
He was buried, and that He rose again the third day according
to the Scriptures.

1 Corinthians 15:3-4

When the apostle Paul wrote the above two verses, the New Testament had not yet been compiled. When he used the word "Scriptures" he was referring to the Old Testament. How is it possible for the Old Testament to speak about the sacrifice of Christ so many years before He was born? As a Pharisee, Paul would have been very familiar with the Old Testament tabernacle rituals, however, over the years, they had become virtually meaningless. Though Israel celebrated those ceremonies religiously, the truths they spoke of eventually were completely lost. Once Paul was converted, the religious scales fell from his eyes, and those Old Testament tabernacle worship stations suddenly took on an exciting new meaning. Instead of worshiping an empty ritual, Paul saw the Lord Jesus symbolized at every station. Yes, Jesus is clearly portrayed throughout the Old Testament and nowhere more clearly than in the tabernacle teachings.

Tabernacle

With the exception of Luke, the New Testament writers were Hebrews who assumed that only small groups of believing Jews would be reading their writings. The thought never entered their minds that many hundreds of years later, their writings would be compiled into one book and read by Gentiles in every corner of the globe. Thinking they were writing to a select few, they felt no need to elaborate on such Jewish words as propitiation, mercy seat, and brazen altar. Jews with an Old Testament background would be familiar with such terms. Today, the vast majority of New Testament readers are converted Gentiles. With little understanding of tabernacle lingo, they are at a disadvantage when reading the Bible. With little Old Testament background, entire portions of the New Testament remain unclear. Paul's writings are filled with words and phrases that are tabernacle based and remain fuzzy and unclear to most Gentile believers. The book of Hebrews was obviously written by a converted Jew, one who was very familiar with tabernacle teachings—perhaps Paul himself. Until we understand what each tabernacle worship station symbolizes, the book of Hebrews is very difficult to understand and, therefore, rarely taught today. With a good understanding of the tabernacle worship stations, Hebrews not only becomes one of the richest books in the Bible, but one of the easiest to understand.

Today, there is a lot of talk about Bible codes, which I personally have not researched, but there is certainly one Bible code that has great validity. That code is unlocked when studying the six stations of worship contained in the tabernacle rituals. Without clearly understanding each worship station, portions of the New Testament remains closed.

I occasionally hear Christians say, "I only read the New Testament, as the Old Testament is just a history book." Yes, in part, the Old Testament is a history book, primarily recording the history of the nation of Israel. It is also the very foundation of the New Testament. The New Testament has its roots in the Old Testament—especially in the tabernacle. Without a grasp of the entire tabernacle teaching, reading Paul's epistles and the book of Hebrews will be like trying to understand calculus with no understanding of basic math. Have you ever turned on the television and tried watching a movie that had already been playing for over an hour? Having missed significant key points, it is difficult to grasp the essence of the story. When reading a large detailed sixty-six chapter book, it is unlikely we would begin our reading at chapter forty, however, that is where many Christians begin their study of the Bible. I expect it will surprise you to know that God's formula for becoming a Christian and even how to mature as a believer, can easily be taught using the Old Testament tabernacle worship stations. Getting a clear overall picture of the Bible is similar to piecing together a large puzzle. As each new piece is added, the overall picture becomes clearer. Not having the pieces of the tabernacle in place, we miss out on much of what the New Testament is saying.

The word *tabernacle* means *dwelling place*. God dwelt among His people, Israel, and through the tabernacle, revealed His attributes to them. Prior to this stage of their exodus, Israel had a limited relationship with God. "I appeared to Abraham, to Isaac, and to Jacob, as God Almighty, but by My name Lord I was not known to them" (Exodus 6:3). Now, through the tabernacle worship stations, Israel's fellowship with Him was to become more intimate. Certainly a much closer relationship than they experienced in the slave camps of Egypt.

Jesus Our Tabernacle

Our fathers had the tabernacle of witness in the wilderness, as He appointed, instructing Moses to make it according to the pattern that he had seen.

Acts 7:44

The Word became flesh and dwelt among us.

John 1:14

The tabernacle spoke of Christ. The rituals performed there were the foundation of the gospel. The word "dwelt" originates from the same Hebrew word as "tabernacle." Approximately fourteen hundred years after the Old Testament tabernacle was erected, Christ tabernacled (dwelt) on earth for a period of thirty-three years. At that time, Christians enjoyed a more intimate relationship with God than at any previous time, for they saw Jesus face-to-face. Jesus said, "He who has seen Me has seen the Father" (John 14:9B).

When Jesus told the disciples He was about to return to the Father, they naturally became concerned. Who would they turn to for guidance and advice? With their leader gone, would the Christian movement fizzle out? With whom would they have intimate conversations, once He departed? When they chose to follow Christ, they were excommunicated from the local temple, and it was unlikely they would ever be welcomed back with open arms.

Jesus set their hearts at ease by reminding them of an Old Testament verse. "I will put My Spirit within you..." (Ezekiel 36:27). He told them another Helper would come who would not only dwell in them, but would remain with them for a long time—forever (John 14:16-17). A comforting promise! Jesus made it pretty clear that once He returned home, the Holy Spirit would shift His headquarters from heaven and tabernacle (dwell) in the hearts of believers. That event took place at Pentecost (Acts 2:1). The Holy Spirit did indeed come, and in this age, He does reside in the hearts of believers, enabling them to experience a more intimate relationship with God than at any previous time in history (1 Corinthians 6:19). I like the way Jesus put it. He said, "We will come to him and make Our home with him" (John 14:23B). Don't hang up the phone, for there is better yet to come!

Once we depart from this world, and throughout all eternity, we will enjoy an even more intimate relationship with Christ. As His bride, we will be forever in His presence—eye to eye! Tabernacling together! Many years ago a Christian friend of mine had a lapel pin that I have always admired, perhaps even coveted just a wee bit. The pin was a replica of one of those long heralding trumpets with an inscription that said, "Perhaps Today." Perhaps today the trumpet will sound and we will be off to the wedding feast!

Successful Tithing

Compared to today's mega churches, the tabernacle erected in the desert was a small dwelling. It was actually a tent—150 feet by 75 feet. Despite its size, it was a most valuable structure. On today's commodities market, the gold and silver used in the furnishings would be worth over twenty million dollars! Where did a ragtag group of ex-slaves obtain such wealth? Did they stumble upon a gold and silver mine during their trek in the desert? No, the good riddance gifts the Egyptians showered upon Israel as they left Egypt were now put to good use (Exodus 12:35-36). All in fulfillment of a promise God made to Abraham—"They shall come out with great possessions" (Genesis 15:14). When it came time to erect the tabernacle, Moses didn't have to locate a mortgage company to raise the necessary funds.

> Speak to the children of Israel, that they bring Me an offering. From everyone who gives it willingly with his heart you shall take My offering.
>
> Exodus 25:2

God called for a free will offering to furnish the tabernacle. The tithe was not to be the legalistic 10 percent figure that is so prevalent in today's church circles, but a heart offering. Each person contributed according to the motivation of his heart. Generally speaking, heart offerings produce the best results. In fact, this method of tithing presented a problem for Moses. The problem was not that they gave too little, they gave too much! Finally, Moses had to say, "Enough already!" (Exodus 36:6-7). Every church board's dream! I can't help but wonder why this seemingly insignificant little detail was recorded in Scripture? Could it be to teach us a lesson on effective tithing? Perhaps!

When a committed congregation is convinced God is behind a program, there will be no problem raising money. There will be no need for guilt-ridden tithing sermons, bingo games, or bake sales to raise funds. Raising money only becomes a problem when the congregation isn't convinced the project is inspired by God, or if they still love their money more than they love God.

> So let each one give as he purposes in his heart, not grudgingly or of necessity; for God loves a cheerful giver.
>
> 2 Corinthians 9:7

It is interesting to note that the current 10 percent tithing rule that exists in most churches today has its origins with Abraham and the Old Testament priest/king Melchizedek. Didn't we recently establish that New Testament Christians are no longer under the law? The legalistic 10 percent we toss on the collection plate is clearly Old Testament law based. In the New Testament age we don't get off that easy. All that we have is His, and as reliable stewards, we are responsible for how we manage our entire bank account. Before casually tossing money on a collection plate, we must make sure Jesus is receiving decent dividends from our gifts. Too often money is tithed without giving any thought as to how and where, or even *if* it will be used to further the Kingdom!

Shadows and Patterns

The writer of Hebrews says the tabernacle rituals were a *shadow* of someone real (Hebrews 8:5). That someone is Christ! A shadow is always inferior to the real! For example, on a sunny day my body casts a shadow which, to some degree, resembles me. However, you cannot have a conversation with my shadow. My shadow has no power to work and earn an income. It is simply a reminder that the real thing is close by. As with any shadow, mine is inferior to the real! Having been married to Ruth for just over fifty years, I don't recall a time when she ever attempted to hug my shadow!

In a similar way, a dress pattern is a shadow of the real. Even with my limited understanding of dressmaking, I can look at a pattern and gain some idea of what the finished garment will look like. However, only a fool would attempt to wear a paper pattern in public. The shadow is inferior to the real! I know little about building a home, but I can examine an architect's plans and visualize, to some extent, what the completed structure will look like. A person cannot find shelter from the weather, however, by crawling under an architect's schematics. The shadow is inferior to the real! In a similar way, a Hebrew father could draw a stick pattern of the tabernacle in the desert sand and explain to his child what each tabernacle worship station symbolized. Studying the pattern in detail, the child could visualize the real coming Lamb of God and how to have a relationship with Him!

Mount Sinai or Mount Zion

In Scripture, Mount Sinai is a pattern—a shadow of the law—for it was on this mountain that Moses was given the Commandments. Symbolically, a nonbeliever resides on Mount Sinai—under the judgmental law. The Bible often makes reference to another mountain—Mount Zion. "You have come to Mount Zion and to the city of the living God, the heavenly Jerusalem" (Hebrews 12:22).

Mount Zion pictures the kingdom of Christ. Once we become a Christian, symbolically, we are translated from Mount Sinai, the law-based mountain, to Mount Zion, the grace-based mountain. Once we make a personal decision to receive Christ as our Savior and Lord, we are permanently removed from Mount

Sinai, no longer under the judgmental law. Every person in this world resides in either Mount Sinai (under the judgmental law), or Mount Zion (under the redeeming blood of Christ). The line in the sand that separates the two is Calvary.

> And it shall come to pass that whoever calls on the name of the Lord shall be saved. For in Mount Zion and Jerusalem there shall be deliverance…
>
> Joel 2:32

There is a definite symbolic relationship between the mount of salvation and Jerusalem.

> Those who trust in the Lord are like Mount Zion, which cannot be moved, but abides forever.
>
> Psalm 125:1

As the above verse states, once we reside in Mount Zion—in the kingdom of Christ—our position remains permanent. Once we become citizens in the kingdom, we come under a new covenant, where *our* conduct cannot cause us to be transferred back to Mount Sinai. Once on Mount Zion always on Mount Zion! The Bible tells us all the kingdoms of this world are going to be severely shaken at some future time, and only the kingdom of Christ will remain intact (Hebrews 12:26-28).

The obvious question is, "Which mountain are you camped upon—Mount Sinai (the law-based mount), or Mount Zion (the grace-based mount)?" Approximately forty years ago Ruth and I moved our base camp to Mt. Zion—Calvary. That is one of the few things in this life I know for sure!

In the next six chapters we will be examining each tabernacle worship stations in detail. Once we have completed that study, I assure you there will never again be a need for you to say, "What's that?

Questions

- Do you find yourself becoming judgmental when others fail to line up with your list of dos and don'ts?

- Do the specks in the eyes of others catch your attention while you view your beams as acceptable?

- Are you beginning to understand why Satan despises the tabernacle and loves the law?

BRAZEN ALTAR

The brazen altar was the first station of worship. Since it was the foundation for the rest of the tabernacle rituals, it was appropriately placed in the courtyard. The annual Passover ritual took place at this worship station. It was the altar of justification.

In order to picture what The Lamb of God would accomplish at Calvary, the Levite high priest selected two lambs (Leviticus 16:8-10). He would carefully inspect the first lamb to ensure it was an acceptable offering with no broken bones, in fact, no imperfections whatsoever. Once he was completely satisfied that was the case, he would slay the lamb on the brazen altar. He would then carry the shed blood into the Holy of Holies (the rear compartment of the tabernacle), where he would sprinkle it on the mercy seat as atonement, first for his sin and then for the sins of the nation of Israel. The ark was the only piece of furniture in the Holy of Holies. It was an elaborately designed box containing the tablets of the law carried off the mount by Moses. Covering the ark was a lid, most appropriately called the mercy seat.

> Into the second part the high priest went alone once a year, not without blood, which he offered for himself (his sins) and for the people's sins.
>
> Hebrews 9:7

When God looked down on this annual ritual, He no longer focused on the judgmental law contained in the ark; instead His gaze fell upon the shed blood of an innocent lamb. You may recall that at the first Passover in Egypt, God proclaimed, "When I see the blood, I will pass over you"—there would be no judgment because the law was obscured by the innocent blood. That truth still prevailed. The shed blood of the Passover lamb didn't actually deal with their sins, but clearly pictured the Lamb of God who one day would. "Christ, our Passover was sacrificed for us" (1 Corinthians 5:7). By placing faith in what the Passover ritual pictured, their position in the kingdom of God was secured. They still went to their graves in their sin, but clutching a promissory note, so to speak, looking forward to the day when the Lamb of God would once and for all time deal with sin (Hebrews 10:11-14). The tabernacle brazen altar ritual clearly pictured what Jesus would accomplish at Calvary's true brazen altar and through His resurrection.

Christ Our Passover Lamb

This is My beloved Son, in whom I am well pleased.

Matthew 3:17B

Of the many spiritual people who have passed through this world, Jesus is the only one who met God's requirements as an acceptable offering for sin. This He did in three unique ways. First, in keeping with the tabernacle Passover ritual, He had no imperfections, physical or otherwise. In order to speed up the death process, it was customary to break the legs of those being crucified. Once their legs were broken, they could no longer elevate themselves on the foot platform and soon died of suffocation. God, Himself, sped up the death process of His Son, for when the soldiers came to break His legs they discovered He was already dead. Had Christ's legs been broken, He would not have fully completed the picture of an acceptable sin offering (Exodus 12:5). How careful God was in the details. Isn't it comforting to know He is always one step ahead?

> The virgin shall conceive and bear a Son, and shall call His name Immanuel.
>
> Isaiah 7:14

The second reason was His unique conception—the virgin birth! Since day one, a child's birth has always resulted from the seed of man, creating a serious problem for every single person born into this world. From the moment a child is conceived, he comes into the world possessing the genes of the first fallen man—Adam. It is clear King David understood this truth, for he wrote, "I was brought forth in iniquity, and in sin did my mother conceived me" (Psalm 51:5). David wasn't implying his mother behaved unseemly, but he knew very well that the moment he was conceived he inherited Adam's sinful DNA. Down through the ages, that sinful nature was passed on from father to son, and in that condition, from day one, man was under judgment (Romans 5:18).

Jesus entered this world in a different manner. His conception was not a result of man, but of the Holy Spirit—the virgin birth. "That which is conceived in her is of the Holy Spirit" (Matthew 1:20B). A miraculous conception! Had Joseph been Christ's father, like King David, Jesus would have been conceived in sin, and in this condition, most certainly would have been an unacceptable offering. His arrival on planet earth would have been no different from the rest of mankind. He too would have possessed Adam's fallen nature and entered as a citizen of Satan's fallen kingdom. For Christ to be *the* acceptable offering for sin, not only was He to have no broken bones, but His virgin birth was an absolute must. This virgin birth was prophesied up front in the Bible and became a reality approximately four thousand years later. "Between your seed [Satan's] and her [Eve's] Seed" (Genesis 3:15). Prior to the conception of Jesus, as well as after, birth has always been a result of the seed of man. This miraculous conception was a one-time-event!

Jesus did not sin in either thought or in deed during his entire time here on earth, and that is the all important third reason. Think about that! In the history of the world, no other person can come close to making that claim! I suppose it's remotely possible for a person to never break the Ten Commandments in deed, but to never sin in thought is a whole different ball game. Only a fool or a liar, would claim to have never sinned in thought. "As he thinks in his heart, so is he" (Proverbs 23:7). Jimmy Carter was right on the money all those years ago, for he was basically quoting the following Scripture. "Whoever looks at a woman to lust for her has already committed adultery with her in his heart" (Matthew 5:28). Unlike the billions of people who have been ushered through this world system, Jesus is the only sinless one! This fact raises an obvious question. Could Jesus have sinned? Prior to his fall, Satan had an intimate relationship with God, and he was obviously convinced Christ, in His humanity, could also be tempted. Otherwise, why would he have wasted so much time trying to get to Him during the forty-day wilderness temptation?

Because of Christ's miraculous conception, His unblemished body, and His sinless life while here on planet earth, God viewed His Lamb as the only acceptable sin offering. After all, didn't He say, "In Him I am well pleased?"

> You were not redeemed with corruptible things, like silver and gold, from your aimless conduct received by tradition from our fathers (the law and religious rituals), but with the precious blood of Christ, as of a lamb without blemish and without spot (sinless).

> 1 Peter 1:18-19

Christ's final words from the cross were profound—"It is finished" (John 19:30). He was not just referring to His physical life being over. That is such a limited view of what was actually taking place. I believe He was announcing to one and all that he had fulfilled, in real time and space, the Old Testament brazen altar ritual. He was saying, "I am that Lamb!" The necessity for ritual and shadows would be no more, for the real had come. Believers this side of the cross can now look back in faith to what Christ accomplished at Calvary's brazen altar. Jesus was the only *just* one, therefore, qualified to justify (Romans 3:26). When Jesus said, "It is finished," He was also saying the Old Testament age was finished, and a new age was about to begin—the church age—the age of the bride—the age of the Gentiles!

> Behold, the Lamb of God who takes away the sin of the world.
>
> John 1:29

When John the Baptist announced the arrival of God's Lamb, the hearts of believing Jews should have been filled with excitement. Knowing the promised Lamb was on the scene should have filled their hearts with joy. John very specifically referred to Jesus as the Lamb of God. Other appropriate titles could have been chosen. For example, he could have referred to Christ as the Lion of God, not only the king of the beasts, but the symbol of the tribe from which Jesus stemmed—the tribe of Judah. John could have labeled Jesus the Elephant of God, speaking of Christ's mighty power and strength, or the Owl of God, speaking of His unparalleled wisdom. John was Jewish and certainly familiar with the tabernacle brazen altar ritual; therefore, he appropriately labeled Jesus, "The Lamb of God."

> Christ came as a High Priest of good things to come, with the greater and more perfect tabernacle not made with hands, that

is, not of this creation. Not with the blood of goats and calves, but with His own blood He entered the Most Holy Place once for all, having obtained eternal redemption.

Hebrews 9:11-12

After His resurrection, Jesus ascended to heaven, where, as our High Priest, He personally sprinkled His shed blood on the heavenly mercy seat—again in fulfillment of the Old Testament brazen altar shadow. Once we place faith in what Jesus accomplished at Calvary, and through His resurrection, the promise God made to Israel at the first Passover in Egypt also becomes a reality in our lives—"When I see the blood I will pass over you." God no longer views us as condemned by the judgmental law; instead He sees us covered by the redeeming blood of His slain Lamb!

Christ Our Scapegoat

The second lamb presented to the tabernacle high priest was not slain, but kept alive. This lamb was referred to as the scapegoat (Leviticus 16:10, 20-22). A scapegoat, as you well know, is one who is unjustly accused. I expect there have been times when we have all attempted to shift our stupid mistakes to a scapegoat—perhaps our spouse or even God! That's exactly what Adam did when he stumbled. He blamed everyone in the phone book—God and Eve.

> The woman whom You gave to be with me, she gave me of the tree, and I ate.

Genesis 3:12

Over the past six thousand years, man hasn't changed one iota. When he stumbles, he is usually quick to look for a scapegoat—often among those closest to him. A good definition of the word frustration is, "Not having anyone to blame but ourselves!" Fortunately, we have a Lamb, who is currently seated at the right hand of the Father, who was willing to be our Scapegoat. After the high priest examined the scapegoat to ensure it contained no imperfections, he placed his hand on the head of the lamb. This ritual pictured an exchange of status. The Israelite's sin status was symbolically imputed to the innocent lamb, and the lamb's innocent status was imputed to the sinner's account. All a picture of what I call the Big Swap verse which says, "He made Him who knew no sin to be sin for us, that we might become the righteousness of God in Him." (2 Corinthians 5:21).

Once the Old Testament high priest performed this symbolic ritual, he released that lamb into the barren desert, never to be seen again. What a beautiful picture of how God views a believer, released from condemnation completely, and forever! We should rejoice continually at the completeness of our salvation! Our God left no stone unturned. As believers we, too, can say with complete confidence, "It is finished."

> As far as the east is from the west, so far has He removed our transgressions from us.
>
> Psalm 103:12

Two Birthdays

Each year I celebrate two birthdays—my physical birth and my spiritual birth. Both births are a result of a supernatural event. In his book *Where is God When it Hurts?* Philip Yancey describes our physical birth in the following most interesting and unusual manner:

> In the womb your world is dark, safe, secure. You are bathed in warm liquid, cushioned from shock. You do nothing for

yourself; you are fed automatically, and a murmuring heart-beat assures you that someone larger than you fills all your needs. Your life consists of simple waiting—you're not sure what you are waiting for, but any change seems far away and scary. You meet no sharp objects, no pain, no threatening adventures. A fine existence. One day you feel a tug. The walls are falling in on you. Those soft cushions are now pulsing and beating against you, crushing you downwards. Your body is bent double, your limbs twisted and wrenched. You're falling, upside down. For the first time in your life, you feel pain. You're in a sea of roiling matter. There is more pressure, almost too intense to bear. Your head is squeezed flat, and you are pushed harder, harder into a dark tunnel. Oh, the pain. Noise. More pressure. You hurt all over. You hear a groaning sound and an awful, sudden fear rushes in you. It is happening—your world is collapsing. You're sure it's the end. You see a piercing, blinding light. Cold, rough hands pull at you. A painful slap. Waaaahhhh! Congratulations! You've just been born.

Most assuredly, I say to you, unless one is born again, he cannot see the kingdom of God.

John 3:3

Our physical birth is undoubtedly a miraculous event. An event worthy of celebrating! However, our spiritual birth is an even more spectacular event! Think about the miracle of being *born again*. One moment we are in our sins. The very next moment, because of a personal decision, the righteousness of the Creator of the universe is imputed to our account. One moment we are under judgment, and the next moment we are totally set free of God's judgmental law! One moment God is on the outside, and in the twinkling of an eye, through the Holy Spirit, the God of the universe takes up residence within our lives! Furthermore, at the moment of our spiritual birth, we are immediately translated from Satan's darkened kingdom to the kingdom of Christ! Being *born again* is the event of a lifetime! An event worthy of celebration! No wonder the Bible tells us the angels break into song every time a sinner is converted! Have you given the angels an opportunity to sing for you?

> He has delivered us from the power of darkness and conveyed us into the kingdom of the Son of His love, in whom we have redemption through His blood, the forgiveness of sins.
>
> Colossians 1:13-14

Obviously, I do not recall the details of my physical birth, but after approximately forty years, I can vividly recall every detail of the number one event in my life—my spiritual birth. I remember the people who were in the room and can even visualize where each sat. I remember the date and time—September 23, 1971, at 4:00 a.m. The decision I made that early morn altered my citizenship forever, and from that moment on, I have always known where I would spend eternity!

Billy Graham was speaking to a group several years ago and told a story about the physicist Albert Einstein who boarded a train in Princeton. When the conductor asked for his ticket, Mr. Einstein was unable to locate it. Recognizing Einstein, the conductor said, "I know who you are, and that you would have purchased a ticket, don't worry about your misplaced ticket." Just before proceeding to the next car, the conductor glanced back and saw Einstein still searching for his ticket. Again, the conductor reassured him. Einstein replied, "Young man, I, too, know who I am. What I don't know is where I'm going." In relating this story, Billy Graham was clearly making a point. That point being, once he departed from this planet, Billy knew his exact destination.

> These things I have written to you who believe in the name of the Son of God, that you may know that you have eternal life.
>
> 1 John 5:13

Death is simply a door to a predetermined destination. Regardless of what unbelievers think lies beyond deaths door, the Creator of the universe says, "There will be a resurrection of the dead, both of the *just* and the *unjust*" (Acts 24:15B). God also makes it clear in His Word that Jesus is the only ticket to heaven—"I am the door of the sheep... If anyone enters by Me, he will be saved" (John 10:7, 9). Once we step through death's door, we are then faced with two possible paths—the path that leads to eternal life with Christ, or the path that leads to eternal life in Satan's camp.

Questions

- If you arrived at heaven's gate and were asked why you felt you were qualified to enter, what would be your reply?

- Would you arrive placing confidence in your earthly accomplishments? Or would you arrive having placed faith in Christ's accomplishments?

LAVER

In the previous chapter we talked about the first worship station—the brazen altar, which pictured how a nonbeliever was set right in the eyes of God. We saw how God viewed a believer who placed faith in what the shed blood of an innocent lamb symbolized—the true Lamb of God. The brazen altar was the place of *justification.* Just as the brazen altar was the foundation for all the other worship stations, Christ is the foundation for our Christian life. Spiritual life begins once Jesus is acknowledged as Savior and Lord. That life is produced by the indwelling Holy Spirit, who enters our lives, upon invitation, at our salvation experience.

The next worship station we come to is the laver. The ritual performed at the laver is a beautiful picture of the ongoing *sanctification* process a believer is meant to experience once he has been justified. The laver was also located in the courtyard, between the brazen altar and the entrance to the tabernacle.

The words lavatory and laver stem from the same Hebrew root word, meaning a place of cleansing. The laver was a highly polished brass bowl which, when filled with water, functioned as a mirror (Exodus 30:17-19, 38:8). Before entering the tabernacle to minister on Israel's behalf, the Levite priests examined themselves in the laver and washed away whatever dirt was exposed.

But be doers of the word, and not hearers only, deceiving yourselves. For if anyone is a hearer of the word and not a doer, he is like a man observing his natural face in a mirror; for he observes himself, goes away, and immediately forgets what kind of man he was. But he who looks into the perfect law of liberty and continues in it, and is not a forgetful hearer but a doer of the work, this one will be blessed in what he does.

James 1:22-25

In a previous chapter, we discussed the two spiritual occupations of a believer. At this point, I'd like to further focus on one of those occupations—our priesthood. As bridge-builders, we fulfill this role when we encourage a nonbeliever to defect from the kingdom of Satan to become a citizen in the kingdom of Christ. We also exercise our priesthood when we encourage a troubled Christian to move from a position of defeat and discouragement to a position of victory. Jesus, our High Priest, is the ultimate bridge-builder, and as His representatives here on earth, one of our main ministries is to encourage and build up the body of Christ—the church. "Let us do good to all, especially to those who are of the household of faith" (Galatians 6:10). If we are to be effective in our role as priest, we too must regularly go to the laver and deal with whenever sin is exposed. As the above verse in James clearly states, our laver is the Word of God.

There is a touching fictional story, where it comes from I do not know, which beautifully illustrates how Christians are to minister one to another. A Christian arrived at heaven's gate where he was met by the gatekeeper. Before entering, he asked the gatekeeper if he could stop by hell and say a final goodbye to some of his old cronies. The gatekeeper gave him permission, but told him he couldn't go beyond the gate of hell, as he possessed the wrong citizenship. He arrived at meal time, and he could see large bowls of stew on long banquet tables. People were sitting around those tables undernourished and in a state of bedlam. He immediately spotted the problem. Each person had a long handled spoon permanently attached to his wrist, which prevented him from getting food from the bowl to his mouth. Despite an abundance of food, everyone was starving. When the man returned to heaven he was amazed to see a similar scene. There were large bowls of food on long tables, and each resident there also had a long handled spoon permanently attached to his wrist. There was one major difference, however. Everyone was well fed and obviously content. It was easy to see why. Each person was patiently feeding his neighbor across the table.

The flight behavior of geese also gives us a pattern from which we Christians could learn much. Despite the superior strength of the eagle, geese are able to fly longer distances. Eagles are lone rangers. They never fly in groups. Geese are able to fly longer distances, not because of their individual strength, but because of group strength. I am sure you have observed the famous V-formations of migrating geese. The lead bird displaces the air, allowing the birds in the rear to exert less energy as they fly. When the lead bird tires he drops back in the formation and is replaced by another that has renewed his strength. Younger less experienced birds remain at the rear, watching and learning as they develop their strength. Wow! If Christianity could only function that way!

Bondservants

In several of his epistles, Paul speaks of himself as a bondservant to Jesus Christ. In Paul's day, there were two categories of servants—a hired servant and a bondservant. Such occupations as teachers, lawyers, doctors, and bookkeepers are examples of hired servants. They were employed for a particular purpose, and for a specific period of time, and had no permanent ties to the household. They simply did the task they were hired to do, and once the job was finished, they went on their way.

A bondservant was different. He was viewed as a permanent member of the household. Thus the term "bond." As proof of his permanent attachment to the family, it was customary for the master to place a mark on the earlobe of the bondservant—a tiny tattoo. The word bondservant tends to picture in our minds a slave. When the master says jump, the bondservant says, "How high, sir?" That was clearly not the case. Over the years, a loving relationship developed between the bondservant and his master. The bondservant was given great liberties and freedom within the family.

Abraham's relationship with Eliezar is a perfect example of that love-trust relationship. All Eliezar's needs were provided; he came under Abraham's protection, and within the household, he enjoyed a life of freedom and authority. When it was time to select a bride for Isaac, Abraham's beloved son, Eliezar, above all others, was given the responsibility of traveling the long distance to Abraham's homeland in order to select a suitable bride. A major responsibility you will agree.

Bondservant is a perfect title for a Christian. A bondservant to Christ should be a coveted position. Instead of living a life of bondage, he is the freest person on earth. If we are not finding freedom in our daily exodus with Christ, it is because we have neither discovered, nor are we inhabiting our role as bondservants. As bondservants, we are promised our daily needs (not wants) will be provided. Additionally, we are meant to enter into a life of freedom and dominion. Upon conversion, we become permanent citizens of Christ's household—permanently bonded to Him. Instead of placing an identifying mark on our earlobes, Christ demonstrates our position in His kingdom by placing an irrevocable mark on our hearts, which the apostle Paul refers to as "circumcision of the heart."

As a bondservant to Christ, it is His desire to use our talents and gifts to edify His kingdom. Knowing our capabilities, He will never assign tasks that will bring about stress, frustration, and burnout. Should these things occur, be assured it is because we have taken on responsibilities He never assigned. Today, many, many Christians are experiencing frustration and burnout for this very reason.

As a new Christian, in my eagerness to serve, I was often too quick to say, "Yes" when offered a position within the Christian community. I have since learned to be more cautious. Unless I am firmly convinced Christ is motivating me to take on a certain responsibility, I have learned to say, "Thanks, but no thanks," despite the guilt trip sometimes laid on me by well meaning Christians (you know, the old guilt trip thing, "God has told me you would be the perfect one to fill this position"). In my early years as a believer, I loaded myself down with so many Christian duties I began experiencing enormous frustration and burnout. I was the director of evangelism in our church, an elder, president of the local Christian Business Men's Association, and to top things off, once a week we held a Bible study in our home for street people. I made a decision. I was in over my head, and it became clear that some of the *good* had to be sacrificed in order to focus on the *best*. I asked myself the question, "What is producing the most fruit?" Guess which activity remained? The Bible study! Some may have thought the Bible study should have been the first to go as that particular ragtag group certainly didn't fit the mold, if you get my drift. Among them were thieves; others were either still in, or fresh out of the drug scene. And at each study, you could cut the smoke with a knife. Certainly not everybody's cup of tea, but God made it Ruth's and mine. People were becoming believers and beginning to see negatives flushed out of their lives. They were so excited about their new found life, they even began inviting their cronies to the meetings. Many in the Christian community were rather puzzled as to why I chose to direct all my attention to that particular group. It simply became clear to us that was where Christ would have us serve, at that particular time in our lives. I have to tell you that once that decision was made, the frustration and burnout disappeared. The effort put forth in the weekly home study was not only fruitful, but enjoyable! I was a fairly new Christian at the time, and that weekly study was about all I could handle. I managed to stay about one page ahead of them each week, learning as I went. Having lived in the world for over thirty years before becoming Christians, we also had an understanding of their plight, and they felt no judgmental attitude in our home. Not only was there fruit from our labors, but both Ruth and I learned so much in those first Bible studies ourselves.

Small groups have always been at the heart of our ministry and remain so to this very day. For the last ten years we lived on the side of a mountain in a little fishing village with cobblestone streets in the heart of Mexico. We were fortunate enough to have a very large terrace, and every Friday morning we held a Bible study there. Ajijic, our little village, is somewhat of an expat community, and gathered on our terrace each Friday were anywhere from thirty to forty hungry souls who gladly sat for an hour being taught the Word. This is probably as good a spot as any to say that the book you hold in your hands comes as a result of all those years and years of small group studies.

Circumcision

In Him you were also circumcised with the circumcision made without hands.

Colossians 2:11

Circumcision is that of the heart.

Romans 2:29

If you are a Christian, regardless of your sex, you have been circumcised. Not the physical circumcision made with hands, but a circumcision of the heart. This operation took place when the Holy Spirit took up residence in your heart. Today, most Jews and Gentiles fail to understand why God instituted the Old Testament ritual of circumcision.

Physical circumcision spoke of a believer's *position* in the kingdom of God (Genesis 17:10-11). During their captivity in Egypt, Israel got away from circumcising their males, and God reminded them to reinstate this ritual once they placed faith in what the Passover blood symbolized (Exodus 12:43-48). Circumcision was another *shadow*, which made several statements. It was a constant reminder to Israel that they were *different*. They were set apart from the other nations. God's chosen. They served a real God and not some impotent pagan idol. They were to live a different quality of life and display that life to the non-believing nations around them. As believers, they looked forward to spending eternity in a different camp than nonbelievers. When a Hebrew lad went skinny dipping everyone watching knew he was different—one of those God kids. They had God's brand of approval on them!

Physical circumcision made another significant statement. It was an *irrevocable* act—impossible to undo. Circumcision was a constant reminder to Israel, that once they placed faith in what the Passover ritual represented, their status with God was fixed. They could never become uncircumcised. As the saying might have gone, once circumcised, always circumcised! When the foreskin was discarded in the desert sand, it was never seen again. "As far as the east is from the west."

The Old Testament saints were taught that the ritual of physical circumcision spoke of a future form of circumcision that would alter a person's status forever. It was a *shadow* of a superior form of circumcision—spiritual circumcision.

> The Lord your God will (future tense) circumcise your heart...
>
> Deuteronomy 30:6

Just as physical circumcision made statements, our spiritual circumcision makes several important statements.

The phrase born again speaks of our change in citizenship. As Christians, we are grafted into the tree of Israel, not as a national Jew, but a spiritual Jew (Romans chapter eleven). We become the seed of Abraham (a Jew)—members of the same eternal family (Galatians 3:29). Jesus Christ (a Jew) becomes our Lord. The writer of the book of Hebrews reminds us our Savior is not ashamed to call us brethren (Hebrews 2:11B). Adam, Abraham, King David, the disciples, and all believers are members of the same family—spiritual Jews. In heaven there will not be Americans, Africans, Canadians, Mexicans, or Russians. There will be only one nationality—spiritual Jews. Heaven's residents will consist of Old Testament saints who placed faith in what the Passover ritual symbolized and New Testament saints who placed faith in Christ the fulfillment of that ritual.

Spiritual circumcision also reminds us we are *different*! As Christians we should begin to think and function differently than we did when we were citizens in the old kingdom. As we examine ourselves in our laver (The Word), we should no longer function as we did in the old kingdom, constantly struggling with stress, worry, fear, and anger. As we mature, our values and attitudes begin to change. Instead of looking to the world to satisfy our inner emptiness, our fulfillment should come as a result of our personal relationship with Christ. We should no longer allow this spiritually darkened world to manipulate our emotions and time. Instead we should begin to soar like an eagle, free from the annoyances of the world (Isaiah 40:31). Eagles fly higher than any bird. Pilots have spotted them at 30,000 feet. Despite their smaller size, crows love to annoy eagles. When an annoying crow approaches, eagles simply rise a little higher.

What a lovely picture of the Christian life as it should be lived! When we are confronted with the annoyances of this fallen world, if we have made digesting God's Word a regular part of our lives, and in turn, are seeking to eliminate the negatives, as they are exposed, we will find ourselves soaring like eagles. Christ clearly stated there would always be annoyances confronting us. Instead of being overcome by them, however, we must simply move on up a little higher. The apostle Paul refers to this soaring as a "renewing of the mind" (Romans 12:2). Unfortunately, many of God's children do little soaring. Instead they flop around like decapitated turkeys kicking up a lot of dust but going nowhere fast.

It's sad to see believers who are still shackled to the world—allowing the world to lead them around by the nose. In his early years as king, Solomon looked to the world for fulfillment. From a worldly point of view, he had everything one could desire: wealth, wisdom, position in the community, and his every fleshly desire catered to. Eventually, Solomon came to the conclusion that the things of this world only provided temporal satisfaction and were nothing more than vanity and vexation (Ecclesiastes 12:8). He finally realized the only thing that truly mattered in life was his relationship with God. Until we come to that same understanding, we will find our emotions manipulated by this fallen world, and our soaring will be sporadic at best.

Our heart circumcision not only reminds us that we are different, it also is a constant reminder that our status in the kingdom of Christ is *irrevocable*. Once heart circumcised—always heart circumcised!

The righteous (believers) will never be removed.

Proverbs 10:30

Blessed are those whose lawless deeds are forgiven (believers), and whose sins are covered (by the blood). Blessed is the man to whom the Lord shall not impute sin.

Romans 4:7-8

Keeping Up Appearances

Just as the Levite priests washed at the laver before ministering within the tabernacle, as priests, we are challenged to take action whenever our mirror, the Word of God, exposes a problem. Whenever negatives are exposed, we should not rest until the bondage is flushed out. Perhaps I should have said, "There will be no rest until the bondage is flushed out!" When sin is exposed, there are two courses of action we can employ. We can be *hearers* only and carry on in the same manner, or we can be *doers*, willing to deal with exposed sin. The Word states that a doer will be blessed (James 1:25). If we could just get it in our heads that dealing with sin in our lives is always for our benefit! It is never meant to deny us or cramp our style, but to set us free in order to soar a little higher.

In today's Christian community, we have let our guard down. The majority of believers have a sin list—acceptable and unacceptable. Murder, drunkenness, rape, smoking, and spousal abuse are usually high on the unacceptable list and often preached about. Fear, anger, worry, depression, envy, and pride seem to be viewed as acceptable behavior and are rarely preached about or called sin. Is it possible that in this lukewarm church age, pastors are afraid of offending their flocks with such preaching only to see them leave the church—taking their pocketbooks with them? As a result, congregations all too often leave their churches Sunday after Sunday in the same spiritual condition as they entered.

Perhaps keeping up appearances externally, but inwardly, living a less than satisfying Christian life.

A few years ago there was a delightful series on British television called, "Keeping Up Appearances." The lead character was the wife—Hyacinth Bucket, which she, of course, pronounced "Bouquet." Struggling to hide her own insecurities, her less than stellar family, her small row house, and the lack of pride in her husband's occupation were the sources of her constant struggle to keep up appearances. She worked very hard to convince one and all that an invitation to one of her Candlelight Suppers was the greatest honor she could bestow. Hyacinth's condescending behavior toward poor Liz, her neighbor, rattled her whenever she was in Hyacinth's presence. She was forever stumbling and bumbling and spilling her tea. Liz and others in the neighborhood went to great lengths to avoid having any contact with Hyacinth. Today, many in the religious community function much the same as Mrs. Bucket, and the world still goes to great lengths to avoid them, not fully understanding why. If anyone in your circle has to put you down in order to raise themselves up, know they are struggling with a poor self image and probably a whole lot more! I find it interesting that Jesus, the King of the Universe, never made those around him feel that way. In fact, He was so approachable that little children, who are always so perceptive, wanted to climb on his lap.

Because of a lack of solid teaching, or reluctance to deal with negative issues in their lives, many of today's Christians have become terribly bogged down. Some feel it is just too much effort to open the can of worms and deal with their infirmities. Others make the mistake of viewing their fleshly negatives as necessary protection. I'm reminded of a Christian man who said he needed his anger in order to demonstrate authority. When others crossed him, he would invariably strike back, thinking only a wimp would turn the other cheek! He failed to understand his explosive anger was not a sign of strength but of weakness. A wise man once said, "Anger and a fool lie in the same bed" (Ecclesiastes 7:9). I have crossed paths with Christian women who use self-pity as a means of attracting sympathy and attention. It's interesting that when they decide to throw a pity-party, their tough love friends rarely get invited.

The Lord cautions us not to compare ourselves among ourselves. Once we do that, there is a danger of complacency creeping in. What we must do is open our Bibles on a regular basis, comparing ourselves to Christ. When we do that, there will never be time for inertia, which my dictionary, the *New Oxford American Dictionary*, explains as, "A tendency to remain in a fixed condition without change." There will always be at least one issue in our lives that needs to be flushed out. With the elimination of each fleshly addiction, we will find ourselves set free from another prison. When the word "addiction" is mentioned, we mostly think of drugs or alcohol. Worry, fear, anger, and depression can also become forms of addiction, a way of life so deeply imbedded that it takes the indwelling power of the Holy Spirit to set us free. Overeating can also be an addiction!

The apostle Paul never did reach that stage of inertia. He said it was his desire to *know* Christ (Philippians 3:10). When Paul wrote this verse, he had been a believer for many years, so he was not referring to a salvation experience. *Know* speaks of intimacy. When a couple marries, they begin a journey of getting to know one another more intimately with each passing year. Ruth and I have been married fifty years now, and as each year passes, I discover more wonderful attributes that my dear wife possesses. Paul's desire was to know Christ more intimately with each passing day. If our relationship with Christ is the same today as it was a year ago, we are definitely dragging our heels!

Remember the man Jesus encountered at the healing pool? For thirty-eight years this man had lived with an infirmity of some sort. When Jesus asked if he wanted to be made whole, one would have expected the man to shout, "Absolutely!" Surprisingly, his initial response was one of reluctance. Perhaps he thought if he were made whole, he would no longer attract the sympathy and the pity he had been accustomed to receiving. His hesitancy may have been because he would have to begin standing on his own two feet and make his own way through life, rather than relying on some sort of welfare system for support. Shockingly, there are many believers today who are somewhat reluctant to be made whole, preferring to lean on their various crutches to get them through life. Anger and self-pity are certainly crutches! There are professing Christians who prefer to wallow in self-pity, because of past mistakes and failures, rather than move beyond their pigpen and get on with life. The question Jesus still asks today is "Do you want to continue to hang on to your debilitating infirmities, or do you *really* want to be made whole?" Are we willing to sit in the pews playing church, constantly leaving in the same spiritual condition as we entered? It is up to us.

> Make straight paths for your feet, so that what is lame may not be dislocated, but rather healed.
>
> Hebrews 12:13

Yucky-Flavored Christianity

> I know your works, that you are neither cold nor hot. I could wish you were cold or hot. So then, because you are lukewarm, and neither cold nor hot, I will vomit you out of My mouth.
>
> Revelation 3:15-16

Chapters two and three in the book of Revelation list the spiritual condition of each of the seven church ages that have existed since Calvary. Most Bible scholars agree that we live in the last church age—the age of the lukewarm church. As the above verse implies, the Lord's opinion of this present church age is anything but complementary.

This idea of *lukewarmness* reminds me of a swelteringly hot day in Florida when I was working in the yard. After working for an hour or so, as you can imagine, I was pretty thirsty. Instead of making the effort to go inside to get a cool drink, I took a large swig from the nearby garden hose. Not a wise decision! As soon as I tasted the yucky lukewarm water, I was quick to spit it out. With few exceptions, the book of Revelation chapter three tells us that is exactly how the Lord feels about the current church age. To put it rather bluntly, it makes Him want to throw up. Now think about that. For many years I sat in the pews of several different churches, getting absolutely nothing out of the Sunday morning service. We were reluctant to leave, knowing we would be criticized and called pew hoppers. Well, that is no longer the case. If I am not being fed from the pulpit and challenged in my faith, I just move on. I am well able to feed myself, and there are many other clubs I can join for friendship. Times have changed I am sad to say. It is now the spiritual Christians who are leaving churches in search of a church home where they can be fed and enjoy true fellowship. But then, if this is the lukewarm church age, why are we so surprised?

> Behold, I stand at the door and knock. If anyone hears My voice and opens the door, I will come into him and dine with him (fellowship), and he with Me.
>
> Revelation 3:20

As long as Christians ignore the Word, there will be little desire for change, and our churches will remain lukewarm. The above portion of Scripture clearly pictures Jesus knocking at the door of today's churches in hopes of being invited into their midst. How can this be? Isn't He the focal point in all churches? Aren't the Bibles stored in the back of most pews an indication that Jesus is in the church? Isn't the steeple on the roof or the cross on the wall an indication of His presence? What about the Communion ritual? Isn't that proof of His presence? What about all the carefully-designed church programs? Surely all these activities indicate He is the center of the organization! All these activities are noble efforts, but *may* not be an indication that the Lord Jesus Christ is the focal point in the inner workings of any particular church.

If Jesus returned to earth today, how would you expect Him to react to the church scene? Would He discover the Holy Spirit was the power behind each activity, or would He find man's desires and ingenuity as the motivating force behind most church programs? Would He once again be kicking over the tables, so to speak? Would He begin abolishing programs that produced puny spiritual results? Would Jesus eliminate rituals and programs that were not Bible based? Would He send pastors packing who preach watered down sermons and remove nonbelievers and carnal Christians from positions of leadership? Would He be pleased by the dividends received from the tithes and offerings, or would He begin directing *His* money in other areas? If Jesus returned today, would He be able to refer to the congregation as "brethren," or would some hear Him say, "You are not a part of My flock?"

> Many will say to Me in that day, Lord, Lord, have we not prophesied in Your name, cast out demons in Your name, done many wonders in Your name? And then I will declare to them, I never knew you; depart from Me, you who practice lawlessness.
>
> Matthew 7:22-23

Harsh words! If Jesus returned today, went on worldwide television, and repeated His above remarks, how do you think He would be received by the church going community? Would He be welcomed with open arms, or excommunicated, or even executed? Let's move closer to home. If Jesus announced He was coming to your house, would you find yourself rushing about making changes before His arrival, or would life continue as normal while you anxiously awaited His appearance? The poem quoted below was given to Ruth and me in pamphlet form in the early days of our Christianity, and I can tell you it made a profound impression on both of us, so much so that we have given out hundreds of copies of that little pamphlet. After all these years, we still have a few on hand to give out, should the occasion arise.

> If Jesus came to your house to spend a day or two.
>
> If He came unexpectedly, I wonder what you'd do.
>
> Oh, I know you'd give your nicest room to such an honored Guest.
>
> And all the food you'd serve to Him would be the very best,
>
> And you would keep assuring Him you're glad to have Him there.
>
> That serving Him in your own home is joy beyond compare.
>
> When you saw Him coming, would you meet Him at the door,
>
> With arms outstretched in welcome to your heavenly Visitor?
>
> Or would you have to change your clothes before you let Him in?
>
> Or hide some magazines and put the Bible where they'd been?
>
> Would you turn off the TV and hope He hadn't heard?
>
> And wish you hadn't uttered that last, loud, hasty word?
>
> Would you hide your worldly music and put some hymn books out?
>
> Could you let Jesus walk right in, or would you rush about?

And I wonder—if the Savior spent a day or two with you,

Would you go right on doing the things you always do?

Would you go right on saying the things you always say?

Would life for you continue as it does from day to day?

Would your family conversation keep up its usual pace?

And would you find it hard each meal to say a table grace?

Would you sing the songs you always sing, and read the books you read,

And let Him know the things on which your mind and spirit feed?

Would you take Jesus with you everywhere you'd planned to go?

Or would you, maybe, change your plans for just a day or so?

Would you be glad to have Him meet your very closest friends?

Or would you hope they'd stay away until His visit ends?

Would you be glad to have Him stay forever on and on?

Or would you sigh with great relief when He at last was gone?

It might be interesting to know the things that you must do.

If Jesus Christ in person came to spend some time with you.

Lois Kendall

Judging

The laver was the only worship station in the tabernacle that had no detailed list of instructions simply because the sanctification process is personal. The Holy Spirit deals with each Christian individually, which is why there is no room for Christians to be judgmental of one another. A good indicator of a judgmental attitude is seeing our sin as insignificant in comparison to the sins of others. Instead of playing Holy Spirit by focusing on the specks in the eyes of others, we are cautioned to focus on the beams in our eyes (Luke 6:41 42). From personal experience, I can assure you, dealing with our personal beams will keep us fully occupied until the trumpets sound. Someone once said, "When we point a judgmental finger at another, there are three others pointing back at us." We are told to refrain from judging until we have *all* the beams removed from our own eyes, which will never leave us time to be judgmental of others, not even our spouses!

> If you judge people, you have no time to love them.
>
> Mother Teresa

At one point in his life, King David was nailed as a judgmental finger pointer. Despite his many wives, he coveted the wife of Uriah and began an affair with her. When Uriah arrived home from the battlefield, he immediately smelled a rat. David thought by sending him back to the front lines, Uriah would be killed and his sin, in turn, swept under the rug. Uriah indeed was killed. Some time later, Nathan, the prophet, met with David. He told him a fictitious story of a poor man who owned one lamb and a rich man who possessed many lambs. Despite his large flock, the rich man coveted the poor man's lamb and eventually took his only lamb into his fold. Assuming the story was true, David instructed Nathan to execute the rich man. Nathan replied, "You are that man" (2 Samuel 12:7). Despite his affair and pre-meditated murder, David never lost his position as a believer, but for a time his relationship with his Maker was definitely tarnished. His family disowned him, and his kingdom never regained the stature it once had. Unfortunately we often do reap what we sow!

A new commandment I give unto you, that you love one
another; as I have loved you, that you also love one another.

John 13:34

Jesus left us with a commandment we would be wise to heed in
our daily pilgrimage. I think you will agree that a commandment
coming from Christ is not meant to be merely a suggestion, but
is to become a reality! His command does not instruct Christians
to judge one another but to love one another. A judgmental
attitude gives nonbelievers such a negative view of Christianity,
while even the most hardened and indifferent person will be hard
pressed not to eventually respond to love. Rather than playing
Holy Spirit, attempting to force others to abide by our list of dos
and don'ts, we should focus on the only person we can change—
ourselves! How we love to go about trying to change the world,
conveniently forgetting to focus on the only person we can actually change. Jesus has always been known as the great fisherman,
and He is well able to clean his own fish! Since He created us,
surely He knows what needs to be done to make us whole and
set us free. The question remains: do we truly want to be made
whole?

Anne Graham tells the story of a man whose Ford car stalled
on the Detroit freeway. After raising the hood and doing some
useless tire kicking, he realized repairing the vehicle was beyond
his ability. Suddenly a limo pulled up and a well-dressed man
stepped out asking if he could help. The owner of the stalled car
thought, "What could this well-heeled dude know about fixing
my car?" With nothing to lose, he offered the man a look under
the hood. After making a few adjustments, the engine suddenly
sprang to life. The owner thanked the gentleman and asked his
name. "Henry Ford," was the reply! Obviously, the designer
knew better than anyone else how to keep his invention running
smoothly. It seems reasonable to think that our Designer is also

the most qualified in the entire universe to keep us in good running order. He makes us whole, not with wrenches and screwdrivers, but by urging us to regularly open His repair manual and heed the instructions recorded therein. A dusty Bible tucked away on some shelf is an indication of little or no desire to be made whole.

We all come into the kingdom of Christ with varying degrees of damaged emotions, and it is the Lord's desire to set us free from those infirmities. The negatives the Holy Spirit exposes in the lives of others will quite likely be different from those He is currently revealing in our lives. We are all at different spiritual levels and dealing with different issues. Relationships within the body of believers would greatly improve if only we would stop judging others and focus exclusively on the one person in the universe we can truly change. Have you ever had anyone say to you, "How kind of you to point that out to me?" I seriously doubt it.

The Potter

A few years back, Ruth and I spent the better part of a year traveling overseas. During that time, we spent almost two months in Turkey. One day we were taken to observe one of the local skilled potters at work. It was fascinating to watch him take what appeared to be a useless lump of clay and begin molding it into the vessel he envisioned. Occasionally he would pause, which I mistakenly assumed was for a rest. No so. He paused in his work to remove hardened particles that were imbedded in the clay. If the particles were allowed to remain, the end product would be somewhat marred and would be a poor reflection of the potter's skill.

We are the clay, and You our potter...

Isaiah 64:8a

Does not the potter have power over the clay...?

Romans 9:21

Surely you have heard that the Holy Spirit is in the pottery business. When He takes up residence in our lives, it is His desire to remodel His dwelling place, surprisingly enough, not for His benefit, but for ours! Through the sanctification process, His intention is to mold us into the image He has in mind—the image of Christ. During the molding process, He will want to remove harmful imperfections from our lives, and if we have any wisdom at all, we will allow Him free rein. As each negative is removed, we not only become more conformed to Christ's image, but with the removal of each negative, we are set free from yet another prison. I repeat, if we could only get it clear in our heads that this molding process is not for Christ's benefit, but for *our* benefit!

Most Christians take the wrong approach when dealing with their fleshly infirmities and, as a result, find little permanent freedom from such crippling emotions as worry, fear, and anger. They have a desire to display unconditional love and experience peace in the midst of a raging storm, but when the dark clouds appear, and their flesh is challenged, they quickly slide back to the old way of life. They long to be more than conquerors, but find themselves constantly celebrating on the wrong side of their Red Seas. Since Christ promised to set us free, there must be a way to find freedom from our various infirmities. There is! The next chapter is one of the most important chapters in this book, as it describes Christ's formula for finding that freedom. If we can make this Bible truth a reality, our Christian journey will be revolutionized, and we will begin to experience the dominion, freedom, and fruitfulness Jesus promised.

Questions

- As a bondservant to Christ, are you enjoying the freedom and joy that is to be found in that relationship?

- Have you been spiritually circumcised? Or are you in the same condition as when you left your mother's womb—possessing the genes of fallen Adam?

- Do you function like Mrs. Bucket—attempting to hide inner insecurities by keeping up appearances? Or are you letting it all hang out—simply displaying your current level of spirituality?

- Are you bogged down in your Christian journey, functioning much the same today as you did a year or two or five years ago?

- Are you a hearer only or both a hearer and a doer of the Word? Are you obedient to the portions of Scripture that suit you, or is your desire to obey the entire Word of God?

- Do you have a judgmental attitude toward others who fail to line up with your little do and don't list?

LAMPSTAND

Having washed at the laver, the Levite priests were now ready to enter the tabernacle holy room to intercede on Israel's behalf.

The door to the tabernacle was an extremely thick veil, which served two purposes. It was a barrier to remind Israel—priests only. Secondly, it prevented outside light from entering the tabernacle.

Within the holy room, there were three worship stations, and each station, in its own unique way, pictured God's formula for achieving spiritual maturity. If we are serious about progressing in our Christian journey and finding freedom from our infirmities, it is imperative we make the teachings represented by these three stations a reality in our lives. Otherwise, we will find ourselves living a substandard brand of Christianity.

The first worship station we will examine is the *lampstand*, the only source of light within the tabernacle. Just as with every other worship station, the lamp was symbolic—a pattern of something real—a shadow. It is a beautiful illustration of how a Christian is to radiate the light of Christ in this spiritually darkened world. This was no ordinary thirty dollar K-Mart lamp, as it was made of pure gold, and on today's commodities market would be valued at approximately six hundred thousand dollars, perhaps the most expensive lamp ever designed (Exodus 25:31-32)! A constant supply of oil was placed in the lamp to ensure continual light

(Exodus 27:20). Jesus made the following two statements about light, which at first, may appear to be contradictory:

> I am the light of the world.
>
> John 8:12

> You are the light of the world…Let your light so shine before men, that they may see your good works and glorify your Father in heaven.
>
> Matthew 5:14, 16

How can Christ and believers both be light? Very simple! Just as the moon reflects the light of the sun, through the power of the indwelling Holy Spirit, Christians have the capacity to radiate the light (life) of the Son. While Jesus was in the world, He was The Light. When He departed, He passed the torch to Christians. By drawing from the power of the indwelling Holy Spirit, we are meant to become a radiant bride for Christ displaying His attributes, His light!

> The Holy Spirit will come upon you; and you shall be witnesses to Me…
>
> Acts 1:8

The early New Testament Christians were apparently anxious to begin sharing the gospel, but Jesus cautioned them to wait until they were empowered by the Holy Spirit. To be a positive light for Christ, it was vital they possess that indwelling generating power (Acts 1:4-5). Prior to Pentecost, the spreading of the gospel was limited to within walking distance of Jerusalem, and surprisingly, there were few conversions. However, once the Holy Spirit descended and empowered believers, the Christian movement suddenly exploded. In one sermon, Peter was responsible for ushering approximately three thousand people into the kingdom of Christ. Shortly after that, through the ministry of Peter and John, another five thousand were reached with the gospel. Sizable numbers! After Paul was converted, he was commissioned to take the gospel further afield, which he obediently did through several well-recorded missionary journeys. In addition, his epistles have been instrumental in motivating millions around the globe to become part of the kingdom of Christ. Today there are empowered Christians in every corner of the globe serving as effective torchbearers for Christ. Being a torchbearer is not restricted to a pastor or missionary. Jesus expects all citizens of His kingdom to display His light in this spiritually darkened world.

We talked in an earlier chapter about the moon being a rather unimpressive orb on its own, and only becomes an object of beauty when radiating light from the sun. We could say a darkened moon is similar to the heart of a nonbeliever. He may believe in various Bible truths and do impressive works in the name of Christ, but still possess a darkened heart (Romans 1:21). In Matthew 7:21-23, Jesus reminds those who proclaimed they did many wonderful works in His name that they were still not citizens of His kingdom. Through his own efforts, a non-believer can generate religious activities, but under his own fleshly power, he is incapable of producing any degree of spiritual light. Living the Christian life, as it is defined in the Bible, is a supernatural way of life and requires a supernatural generator. The Bible makes it pretty clear the flesh of man is not that generator. I think Jesus made it abundantly clear when he said, "Without Me you can do nothing!" Your reply might be, "What do you mean? I can do lots of things!" And rightfully so! Man has proven down through the ages that he can do many wonderful things. He has built many great monuments to or for *himself*. He has done many charitable deeds to bring glory to *himself*, directly or indirectly. I could go on and on. This statement by Christ makes it clear that we can do nothing, spiritually, through our own efforts. At best, we can counterfeit or imitate His life, nothing more!

A lamp, or perhaps a word that paints a clearer picture for us is lantern, has three distinct parts—the base, the oil container, and the wick. If a bright light is to be displayed, each part must be functioning properly, and working in unison with the others. If any one of the three parts is missing, or not functioning properly, there will be no light displayed, or at best, a dim unimpressive light. The tabernacle lampstand is a beautiful picture of Christ and His formula for radiating spiritual light, or put another way, being a positive witness.

The *base* was the foundation, and pictured Christ as the foundation of the Christian life—our rock—our cornerstone. It was made of pure gold and contained no impurities. Just as the base of the lamp was a constant, Jesus is also a constant. He remains the same yesterday, today, and forever. He never changes, which is a fantastic benefit for believers. It means the promises made hundreds, even thousands of years ago, are 100 percent reliable to this very day. The writer of the book of Hebrews refers to Jesus as an "anchor that is both sure and steadfast." A constant in a world where constants are fast slipping away.

Oil was the source of power for the tabernacle lampstand. The oil in the lamp was also a constant—always present as a source of energy (Exodus 27:20). In the Scripture, oil always speaks of the Holy Spirit. Since Pentecost, the Holy Spirit has been a constant source of power enabling believers to radiate spiritual light (fruit). I think it is safe to say the Holy Spirit is the only influence in today's world that keeps sin somewhat in check. Once the Holy Spirit ascends with the raptured church, His spiritual influence will no longer be present, and I assure you, at that point, all hell will break loose!

The third part of the lamp was the *wick*. The wick simply needed to be saturated with oil to display a bright light. Of the three parts of the lamp, the lighted wick was the only part that was not a constant. The condition of the wick could change. For example, it is impossible for an unsaturated wick to display light. It is also impossible for a charred wick to display a bright odorless light. The wick is symbolic of man. From God's perspective, there are only two types of wicks in the world—saturated and unsaturated. Light-bearing wicks and spiritually darkened wicks.

An individual can know about and even believe such Biblical truths as the virgin birth, the miracles of Christ, His crucifixion, and resurrection, but still have a darkened heart—a heart that has not been illuminated by the Holy Spirit. Simply put, no Oil in his wick! In his epistle to the Corinthian church, Paul reminded them of this doctrinal truth, for he wrote that it was possible to *believe in vain* (1 Corinthians 15:2B). Apparently he was concerned about people in the congregation who professed to be Christians, but whose hearts were not yet illuminated. You may be astounded to know that one of today's top evangelists estimates that 50 percent of people in pews who hear the gospel preached on a regular basis sit with darkened hearts, believing but never receiving (John 1:12). One has to wonder what the percentage is in liberal churches where a watered down version of the gospel is preached.

A person lacking this indwelling power could be compared to an empty glove. Picture a glove lying on the table. You can command it to do certain chores, but it will just lie there showing no sign of life. If the glove is to be of value, the owner's hand must be inserted. If the glove could speak, I picture it saying, "Look what I can do once my master's power is within!"

Today, both saturated and unsaturated wicks can be found seated in the pews of every church and Bible study group. Externally, both may look presentable, perhaps performing similar tasks within the organization. Church boards are often made up of both kinds of wicks. An unsaturated wick can graduate from a seminary, stand behind a pulpit and minister to a sizable congregation. Through his own efforts, an unsaturated wick is even able to counterfeit spiritual fruit. However, when tribulations surface, the false light will quickly sputter out, only to be replaced by anger, worry, fear, etc. Have you ever attempted to light an unsaturated wick? A frustrating useless effort. What the Lord longs for today is spiritual fruit—not religious nuts!

In another place, the Scripture refers to these two categories of people as wheat and tares (Webster defines tares as, "noxious weeds"). Until harvest time, both wheat and tares have a similar external appearance. In today's lukewarm church age, it is extremely difficult to separate the two, as both often function in a similar manner. In fact, longing for recognition and pats on the back, it is common to find the tares more active in Christian circles than the wheat. When there is a need to fill a position in the church, because of his much activity within the organization, the tare's name will often surface quickly. Soon he will have wormed his way into a leadership position. Believe me, it is much easier to get a tare installed in a position of power and authority than it is to have him removed!

Trimming Our Wicks

Part of my growing up years was spent on a farm where oil lamps were still occasionally used. Does that date me? I suppose. Whenever I entered a room and detected an unpleasant smoky odor, from past experience, I knew the source of the odor. The lamp's wick was charred and needed trimming. There are two methods of dealing with a charred wick. One method produces positive results, while the other method would only be attempted by the village idiot. The useless way of trying to eliminate the odor would be to locate scissors and begin snipping at the smoke. As long as the focus is on the smoke, despite much effort, the unpleasant odor and dim light remained. Moreover, if a person were seen snipping away at the smoke, he would likely be hauled off to the funny farm.

Anyone with half a brain would know how to eliminate the unpleasant odor. Instead of attempting to deal with the *symptom* (the smoke), the *cause* has to be dealt with—the char. Once the char is removed, the wick can then be raised to a new level, and now completely saturated with oil it will, once again, display a bright odorless light. In the tabernacle, trimmers were on hand to remove char whenever it accumulated (Exodus 25:37-38).

In this beautiful picture, the char clearly represents our flesh. Let's face it, our flesh is not capable of generating one ounce of spiritual light and can only generate such foul smelling activity as anger, worry, fear, self-pity, and gossip to name a few. "It is the Spirit who gives life; the flesh profits nothing" (John 6:63).

Sad to say, in this day and age many believers spend way too much time snipping smoke! When fleshly negatives surface, instead of dealing with the cause (their flesh), they waste time and energy focusing on the symptoms. Attacking symptoms may seem like a noble effort, but it is a total waste of time. As long as a believer focuses on his negative symptoms, there will be little spiritual growth or freedom experienced. Like the first generation of Israelites, he will find himself continually going around the same mountain—constantly dealing with puffs of smoke. Just to make it abundantly clear, other terms for snipping at smoke are flesh polishing or improving one's acting ability. Many in today's pews are doing just that. They learn the church drill and then struggle to live up to the expectations of the congregation. As long as the focus is on self-improvement, there will be little forward movement in their spiritual journey. Just as with the tabernacle lamp, focusing on the cause is the only thing that will produce results.

Show Me Praying

If we are to truly break free, we must drastically alter our thinking. We must stop attempting to educate our flesh and improving our acting ability. We must cease praying for more faith and peace. We must stop struggling to eliminate worry, fear, and anger from our lives, as that is simply snipping smoke. Instead, we must begin to pray *show me* prayers. "Show me why I am feeling this way. Why am I afraid? Why am I angry? Show me why I have so little faith in Your promises? Show me the *cause*, Lord."

When we begin praying sincerely in this manner, God will honor our prayer and quickly reveal the underlying cause. Once we deal properly with the cause, the fleshly traits will begin to fade, and we will then find ourselves becoming a radiant bride to Christ. If we are open to receiving an answer to *show me* praying, we will soon discover the force that generates the unpleasant odor in our lives. It is our dominating flesh that constantly wants things to go *my* way. When life doesn't cater to the desires of our flesh, that is when the beast generates smelly old anger, depression, fear, and worry. Simply put, if we are to experience the Christian life as it is defined in our Bibles, we must cease from being self-centered and self-focused Christians.

Many make the mistake of blaming the world and its residents for their fears and lack of peace. The thinking usually goes something like this:

- *If* the world would just shape up and begin treating me right, I would have no problem experiencing peace.

- *If* that obnoxious person would stop taking shots at me, I would never have to respond in anger.

- *If* unforeseen expenses would stop surfacing, I would never have to struggle with fear, worry, and anxiety.

- *If* my spouse would stop challenging me, I'd have no problem lavishing on him/her unconditional love and affection.

- *If, if, if...*

Such thinking is not only foolish, but a waste of time. It is proof that we are still baby Christians flopping around in the playpen. If our peace and joy are determined by how the world and its residents treat us, we are going to experience little peace. Jesus made it clear that we *will* experience tribulation in this fallen world, but in the midst of negatives, we *may* enjoy peace (John 16:33). This is a promise we can take to the bank. Tribulation will continue to bombard our lives! The sixty-four thousand dollar question is how to find peace in the midst of the pressures, whatever they may be?

Show me praying accomplishes two things. First of all, it gets our focus off the world and other people, and puts the focus where it belongs—on me. The truth is, we can't stop the tribulations of life from surfacing, but we can change how we react to those tribulations. Each of us must face, once and for all, the fact that the only person we can truly change is *me*! Secondly, *show me* praying will reveal the cause of the unpleasant odor. Once we clearly understand the cause of our negative behavior and the resulting lack of freedom, we should then be willing and able to deal with that cause. Only with this kind of thinking and action can we begin living the normal Christian life. Just as trimming the lamp's charred wick required decisive action, dealing with our flesh requires that same sort of action. Until we get to the root of whatever particular problem confronts us, we can never make any lasting changes. Understanding *why* is the key. "Why am I afraid? Why does he make me mad? Why am I depressed?" These are the kinds of questions we need to be asking ourselves. The char on the wick must be removed, which seems to me a clear picture of what must happen in order to become a spiritual power in this world. That old flesh and its desires must, in a sense, be cut off. Paul says to reckon it dead, which to me means no longer being lead around by the nose, heeding its dictates day and night.

Buck Stops Here

Put on the Lord Jesus Christ, and make no provision for the flesh, to fulfill its lusts.

Romans 13:14

This verse gives us the key to living the Christian life, as it is defined in our Bibles, and enjoying the freedom and abundant life Jesus promised. It is one of those verses that can be easily skipped over, without giving much thought to what Paul actually meant by "Make no provision for the flesh." Paul is saying there must come a time in the life of a believer when a dethroning ceremony takes place. Our corrupt flesh must be removed from its dominating position, and Christ must be invited to reign in our lives. Believe it or not, that's Christianity 101! Until we acknowledge Christ as the most qualified person in the universe to manage our lives and give Him that position, we can forget about being more than conquerors. We can also forget about finding permanent freedom from the bondage of our flesh. Until Christ becomes the designated driver, so to speak, we will find ourselves on a spiritual roller coaster, going nowhere fast!

Do not let sin reign in your mortal body, that you should obey it in its lusts.

Romans 6:12

Sin shall not have dominion over you...

Romans 6:14

In Romans 12:1-2, Paul condenses the normal Christian life into two short verses. Since we have been purchased by the redeeming blood of Christ, it is our reasonable duty to present our lives to Him as a *living sacrifice*. Simply put, acknowledging Him as our new manager. We can make the mistake of dedicating our lives to Christ on the installment plan. For example, we can dedicate our singing voice or teaching abilities. At a later time, we decide to present Him with a certain percentage of our income. While such endeavors are noble, this is not what Jesus had in mind when He went to the cross. It is vital that we present our life in its entirety to Him. Only then does He have access to all the many and varied parts. If we purchased a new car, and the salesman presented us with four tires and a jack, we would feel short changed. Not much to work with! Wouldn't we expect to be presented with what we paid for—the entire vehicle. Once we take possession of the car, we would then have access to everything connected to the vehicle—including the tires and jack!

This is exactly the spot where Satan has managed to put his negative spin on the victorious Christian life. All too often we get the mistaken idea that if we give our all to Christ, all the fun will go out of life, and we will be expected to function like little *do good* robots for the rest of our days. Nothing could be further from the truth! Should man fall, which we did, God knew beforehand the only way we would be able to function successfully on this fallen planet was if He took up residence in our redeemed lives. Think of it! The God of the universe, by His Holy Spirit, willingly inhabits our lives at our conversion solely for the purpose of safely navigating our way through life's minefields. How can we be so foolish as to not let Him do so? Anything less is much like that infamous old turkey flopping around with his head cut off.

> Do not be conformed to this world, but be transformed by the renewing of your mind, that you may prove what is that good and acceptable and perfect will of God.
>
> Romans 12:2

Once Romans 12:1 becomes a reality in our lives, the above verse will become a natural byproduct of that decision. Once we have presented our lives to Christ, the sanctification process (the renewing of our minds) we are meant to experience will accelerate. We will find ourselves functioning and thinking differently than we did as citizens of the old kingdom. Instead of displaying the same set of boring fleshly symptoms, life will become exciting and vibrant, and we will find ourselves functioning as a radiant bride—displaying a bright odorless spiritual light! Instead of attempting to satisfy the law of Moses in our own energy, without any conscious effort, we will begin fulfilling the very laws from which we have been set free. Despite external pressures, we will begin to radiate a life filled with peace, joy, patience, and unconditional love. Yes, we will find ourselves soaring like eagles (Isaiah 40:31). A Christ-managed life can be summed up in three wonderful words—freedom, dominion, and fruitfulness! On the other hand, holding a grudge and staying mad at a person keeps me tied up in knots, and most times that person has gone merrily on his/her way, not even aware that I am still mad. Such a waste and certainly a form of bondage!

Asking Christ to reign as Lord in our lives can actually require more faith than inviting Him to be our Savior. This is why so many Christians are reluctant to take this vital step. Making Christ Lord of our lives strikes out at our fleshly pride. It means acknowledging Him as the only truly qualified one to manage our lives. A truth our flesh despises. Our flesh hates to admit the Christian life, as it is defined in the Bible, is a supernatural life and requires a supernatural force to generate that life. Our flesh loves being on center stage. Admitting our flesh is nothing but a sin generator is not an easy truth for most to accept.

> What comes out of a man, that defiles a man. For from within,
> out of the heart of men, proceed evil thoughts, adulteries, for-

nications, murders, thefts, covetousness, wickedness, deceit, lewdness, an evil eye, blasphemy, pride, foolishness. All these evil things come from within and defile a man.

Mark 7:20-23

For I know that in me (that is my flesh) nothing good dwells...

Romans 7:18

Cart Before the Horse

When a Christian focuses on his negative *symptoms*, rather than the *cause* (his flesh), he is, in effect, placing the cart before the horse. For years, many of us have disagreed with our Roman Catholic friends concerning the ritual of confession where they appear to deal with the same set of sins week after week. Today, many of the rest of us, perhaps without realizing the comparison, are doing much the same thing. Often we go around the same mountain confessing the same set of sins time and time again—constantly snipping smoke. Just as a headache is a symptom of an inner problem, the sins we display have their roots in an inner problem—our flesh. Only a fool would tape an aspirin to his forehead when he has a headache.

Trying to educate or polish our flesh is a total waste of time. If we are to mature spiritually, it is imperative we stop putting the cart before the horse and begin focusing on the generator of our negative symptoms—our flesh. Once the generator is properly dealt with, the negative symptoms will begin to vanish.

If I had a well where the water had been poisoned, would you drink from that well? No way! What if I devoted an entire year to cleaning up the well? Would you drink? Unlikely! Despite my sincere efforts to clean up the well, there would always be a trace of poison remaining. The best course of action would be to erect a sign saying, "Contaminated—Unfit to Drink," and dig a new well!

Digging a new well is what Christianity is all about—being born again—starting over! When we become a believer, positionally speaking, God no longer sees our old poisoned well (our sins are no longer recorded), but views us as a new creation in Jesus Christ—possessing His righteousness. As Christians, we simply must learn to walk our newfound position with Christ as our manager.

> Therefore, if anyone is in Christ, he is a new creation; old things have passed away; behold, all things have become new.
>
> 2 Corinthians 5:17

As Christians, we must face the fact that our flesh is so corrupt, it is beyond being sanctified. Our flesh is so vile that Almighty God cannot improve the old well we inherited from fallen Adam. It is beyond repair, and no matter how much polishing we do, it still remains a poisoned well. In the Old Testament, God instructed Israel not to anoint the flesh with oil (Exodus 30:31-32). Remember, we pointed out earlier, oil in Scripture always pictures the Holy Spirit. This is the God of the universe saying the flesh of man is beyond being sanctified! If the Holy Spirit does not have the power to make improvements in our flesh, why do we waste so much time and energy attempting to educate and polish the beast?

> Our old man (flesh) was crucified with Him, that the body of sin might be done away with, that we should no longer be slaves of sin (flesh). For he who has died has been freed from sin.
>
> Romans 6:6-7

In Paul's day, the word "crucify" painted a vivid picture. It spoke of a life that was in the process of dying. Just as being crucified was a painful experience, dying to our fleshly desires can also be a painful experience. To admit we are a self-centered Christian, wanting things to go *my* way, can be painful. Admitting our flesh cannot generate any degree of spiritual activity, and instead only spews out sin, however well it might be disguised, seems terribly humiliating. Many of our actions look so good on the outside, but it takes a totally honest person to admit the often selfish and self-centered reasons hidden behind the act. If we are honest with ourselves, much of what we do is for the praise or approval of man. Making ourselves look wonderful. Fighting our way free from that bondage can take a lifetime for many, and it never does happen for many more. What freedom there is in being led by the Spirit in these matters and being able to say no when necessary! How do I know that? Because both Ruth and I walked the former way for many years, and I can tell you the latter way produces so much more daily peace and freedom. It is our deepest desire not to be "entangled" in the former ways ever again (Galatians 5:1). What an inspired choice of word! It paints such a vivid picture. Ruth and I have been avid SCUBA divers for many years. I can tell you it is a very sad sight to see a beautiful fish entangled in monofilament fishing wire. It is not able to swim freely or do much of anything. Often there is a fishhook festering in his mouth which, unless removed, will eventually do him in. Also you have probably also seen those awful pictures of a beautiful bottle-nosed dolphin entangled in a fisherman's net. We both try to keep those pictures fresh in our minds in order to keep from falling back.

No, we are not perfect in our daily walk, but we have found a great deal of freedom already in our walk with the Lord, so much so that we never want to go back to the old ways. When we do fall prey to the enemy, we are pretty quick to detect the smelly smoke, and also pretty quick to once again get ourselves on the high road. Direct and blatant sin does not trip us up too often, as Christians, but it is that subtle hidden behavior that will trip us up, again and again, if we are not watchful. For example, most of us are not going to be robbing banks, murdering, or even cursing, but look out for envy, pride, fear, hidden anger, and self pity just to name a few.

Our first Bible teacher, Pastor Cliff Dietrick, told the story of a farmer who began harvesting a crop of potatoes. From the surface, all the plants were similar in appearance. The differences were below ground. When the farmer dug up the first plant, he was surprised to find no potatoes. When he searched around for the seed potato, he discovered it was still firm. It hadn't died. The next plant produced a few rather small potatoes, and when the farmer found the seed potato, he discovered it was partially decayed. The third plant produced an abundance of large Idaho potatoes. When he searched for the seed potato, all he found was a mushy empty shell. It was dead! The fruit produced by each seed potato was determined by the degree it had died. Such a great illustration, and he was full of them. It is the same in the spiritual realm! The more we die to the desires of our flesh, the less influence it will have in our lives and the more spiritual fruit we will display.

> Unless a grain of wheat falls into the ground and dies, it remains alone; but if it dies, it produces much grain.
>
> John 12:24

Educating the Flesh

> The wicked are estranged from the womb; they go astray as soon as they are born, speaking lies.
>
> Psalm 58:3

We discussed in an earlier chapter, but it bears repeating here, that we were all born possessing the fallen genes of Adam and without the Holy Spirit. Remember the verse, "Behold I was brought forth in iniquity, and in sin my mother conceived me" (Psalm 51:5)? In this condition, we are forced to lean unto our own understanding for direction and wisdom, with our flesh as our only guiding force. That is a formula for disaster! It leaves a lot of room for costly mistakes! The following illustration describes our journey through life and the educating of our flesh. See if you identify with the various stages.

As a baby, the desires of our flesh were completely catered to. A cry quickly brought attention in the form of feeding, diaper changing, and cuddling. When we began crawling and attempting to form words, we were applauded for our effort. Our flesh was trained to think, "I must be the center of the universe. Everyone caters to my every whim." Once we started walking things began to change. When we reached out to touch a fragile dish or ornament, and our parents said "Don't touch," we often burst into tears and may have even thrown the occasional tantrum. Since no physical pain had been inflicted, why the tears and tantrum? Our *will* had been violated. Plain and simple. Another person's will overrode our fleshly desires, thus the tears and tantrum. Someone dared to go against the desires of the center of the universe!

By the time we entered our teens, our flesh became a little more cunning. Whenever the desires of others went contrary to our will, it is unlikely that we rolled on the floor kicking and screaming. Instead, we showed our displeasure in other ways—often by sulking, shouting, and slamming doors.

As an adult, many of us met a person whom we viewed as the most wonderful person in the world. In fact, that person was so wonderful we decided we wanted to marry him/her—making them our lifelong partner. Shortly after the honeymoon phase, life with our wonderful new partner began to change. They too began to challenge and violate our will. To display our annoyance, we showed our displeasure in more *mature* ways than rolling on the floor throwing tantrums. We experienced a voice change, sometimes speaking to our wonderful new partner in a harsh and cutting tone. Grown men have been known to demonstrate their displeasure by pouting and giving their wonderful partner the silent treatment. Certainly childish behavior. Wives have been known to show their displeasure by shedding tears and screaming whenever their wonderful husbands violated their will. Also childish behavior. When battle stations have existed for several years, and bickering becomes a way of life, it is just a matter of time before thoughts of divorce surface. Alternately, many couples continue to live under the same roof for many years, perhaps even a lifetime, with another kind of divorce—a divorce of the heart! If the battle becomes too intense, they will end up contacting a lawyer, eventually contributing to the high Christian divorce rate. Until our flesh is removed from its dominating position, life is going to be a constant struggle. The world, its residents, and even our wonderful spouse will constantly violate our will and we will respond negatively—displaying such childish fleshly traits as anger, screaming, and pouting. Daily life will resemble a battleground filled with varying degrees of conflict. Little rest and freedom will ever be experienced.

As Christians, we must resign as general manager of the universe and invite Christ to be the reigning force in our lives. Only then will we cease from acting negatively when our will is violated. Only then, despite the trials of life, will we have peace. Only then will the freedom Jesus promised begin to become a way of life. Only then will we be "more than conquerors," displaying peace in the midst of dark clouds.

> I've had more trouble with myself, than with any other person I've met.
>
> Dwight Moody

Don't Feed the Lion

A man was traveling in the heart of Africa and came upon a small native settlement. Shortly after arriving, a marauding lion entered the village, and the natives fled to their huts in fear. The village chief explained to the man that the lion came to the village daily in search of food and was a constant aggravation to the villagers. When the visitor told the chief he could eliminate the problem, the chief was quick to give him permission to deal with the annoying lion. The man built a sturdy cage, and then placed a piece of raw meat within the cage, leaving the door open. The next day the lion returned, smelled the meat, and entered the cage. The man quickly locked the door and placed a sign on the cage, which read, "The lion is dead—Don't feed the lion!"

When the man assured the villagers the lion would no longer be a dominating force in their lives, the villagers timidly left the safety of their huts. Seeing the villagers, the lion soon let out a vicious roar, causing the natives to, once again, flee to their huts shouting, "The lion is alive! The lion is alive!" The man assured them the lion had been caged, and they should view the lion as if he were dead. He also cautioned them not to feed the lion as that would only prolong the death process. As long as they ignored the lion, day by day, its roar would diminish.

Just as the man removed the lion from its dominating position in the village, we need to remove our flesh from its dominating position. Once we make a personal decision to invite Christ to reign in our lives, we will begin to enjoy the freedom and abundant life He promised. Unfortunately, even though our flesh is dethroned, as long as we are in our earthly bodies, our flesh will continue to be a force to reckon with. It is not eradicated when we become a Christian. That only becomes a reality once we receive our eternal bodies. However, once we stop feeding it and catering to its desires, its roar will gradually weaken and we will find ourselves free from its dominating influence.

Rather than catering to the desires of our flesh, we should be feeding the spiritual side of our lives. That can only be accomplished by sitting under solid Bible teaching with hearing ears. As we begin to mature spiritually, our flesh will weaken, and instead of tantrums, whether large and small, we will begin to function like wise and kind Christian adults. You may have heard the old Indian proverb about the man who had a white dog and a black dog. In an attempt to establish dominance, the dogs were always scrapping. When the man was asked which dog would win, he replied, "The one that is best fed."

If we find ourselves displaying much the same spiritual quality of life as we did a year ago, it is for one or the other, or perhaps both, of the following reasons. First of all, our flesh is still in a dominating position. Secondly, we are catering to the wrong force in our lives—constantly satisfying the desires of our flesh. Once we are in the right spiritual condition, instead of responding in a negative fleshly manner when our will is violated, we will find ourselves displaying the light of Christ—spiritual fruit. When we find ourselves boxed in with a Red Sea type situation, instead of seeing fear and worry surface, we should be able to put into motion the Three-Step Program and become more than conquerors. If we continue catering to the desires of our flesh, we are in fact, feeding the lion—keeping the beast strong and active. In this condition, it is just a matter of time before our flesh, with all its negatives, (fear, anger, worry, and depression, to name a few) overwhelms us once again.

Legal Heir

In the book of Galatians, the apostle Paul used a familiar Old Testament event to illustrate why a dethroning ceremony is necessary in the life of a Christian. It is found in Genesis 15. God promised Abraham and Sarah a son who would become the legal heir of Israel. After waiting ten years for Sarah to conceive, they decided to help move things along. With his wife's encouragement, Abraham fathered a son through their Egyptian hand-maiden, Hagar. The child was given the name Ishmael. The law of the land stated that the firstborn son was the legal heir in the camp. Consequently, Ishmael was viewed as the legal heir in Canaan.

When God's timing was right, despite the fact that Sara was a barren ninety-year-old, and Abraham even older, at age one hundred, she gave birth to Isaac. Without a doubt, a supernatural conception! The minute Isaac arrived on the scene, conflict surfaced. Who was the true heir in the land of Canaan—Ishmael the first born, or the promised one, Isaac? If you read the complete story, God Himself, stepped in and settled the dispute by removing Ishmael from the camp, leaving Isaac to assume his rightful position.

Today's Arab nations are descended from the loins of Ishmael, while the Jewish nation descended from Isaac. Beginning with the birth of Isaac, conflict has prevailed between the Hebrew and Arab communities. Today, the media, and most everyone else, fails to understand why there is such ongoing conflict. Despite popular belief, the conflict is not over oil, but over *land!* The Arab world claims Abraham as their father, and according to the law of the land, Ishmael is the legal heir of Canaan (modern day Israel). With this thinking, the Arab community views the Jews as illegal squatters on their land and are committed to their removal.

The Jews have a different view. They also claim Abraham as their father. The land of Canaan was given to Abraham and passed on from Abraham to God's appointed heir—Isaac. From God's perspective the land of Canaan does belong to the Jews. Despite the many peace treaties between these two camps, this conflict over the land will continue until the Lord returns, confirming Isaac as the legal heir to the Promised Land. Biblical records in the first chapter of Matthew definitely verify that the

Lord Jesus, the ultimate Child of Promise, did come through the loins of Isaac.

> He who was born according to the flesh (Ishmael) then perse-
> cuted him who was born according to the Spirit (Isaac), even
> so it is now.
>
> Galatians 4:29

Paul uses the conflict that arose between Isaac and Ishmael as a symbolic picture of the warfare that exists between the two forces within the life of a believer—the battle between the flesh and the indwelling Holy Spirit. Ishmael pictures our first birth—our fleshly physical birth. Isaac is symbolic of our second birth—our supernatural birth. The ongoing conflict between the two forces is over dominance.

Ishmael (our flesh) has been a part of our lives since the day we were born, and desires to remain the dominating force. When we become Christians, the Holy Spirit (represented in this illus-tration by Isaac, the Child of Promise) takes up residence in our lives, and it is His desire to be the guiding force in the life Christ purchased.

> For the flesh lusts against the Spirit, and the Spirit against the
> flesh, and these are contrary to one another, so that you do not
> do the things that you wish.
>
> Galatians 5:17

The question that confronts every Christian is whether our flesh will be allowed to continue reigning in our lives, or will we invite Christ to reign? As long as our flesh remains the dominating force, there will be constant conflict. The freedom and dominion Jesus promised will be fleeting. As long as our flesh is in the driver's seat, the Holy Spirit will be relegated to the rear, having little influence in our lives. In Galatians 4:30, the apostle Paul asks a question, and quickly answers his own question. "What does the Scripture say about these two forces?" His answer is, "Cast out the bondwoman (Hagar) and her son (Ishmael), for the son of the bondwoman shall not be heir with the son of the free woman."

Until Christ is reigning as Lord over His purchased possession, the light we radiate, as His bride, will be dim. Smelly fleshly odors will constantly surface. I promise you it is only when we are radiating His light that we experience the peace and joy we so long for in this harsh old world.

Questions

- As the bride of Christ do you find yourself radiating His light whenever tribulations surface? Or do the works of the flesh still prevail?

- Are you making a mark on the world? Or is the world making its mark on you?

- Are you continually snipping smoke? Or are you learning to deal with the cause?

- Have you entertained the thought of putting into action "show me" praying?

- Do you find yourself still blaming the world, and those around you, for causing your worry, fear and anger, or have you learned to place the blame where it belongs?

- Are you still catering to the roar of your fleshly lion? Or have you learned to ignore its roar, endeavoring, instead, to feed yourself spiritually?

- Is Ishmael still in a reigning position in your life? Or have you made the decision to invite the legal heir to reign?

- Are you just growing old in the Lord, or are you growing up?

TABLE OF BREAD

The table of bread was the next worship station in the tabernacle holy room (Leviticus 24:5-9). The bread was placed there to provide the priests with the necessary nourishment to sustain their physical strength while ministering on Israel's behalf. Just as we observed in the previous tabernacle rituals, this worship station was also symbolic. It pictured the Word of God, which provides a believer with spiritual strength. Countries such as Italy, Greece, Germany, China, and Mexico all have their own specialty foods. The kingdom of Christ is no different. Its specialty food is the bread of heaven—the Word of God!

> I am the bread of life. Your fathers ate the manna in the wilderness, and are dead. This is the bread which comes down from heaven, that one may eat of it and not die. I am the living bread, which came down from heaven. If anyone eats of this bread, he will live forever.
>
> John 6:48-51

Jesus and the Word are inseparable—one and the same. If we neglect the Word, we are in fact neglecting our relationship with Christ. A Bible placed on some out-of-the-way dusty shelf is usually an indication of a flagging relationship with Jesus.

> The Word became flesh and dwelt among us.
>
> John 1:14

His name is called The Word of God.

Revelation 19:13B

Frankincense was mixed in with the dough, giving the tabernacle bread a sweet flavor. Perhaps Ezekiel had this worship station in mind when he wrote that the Word was like honey to his lips (Ezekiel 3:3B). David expressed the same thought when he wrote, "How sweet are Your words to my taste, sweeter than honey to my mouth" (Psalm 119:103).

For obvious reasons the tabernacle bread was replenished weekly; in the desert heat it soon became stale. It is the same with the Word. If our digesting of the Word of God is limited to a brief twenty or thirty minute sermon each week, we will not only find ourselves spiritually weak (undernourished), but our Christian lives will become stale and flavorless. Just as a sailboat cannot run on yesterday's wind, without digesting heavenly manna on a regular basis, we will find ourselves making wrong and sometimes costly decisions (Matthew 22:29). Too often we think our calendar is just too full to bother spending time in the Word, when in actual fact, the busier we are, the more spiritual strength we require.

He who heeds the word wisely will find good.

Proverbs 16:20

Is the Bible Reliable?

Have you ever had someone say they don't believe the Bible to be 100 percent true and that it contains many fictitious stories and fables? Humanly speaking, logical reasoning! After all, every historical book in the libraries of the world contains discrepancies. For example, take any two history books covering the brief period of World War II, and you will find contradictions over dates, events, and city names. How is it possible then for forty men to record the Bible and not have it contain contradictions? These recorded events didn't cover a period of just a few years, but hundreds of years—in some cases, nearly four thousand. Much of the early Biblical history was passed down verbally, from generation to generation. It would seem reasonable to think that, along the way, original truths would have been somewhat altered and distorted. Try placing forty people in a line and tell the first person a detailed story. Then instruct him to pass the story down the line. For the story to reach the ear of the last person wouldn't take hundreds of years, but less than an hour. Regardless of the time, I can promise you, the fortieth person's version would contain distortions of the original. How could the events recorded in the Bible not contain errors and contradictions? The Bible is infallible from cover to cover because there were not forty authors, but *one*! The Holy Spirit inspired forty secretaries to record His dictated Word.

> All Scripture is given by inspiration of God...
>
> 2 Timothy 3:16

> Prophecy never came by the will of man, but holy men of God spoke as they were moved by the Holy Spirit.
>
> 2 Peter 1:21

When people suggest certain characters in the Bible are fictional, I always ask them to give me an example. They almost always mention Adam and Noah. When I ask if they believe the teaching/writings of Jesus and Paul to be infallible, their reply is usually, "Yes." When I point out that Christ referred to Noah as a real person and that Paul wrote about Adam being a real person, the discussion usually gets shifted to another topic. If Adam and

Noah were fictional people, then both Jesus and Paul lied, which places a cloud of doubt over everything they said or wrote.

I have been studying and teaching the Word for nearly forty years, and there have been times when I thought the Bible contained contradictions. However, as I gained more insight into the Word, suddenly those puzzling verses fell into place. Reading the Bible is similar to putting together a large jigsaw puzzle. When we first begin studying, it appears to be an enormous book to comprehend, but eventually the pieces begin to dovetail together, and many troubling verses suddenly become clear. Many make the mistake of reading only the New Testament, which is like putting together a small corner of a puzzle. You never get to see the total picture. The Old Testament is the foundation to the New, and without that solid foundation, much of the New Testament will remain fuzzy. Paul writes that the lives of the Old Testament saints are to be an example, and that we should learn from their positives as well as their negatives (1 Corinthians 10:11).

Satan despises the Word, and over the centuries, he has made a major effort to discredit the Bible. Remember, it was the Word that banished Satan from heaven (Revelation 12:9). Michael and his angels, as Christ's representatives, defeated Satan, and on behalf of Jesus, sent Satan packing. The Word announced the fatal blow to Satan's head (Genesis 3:15). The Word defeated the Deceiver in the wilderness (Luke 4:5-8). When everything is stripped aside, it is the Word that motivates sinners to defect from Satan's kingdom to the kingdom of Christ (Romans 10:17). The Word matures Christians and enables them to stand victorious against Satan in all his deceiving forms (John 17:17). It will be the Word that will eventually dethrone Satan as the prince of this world once and for all. Yes, you can safely say Satan despises the Word! Do I need to repeat that the Word and Christ are one and the same? For the past six thousand years, the Word has been a constant source of aggravation to Satan, which is why he has gone to great lengths to discredit the Bible. One has to admit he has been fairly successful in his endeavor, as many of today's pulpits deliver a watered down version of the Word—a social gospel. He has successfully diluted the Word being taught in many of today's seminaries, resulting in many students graduating in either a lost condition, or as believers, ill-equipped to strengthen their congregations.

Here is something that puzzles me, and I expect it will puzzle you as well. The Bible cannot be taught to impressionable minds in our schools, yet prison inmates are allowed to read the Word in their cells! Go figure! Here is another puzzling fact. Prior to testifying in a courtroom, we are required to swear on the Bible, yet the Ten Commandments can't be displayed in that same courtroom, or for that matter, in any federal building!

In many religious circles, such truths as the virgin birth, God's provision for sin (Calvary), and the resurrection of Christ have been ridiculed and discredited. Once we begin tossing out portions of the Bible, where does it end? Whether we trash one tiny verse, or an entire chapter of the Bible, we may as well trash the entire Book. How can we place faith in a book which we believe contains discrepancies?

The emphasis in many of today's seminaries is on the historical part of the Bible, and more importantly, how to organize and build a megachurch with all the trappings. There seems to be less and less focus on students' personal lives lining up with the Word of God. Since a pastor cannot lead his flock beyond his own spiritual level, many are ill-equipped to speak to the spiritual needs of their congregations. Sadly, the Scripture that talks about the blind leading the blind seems to be more and more applicable. Despite Satan's attempt to discredit and water down the Word, year after year the Bible remains the number one best seller! No other author in the history of the world can come close to claiming that success. Someone should remind the New York Times of this fact. Will you do it or shall I?

> The words of the Lord are pure words, like silver tried in a furnace of earth, purified seven times.
>
> Psalm 12:6

> The entirety of Your word is truth.
>
> Psalm 119:160

Why No Appetite?

Since it is natural for a healthy body to have an appetite for food, why do so many Christians have little appetite for God's Word—spiritual food? Why is the Word not sweet to their lips? Why are there professing Christians holding responsible positions in churches who rarely open their Bibles outside the church building? Why do people attend church carrying Bibles with worn out covers but with inner pages looking as though they just came off the press? Why do these same people come up with feeble excuses when they are invited to attend a solid Bible study, yet will rearrange their entire schedule to accommodate a football game or a fashion show? Why are people content to sit in a pew week after week being fed a watered down version of the Word and leave the meeting in the same sad spiritual condition as they entered? Why? Why? Why?

> The natural man (nonbeliever) does not receive the things of the Spirit of God, for they are foolishness to him; nor can he know them, because they are spiritually discerned.
>
> 1 Corinthians 2:14

> He who is of God hears God's words; therefore you do not
> hear, because you are not of God.

John 8:47

It is understandable that a nonbeliever has little appetite for the Word, for the author, the Holy Spirit, while still outside his life, is unable to illuminate the truth or stimulate his spiritual taste buds. He may attempt to read the Bible, but will quickly tire of the boring effort. Prior to becoming a Christian, I made a few feeble attempts myself. After a few chapters, I soon lost interest. Let me tell you, when the Holy Spirit took up residence in my life, I suddenly had an insatiable appetite for the Word that nothing else would satisfy.

There are several possible reasons why a Christian has little appetite for the heavenly manna. His spiritual taste buds may rarely be stimulated by solid Bible teaching. In this condition, it is just a matter of time before he slides into a state of apathy, expecting to exit each church meeting in the same spiritual condition as he entered. Instead of anxiously looking forward to being fed, he sits in the pew watching the clock, looking forward to the highlight of his day—lunch! Once he finds himself in this spiritual rut, he readily accepts envy, anger, worry, fear, and stress as the norm. In this condition, rather than have his carnal corns stepped on, he will avoid solid Bible teaching like the plague.

Another reason for having little appetite for the Word was covered in the chapter entitled Eating Lamb. If a person sits under a watered down ministry for a long period of time, he will slowly, and unconsciously, slide into a state of spiritual malnutrition. Once a person falls into this sad state, it is nearly impossible to get his spiritual taste buds stimulated. Fear of exposure will also cause this person to use any and every excuse to avoid solid teaching.

The gospel was preached to us as well as to them, but the word which they heard did not profit them, not being mixed with faith in those who heard it.

Hebrews 4:2

Value of the Bible

The best compliment we can pay any author is to read his book. An even greater compliment is to take the contents seriously. We please the author every time we open our Bibles, and even more so, when we allow His Word to make positive changes in our lives. We must get it through our thick skulls that the Bible is not for the Lord's benefit, but for our benefit. He is unchangeable; we are the ones who desperately need change! The degree of spiritual prosperity, freedom, and spiritual fruit we display will be directly related to the degree we digest God's Word and make the teachings contained therein a part of our daily lives.

This Book of the law shall not depart from your mouth, but you shall meditate in it day and night, that you may observe to do according to all that is written in it. For then you will make your way prosperous and then you will have good success.

Joshua 1:8

This verse makes it clear that Joshua did not instruct his readers to store the Word in their minds, but to make it a part of their daily lives. *Mouth* speaks of digesting. Accumulating head knowledge is not only a waste of time, it can actually be dangerous. For example, when the pressures of life surface, head knowledge will let us down every time. The tendency is to quickly offer our wisdom (head knowledge) to others, while we ourselves flounder at every turn. Instead of being more than conquerors, we are constantly overcome with fear and worry. Head knowledge tends to puff up our flesh. All too often that person finds himself quoting Scripture *at* others in order to demonstrate his holiness—always a major turn off. The apostle Paul cautioned that head knowledge alone would keep seekers from the Kingdom. Unless head knowledge becomes a heart reality there is no internal change and the heart remains spiritually darkened (Romans 1:21-22).

The degree to which we internalize the Word determines the degree of prosperity and good success we will experience. It's that simple! When Joshua wrote about prosperity and success, he was speaking of every area of our lives. Our marriages will blossom. We will be successful parents. We will be viewed as reliable and trustworthy workers. Wrong and costly decisions will be avoided. The freedom we experience will be directly related to the degree God's Word abides within. Instead of the world and its inhabitants constantly manipulating our emotions and time, we will begin exercising dominion. Our spiritual discernment will be sharpened and we will no longer find ourselves tossed to and fro by every new false doctrine that surfaces. We will enjoy a more intimate relationship with Christ and display a positive spiritual light to those around us.

Questions

- How do you view the Word of God? Do you place confidence in the Book cover to cover, or do you doubt certain portions? Since Christ and the Word are one and the same, anyone who doubts portions of the Bible will find all their relationships on shaky ground, both vertical and horizontal.

- Do you have a natural appetite for the Word, or are you somewhat indifferent? If so, why?

ALTAR OF INCENSE

The last worship station in the holy room was the altar of incense located just before the thin veil separating the holy room from the holy of holies (Exodus 30:1, 6-8). The holy of holies represented the throne of God located in the heavenly Holy of Holies (Hebrews 9:7-9). In the earthly tabernacle, sweet incense was ignited, and the aroma rose from the altar flowing through the thin veil into the holy of holies—such a beautiful picture of the prayers of the saints rising to the throne of God. Throughout the day, a Levite priest would perform this ritual which eventually became known as the "hour of incense" (Luke 1:8-10). I find it intriguing that the burning of incense has made its way into the rituals and practices of many of today's religions and cults. Do you think they have any earthly idea where the ritual originated? I don't think so!

When the apostle John was given a vision of heaven, he viewed golden bowls full of incense, which are the prayers of the saints (Revelation 5:8). Can you believe God actually stores the prayers that reach the throne in bowls? Apparently they are of great importance to Him! With this beautiful picture, we can see that prayer is the highest office of a believer, a direct pipeline to God and the closest we can get to Him while still in this world.

The altar of incense did not have a long detailed list of instructions simply because prayer is meant to be a personal chat with the Lord. For this reason, it is difficult to teach another person how they should pray. However, Jesus did leave us with a few important thoughts concerning an effective prayer life.

Self-Focused Prayer

> When you pray, you shall not be like the hypocrites. For they love to pray standing in the synagogues and on the corners of the streets, that they may be seen by men. Assuredly, I say to you, they have their reward. But you, when you pray, go into your room, and when you have shut your door, pray to your Father who is in the secret place.
>
> Matthew 6:5-6

In this verse, Jesus was not discouraging public prayer but was cautioning Christians about the possible pitfalls of public prayer. When we pray publicly, there is the potential danger of attempting to impress others around us rather than simply talking to God. Such praying is pretty self-centered! When we pray with the intent of impressing others in the room, it is unlikely our petitions will get beyond the ceiling. Have you ever heard someone in a group begin praying and their voice suddenly takes on a holy syrupy tone? Have you ever heard someone preach a mini-sermon when praying in a group? It is also fairly common to hear guilt-ridden sermons preached in public prayers, with the intent of convicting someone within the room—often a spouse. These self-generated prayers are a turnoff to those in the room, and based on Christ's advice, they are totally ineffective. Another most ineffective method of praying is to quote Scripture back at the Lord. After all, He did write the Book. I know I may sound a bit flip and rather harsh here, but it is just so important to see that praying is simply talking to the God of the universe and telling Him our concerns. Picture in your mind the kindest of fathers who loves you unconditionally every hour of every day. Praying should feel like having a chat with your very best friend, for that is who He is. Give Him your full attention, and I promise He will always give you His!

> When you pray, do not use vain repetitions as the heathen do.
> For they think that they will be heard for their many words.
>
> Matthew 6:7

It seems to me it would also be wise to refrain from inserting worn out Christian platitudes in our prayers in order to impress those around us. Overused Christian phrases should not only be eliminated from our public prayer life, but also from normal conversation—especially around non-Christians. Over the years, I have met Christians who have difficulty praying, or for that matter, even talking, without constantly inserting such platitudes. I wonder if they actually talk this way behind closed doors? I doubt it! Jesus is telling us in the above verse that our public prayer life should be no different than when we pray in private—an intimate and personal conversation with Him. When alone with the Lord, it is unlikely we will pray with an affected holy voice, quoting Christian platitudes and preaching mini sermons.

How the Lord Answers Prayer

There are three ways the Lord answers prayer—immediately, later, and sometimes His answer is simply "No":

1. *Immediately*: Have you ever prayed and received an immediate answer? *Show me* praying, for instance, usually brings about a quick response.

2. *Later*: Wouldn't it be wonderful if we could pray for someone to become a Christian or for a troubled believer to find

victory and have our prayer answered immediately? Often this is not the case. Sometimes the Lord has to get several ducks lined up in that person's life before they consider looking up. God promised Abraham a legal heir. Yet it took twenty-five years before the timing was right to usher Isaac into the world. During that time, I expect Abraham and Sarah were in prayer almost daily asking the Lord to fulfill His promise.

When Joseph was a teen, the Lord told him he would eventually rule over the nation of Israel. Shortly after he was given that promise, Joseph was sold by his brothers to an Egyptian, and because of a bad rap, found himself incarcerated in a hot Egyptian prison. During his time in prison, I expect he was fervently in prayer asking God to fulfill His promise. When the timing was right, the Lord did free Joseph from prison, and he eventually did become a ruler over Israel.

In this fast paced, quick fix world, we tend to look for immediate answers to our prayers. When the Lord fails to answer immediately, there is a danger of thinking He is unconcerned, or that He is just too busy running the universe to bother responding. When we are praying for a nonbeliever, the Lord may have to allow him to experience some hard knocks before he begins to be open to a spiritual change. When we are praying for a troubled Christian, it may take time before he sorts things out and makes a decision to get right with the Lord. In the parable of the Prodigal Son, Jesus leaves us with an illustration of a believer who had to hit rock bottom before he came to his senses. During his absence, I expect his father was in constant prayer for the quick return of his wayward son. Before that happened, the son found himself not only broke, but tending pigs. Certainly a low point for a Jewish lad. Eventually, he did decide to climb out of the pig pen and return to his loving father. As New Testament priests, it is our responsibility to pray for people and situations, waiting expectantly for the Lord to bring things to a head, in *His* time.

3. *No*: No can also be an answer to prayer. It is unlikely that self-centered prayers will be answered—"You ask and do not receive, because you ask amiss" (James 4:3). "Lord, please change my spouse" (so that life will be easier for me) probably will not get the requested results. Neither will "Help my child to do well in school" (so that I can brag about her to my friends). "Help me get that raise" (so I can move up a little higher on the social scale) will go nowhere fast, as well. We usually don't pray the above sentences in their entirety, but if we are honest, the last half of the sentences, though unexpressed, are often the motivating factors behind the prayers.

When Jesus told the disciples He was about to depart from this world, they were very concerned. They feared what would happen to the Christian movement once their leader departed? Who would they turn to for spiritual advice and direction? When they were having a bad day, who would they turn to for comfort? Realizing their concern, Jesus told them once He returned home, a new line of communication would be established so that whenever they were troubled, needed advice, or simply wanted to chat, they could place a long distance call to Him. I am told the U.S. president has a red phone, a hot line, on his desk, which enables him to immediately make a direct call to key people around the world. As Christians, we have such a phone. At any hour of the day or night, we can place an absolutely free person-to-person call to *the* key person—the Creator of the universe. Just as the tabernacle incense rose and flowed into God's presence in the holy of holies, our prayers rise straight to the throne of God, and we can expect His response when the time is right.

The effective, fervent prayer of a righteous man avails much.

James 5:16B

Christ's Prayer

We can also learn a lot about effective prayer by examining how Jesus prayed. In the seventeenth chapter of the book of John, we are privileged to have Christ's final recorded in-depth prayer. His prayer not only gives us insight into effective praying, but it also reveals the concerns that were on His heart.

> I pray for them. I do not pray for the world but for those whom You have given Me, for they are Yours.
>
> John 17:9

At the top of His prayer list was "them"—Christians. When the Levite high priest entered the holy of holies during the Passover Feast, he wore a breastplate. Imbedded in the breastplate were twelve precious gems—each representing one of the tribes of Israel, clearly indicating that he had the concerns of Israel on his heart. Such a beautiful picture. Jesus, our High Priest sits, this very day, at the right hand of the Father in the heavenly Holy of Holies with believers on His heart. I find that so very comforting and so should every believer!

> The eyes of the Lord are on the righteous…
>
> 1 Peter 3:12

Jesus prayed that Christians would be "one as We are"—unity (John 17:11, 22). Apparently Jesus spotted disunity within the Christian community even then, for He prayed they would be unified as one spiritual body. He must find the slandering, back-stabbing, and infighting that too often takes place in this luke-warm church age heartbreaking. Not only does disunity harm the Christian community, but it also makes for a negative testimony to the world around us.

When Jesus prayed for unity, His desire was that Christians would get on the same spiritual page—the same side of the fence. Carnal and spiritual believers are both born again, but on different pages. They have a different focus. A carnal believer is self-focused, and in this condition, is forced to lean unto his own understanding for direction and wisdom. He still views himself as the center of the universe, while the spiritual believer views Christ as the focal point of his life. A carnal Christian will usually feel somewhat uncomfortable around a spiritual believer and will avoid developing a personal relationship with that person. Instead, he will gravitate towards other self-focused believers. The "birds of a feather" slogan is alive and well within Christian circles! A spiritual Christian does not walk on water, nor is there a halo above his head, but he does have a different focus. He has acknowledged Christ as his Lord and looks to His Word for direction and motivation—his desire is to live *under the cloud.*

When Jesus prayed for unity among Christians, I think we can all agree that He was not praying for the spiritual to backslide and begin functioning like the carnal but for the carnal to line up with the spiritual—get on the same page. "If we walk in the light as He is in the light, we have fellowship with one another" (1 John 1:7). The only way unity will be experienced in the Christian community is for pastors to begin emphasizing the Lordship of Christ and for their congregations to make that teaching a reality in their lives. Otherwise, disunity will continue to run rampant.

> Now I come to You, and these things I speak in the world, that they may have My joy fulfilled in themselves.
>
> John 17:13

Did you notice in this verse that Jesus didn't pray for tribulations to be eliminated from a believer's life, but that in the midst of negatives, Christians would have joy? Such thinking is puzzling to a carnal Christian, as his limited view of life has taught him peace can only be experienced when there is an absence of negatives. Only a Christ-focused person can experience peace when dark clouds are approaching. Only a spiritual Christian can implement the Three-Step Program when confronted with a Red Sea. Jesus is well aware that we live in a fallen world filled with turmoil and negatives, which will not be completely dispelled until the Millennium. He came not only to provide an eternally safe home for us, but also to provide a way for us to experience peace and joy in the midst of our journey through this life.

> My peace I give to you; not as the world gives do I give to you. Let not your heart be troubled, neither let it be afraid.
>
> John 14:27

> Sanctify them by Your truth. Your word is truth.
>
> John 17:17

Since the sanctification process is a result of digesting the Word (truth), the thought behind this portion of Christ's prayer is for Christians to be seated under solid spiritual teaching and become doers of the taught Word.

> As you have sent Me into the world, I also have sent them into the world.
>
> John 17:18

As priests, we are sent into this spiritually darkened world to radiate the light of Christ, displaying His attributes—His fruit. Once our lives are in the right spiritual condition, we will find ourselves doing just that.

> I do not pray for these alone, but also for those who will believe in Me through their word.
>
> John 17:20

Jesus was about to depart and would no longer be able to personally spread the gospel. He passed the ball to believers whom he hoped would be a positive epistle for Him. I am once again reminded of the woman at the well who effectively witnessed to the people of her village after her conversion.

> You are our epistle written in our hearts, known and read by all men; clearly you are an epistle of Christ...
>
> 2 Corinthians 3:2-3

As Christ's epistles in this spiritually darkened world, nonbelievers should be able to read our lives and form a favorable impression of Christianity. Peter wrote that Christians are to have their "conduct honorable among the Gentiles (nonbelievers)" (1 Peter 2:12). Once we label ourselves as Christians, nonbelievers begin to scrutinize our walk. They are not impressed with our church position or by how much we tithe. We do catch their attention, however, when we walk the talk, radiating a quality of life they so long for. Paul says we are to "Walk in wisdom toward those who are outside (nonbelievers)" and that our "speech always be with grace, seasoned with salt" (Colossians 4:5-6).

> I am my neighbor's Bible, He reads me when we meet, Today he reads me in my home, Tomorrow in the street. He may be a relative or friend, Or slight acquaintance be, He may not even know my name, Yet he is reading me.
>
> Author Unknown

If Jesus considered it important enough to pray for us as believers, as well as those we might reach in our lifetime, surely it is an important part of our priesthood as well. When Ruth and I became a part of Pastor Dietrich's church all those years ago, they had a full-fledged prayer meeting every Wednesday evening. We had a short Bible study first, but the main focus was the actual prayer time. We broke off in groups of threes and fours all over the sanctuary and prayed together about the concerns of the church, missions, and our personal concerns. It was a wonderful feeling to just hear a hum of prayer all over the sanctuary. We are both so very thankful for those times together with some of the senior saints in that congregation, who took us under their wing, for that is where we truly learned to pray. Where are those prayer meetings in the churches of today? In many cases, few and far between. Christians should not be missing out on this vital part of their priesthood. We have come to believe, and Scripture certainly backs this up, that prayer is the most powerful weapon we have in our entire arsenal as we journey through this old world.

> The less I pray, the harder it gets; the more I pray the better it goes.
>
> Martin Luther

Questions

- Are you praying self-focused prayers, no matter how subtle? Or is the motive behind your praying Christ focused?

- In public prayer, are you sometimes more aware of what those around you might be thinking rather than focusing on your conversation with God?

- In public, do you pray in a natural voice, or do you experience a voice change?

HOLY OF HOLIES

Veil Is Rent

In a previous chapter, we talked briefly about the thick veil which separated the outer courtyard from the holy room, permitting priests only to enter. During the time while Jesus hung on the cross, an event took place in Jerusalem, which to most in the area would appear to have no connection whatsoever with His crucifixion. Nevertheless, this event ushered in a totally new age resulting in astounding changes in the lives of the Jewish believers of that day. The heavy veil at the entrance of the Jerusalem temple was rent from top to bottom (Matthew 27:51). This act of God, and God alone, proclaimed far and wide that the Old Testament priesthood was to be abolished for Christians. Our true High Priest, Jesus Christ, was about to take up his permanent abode in the heavenly Holy of Holies where He would forevermore intercede on our behalf. Jesus confirmed this truth with His announcement from the cross, "It is finished" (John 19:30). For believers, all the Old Testament tabernacle shadows could now be abolished—the *Real* had come. First of all, instead of having a Levite priest enter the holy room and minister on behalf of the flock, once the veil was rent, believers could now personally experience the reality symbolized by the three worship stations— the lampstand, the table of bread, and the altar of incense.

Through the power of the indwelling Holy Spirit, believers could now fulfill the beautiful picture symbolized by the tabernacle lampstand and serve as a light for Christ in this spiritually darkened world—"You are the light of the world" (Matthew 5:14). In addition to that, a Levite priest was no longer necessary to interpret the Word. With the author residing within, Christians would now be able to experience spiritual strength and direction from personally studying the written Word. Perhaps most important of all, instead of a priest offering up prayers daily on Israel's behalf at the altar of incense, the way was now open for believers to go directly to the Lord in prayer. We will probably never fully understand all that was incorporated in that last phrase uttered by our Lord on Calvary's Cross, "*It is finished.*"

Behind the Veil

Into the second part the high priest went alone once a year, not without blood, which he offered for himself and for the people's sins...

Hebrews 9:7

Unlike the thick veil that covered the outer door of the tabernacle, a thin veil separated the holy room from the holy of holies, which restricted entry to all but the high priest, and he was only allowed to enter during the annual Passover. Because of the sheerness of the veil, the other priests could peer through the thin curtain from the holy room and get a vague idea of what took place behind the veil. As long as we are on this planet, similar to those Levite priests, we are limited in our understanding of what life will be like beyond the veil in our eternal home.

Now we see in a mirror, dimly, but then face to face.

1 Corinthians 13:12

I think it is safe to say that at one time or another we have all wondered what life will be like in heaven. In the chapter entitled "The Rock," I mentioned several aspects of heaven. Because of the presence of the Holy Spirit, the river that flows from the throne will carry only spiritual activity. Such sins as worry, fear, anger, and pride will be nonexistent. Tears, sorrow, and illness will be history. There will be no hospitals, doctors, insurance companies, funeral parlors, nor politicians. If heaven offers nothing more than those benefits, it sounds like an okay place to me! The icing on the cake is that Jesus will be present, and as His bride, we will always be in His company. We also know that the number one wedding of the universe will take place shortly after our arrival.

Our Anchor

We have an anchor of the soul, both sure and steadfast, and which enters the Presence behind the veil, where the forerunner has entered for us, even Jesus.

Hebrews 6:19-20

We have a reliable anchor who is currently seated behind the heavenly veil—the Lamb of God. Throughout our life here on earth, most people have various anchors (institutions) they place faith in, but unless they are asleep at the wheel, they have to admit their anchors are fast slipping. Job security used to be a fairly solid anchor, but today job security is a joke. It used to be that when a company tried to cut overhead, they began by laying off employees on the lower rungs. Today, in order to cut costs, the layoffs often begin at the top of the corporate ladder. In times past, pension plans were something we could count on. That is no longer the case. Today, there is the danger of these funds finding their way into some offshore account, or worse still, being liquidated to keep a troubled corporation solvent.

There was a time when we felt like we could trust in the promises made by most of our politicians. Need I elaborate? Their main focus these days seems to be the best and most efficient way to raise reelection funds. Serving the needs of those who placed them in office has been relegated to pretty much the bottom of the list. Our Social Security system was once viewed as a reliable anchor, but I fear that anchor is also beginning to slip. With politicians continually adding to the enormous national debt, the Social Security fund is now facing financial problems. In an attempt to keep it solvent, they will continue moving the retirement age to higher levels.

Marriage used to be a fairly solid anchor, but today the divorce rate among Christians is in the 50 percent range—nearly equal to the non-believing world. Similarly, education once pretty much guaranteed the possessor a good and secure job. Not the case today.

Yes, our anchors are fast slipping, leaving us, one and all, with a very uneasy feeling, somewhat like trying to hang on to a handful of Jell-O.

I vividly recall an anchor that let Ruth and me down miserably. Whenever we SCUBA dive from a boat, it is customary to follow the boat's anchor chain to the bottom. Once on the bottom we mark in our minds the location of the anchor, and at the end of our dive return to that spot, following the chain back up to the boat. Simple! On one memorable dive in the Florida Keys, we returned to where the anchor should have been, but no anchor! We surfaced and spotted the dive boat close to a mile away. The anchor failed to hold during our hour-long dive, and the boat drifted downstream. The anchor had let us down. Fortunately, I always carry a small back-up system for just such an occasion. It is a small horn that is activated by air pressure from the dive tank.

When the boat captain heard my shrill horn, he immediately headed our way. Unfortunately, the majority of people have neither a reliable anchor, nor a back-up plan. As Christians, despite the anchors of this world slipping, we do have a solid and reliable anchor—our anchor behind the veil! The only one necessary!

There is another boat story that bears repeating. A small fishing boat was anchored off shore. Those on board were not the sharpest knives in the drawer. They dropped anchor during low tide but forgot to allow slack in the anchor chain to compensate for high tide. When high tide arrived, the crew attempted to let out additional cable, but the winch failed. The very same anchor they trusted in eventually pulled the boat to the ocean floor, and several of the crew perished.

The Bible tells us that one day this old world is going to be severely shaken, and those who place faith in this world's so-called anchors will find themselves going down with the ship (Hebrews 12:26-28). Only those who cling to The Anchor will find their names preserved in the Lamb's Book of Life.

In the Holy of Holies there was just one worship station—the ark of the covenant. The ark was an elaborate wooden box and inside were three extremely significant articles—a pot of manna, Aaron's rod, and the tablets of the law of Moses (Hebrews 9:4). Since each of these items speak of a vital aspect of Christianity, we must examine them separately.

Pot of Manna

In the chapter entitled "Table of Bread" we covered the manna in detail, so allow me at this time to quickly review. After a month on the road, Israel exhausted their food supply, and to sustain their physical needs, from that point on, God supplied them with manna daily (Exodus 16:14-16). The Psalmist referred to the manna as "bread of heaven" (Psalm 105:40). The Word of God. Manna decayed quickly in the desert heat, so each morning God sent them a fresh supply. The manna placed in the ark never decayed. What a beautiful picture of the Word of God, which can always be counted on to provide believers with spiritual strength, direction, and wisdom. Jesus said the manna was a picture of Himself (John 6:48-51). Remember, Christ and the Word are one and the same—inseparable.

The wisest person in the world is not necessarily the one who has the most diplomas on the wall, but the one who acts on the Word of God, which he has hidden deep in his heart. Solomon is spoken of as a wise king. As is so often the case, however, in his early years he was anything but wise. For example, he ignored God's warning against marrying pagan women, and not too far down that road, he actually found himself erecting their pagan idols in the Promised Land! Can you believe it?

Just as the manna in the ark never decayed, the Word will always prevail. "The Word of our God stands forever" (Isaiah 40:8b). The promises given to the Old Testament saints are still in force. God's provision for both justification and sanctification is clearly pictured in the tabernacle. His purpose for believers remains the same today as it was for Israel—His desire was to get them *out of* bondage and *into* the land of rest.

> To him who overcomes I will give some of the hidden manna to eat.
>
> Revelation 2:17

If there is *hidden* manna, there must also be *exposed* manna. When the Israelites came out of their tents each morning, they found manna lying exposed on the ground. The hidden manna was in the ark—out of sight of everyone. There is another type of manna that remains hidden, which the above verse makes reference to—

the Word. It is difficult to determine how much of God's Word is stored in the hearts of others. A person can hold an impressive position in church, sing in the choir, teach Sunday school, and even stand behind a pulpit, but those activities are no indication of how much of God's Word is hidden in his heart. A person may have Scripture stored in his mind, and be found quoting verses at every opportunity, but even that is no indication of how much of that same Word is abiding in his heart. The only indicator of what is truly stored in our hearts is the quality of the fruit displayed when under pressure.

> If you abide in Me, and My words abide in you, you shall ask what you desire, and it shall be done for you. By this My Father is glorified, that you bear much fruit.
>
> John 15:7-8

Aaron's Rod

The second article in the ark was Aaron's rod. During most of Israel's wilderness phase, Aaron was Israel's high priest, and it was his staff that was placed in the ark. Prior to being placed in the ark, it was simply a dead stick—incapable of bearing fruit. His lifeless rod pictures a nonbeliever, who without the indwelling Holy Spirit, is incapable of displaying any degree of spiritual fruit. As long as a person remains in this condition, God views him as spiritually dead and outside His fold. Oh, he may counterfeit the Christian life, but as far as displaying spiritual fruit, he is no different than Aaron's dead rod.

> Just as through one man [Adam] sin entered the world, and death through sin, and thus death spread to all men, because all have sinned... For by one man's [Adam's] offense death reigned through the one.
>
> Romans 5:12, 17

Once Aaron's rod was placed in the ark, amazingly it sprang to life and displayed fruit. By the same token, once we abide in Christ (our Ark) we become a new creation—springing to life! For the first time in our lives, through the power of the indwelling Spirit, we have the capacity to display spiritual fruit. "If anyone is in Christ, he is a new creation" (2 Corinthians 5:17).

> In Him was life...
>
> John 1:4

The Law

Lastly, the ark contained the law of Moses—the Commandments. The law has always been God's only means of judging, and as long as the law remained exposed, Israel was under judgment. During the annual Passover, the high priest took the blood of the slain lamb from the brazen altar and sprinkled it on the mercy seat above the ark to atone for both his own and Israel's sin (Hebrews 9:7). When God looked down upon this ritual, He no longer saw the judgmental law, but the sprinkled blood of the slain lamb. Now we know the Passover ritual did not actually deal with a person's sin, but beautifully pictured the coming Lamb of God who one day would.

> Christ came as a High Priest of the good things to come, with the greater and more perfect tabernacle not made with hands, that is, not of this creation (world). Not with the blood of goats and calves, but with His own blood He entered the Most Holy Place once for all, having obtained eternal redemption.
>
> Hebrews 9:11-12

When Christ, our Passover Lamb, was resurrected, He ascended to heaven where, as our High Priest, He sprinkled Calvary's blood on the heavenly mercy seat for the sins of the world. Once this event took place, believers no longer possessed a sin status, but were in the right spiritual condition to proceed to heaven. "If Christ is not risen, your faith is futile; and you are still in your sins" (1 Corinthians 15:17). From God's perspective, every person in this world is either under the exposed judgmental law, or the atoning blood of Christ. Either under the judgmental Old Testament covenant, or under the New Testament blood based covenant. Either set wrong, or set right. The decision is ours.

Once Jesus fulfilled the Old Testament brazen altar ritual, He sat down at the right hand of the Father—His job was finished! Instead of looking ahead in faith to the coming Lamb of God, as did the Old Testament saints, we look back to what our Savior accomplished at Calvary. "Christ, our Passover was sacrificed for us" (1 Corinthians 5:7B).

> And He Himself is the propitiation for our sins, and not for ours only but for the whole world.
>
> 1 John 2:2

> He loved us and sent His Son to be the propitiation for our sins.
>
> 1 John 4:10

Propitiation is an interesting word. The words mercy seat and propitiation stem from the same Hebrew word *kaphar*. A propitiator is one who unites two opposed parties. Today, the word is rarely used and has been replaced by arbitrator or mediator. Jesus, our Mediator, came to earth approximately two thousand years ago to settle a feud, one could say, which existed between two parties, man and God. We all entered this world possessing Adam's fallen genes and a citizen of Satan's kingdom—separated from our Creator. The feud that exists between God and fallen man not only concerns our wrong citizenship, but *how* our citizenship can be changed. In other words, how we are set right with God—justified.

Since the Fall, the vast majority have placed faith in various types of religious leaves to make themselves presentable before God, trying to act as their own propitiator. Just as God did with Adam, Eve, and Cain, He will always reject man's foolish efforts to self-justify. "Though you wash yourself with lye, and use much soap, yet your iniquity is marked before Me, says the Lord God" (Jeremiah 2:22). As our propitiator and/or mediator, Jesus placed Himself between God and sinners, imputing the sin of the entire world to His own account. When a sinner places faith in what Jesus accomplished at Calvary, he then receives the free gift of salvation, and the feud is settled for all times. From God's perspective, he stands forever 100 percent justified, possessing the righteousness of Christ.

> Nor is there salvation in any other, for there is no other name under heaven given among men by which we must be saved.
>
> Acts 4:12

> There is one God and one Mediator between God and men, the Man Christ Jesus.
>
> 1 Timothy 2:5

After His resurrection, our mediator, Jesus Christ, sprinkled His own blood on the heavenly mercy seat. Jesus is unique in many ways. To my knowledge, He is the only mediator who ever settled a feud by dying. Today, we still have mediators, but I have yet to hear of one who settled a dispute by sacrificing his own life! Also, it is customary for an earthly mediator to charge for his services, while Christ, Himself, paid a huge price to settle the feud that existed between God and sinners.

Every priest stands ministering daily and offering repeatedly the same sacrifices, which can never take away sins. But this Man, after He had offered one sacrifice for sins forever, sat down at the right hand of God... For by one offering He has perfected forever those who are being sanctified.

Hebrews 10:11-12, 14

One would be foolish to think the animals slain during Old Testament Passover rituals could actually deal with sin. They simply pictured the Lamb, who, through *one* offering, Himself, would deal with our sin status forever. Don't you love the last sentence in the above Scripture—"perfected forever those who are being sanctified"? Only a Christian can be sanctified and be viewed as perfected by placing faith in what Jesus accomplished on our behalf. Isn't it comforting to know that we possess that status for a long time—forever!

Full Calendar Day

Have you ever thought about what was actually accomplished on resurrection day? For Jesus, it was a full calendar day. He was required to travel vast distances in order to participate in three key appointments. Even if He traveled at the speed of light, He would never have had time to make all three appointments in one single day. It seems Jesus must have traveled, not at the speed of *light*, but at the speed of *thought*. Just as He thought the universe into existence, He could think of being anywhere in the universe, and immediately He was there! Will that be our mode of transportation once we step into eternity? Perhaps!

The first person Jesus met after leaving the tomb was Mary Magdalene. In order to discredit Christ, His critics have attempted to make a sexual connection between Christ and Mary Magdalene. Clearly, that was not the case. To understand her love for Jesus we must look at her background. Magdalene was not her surname. She came from the village of Magdala, thus the name Magdalene to differentiate from the other Mary's among His circle of friends, and there were several. Her village was a hot bed for demonic activity, and prior to meeting Jesus, she had been demon possessed, probably for a very long time. Christ set her completely free. No wonder she was forever grateful and loved Him from the very depths of her being.

When she saw Jesus that morning beside the tomb, her natural reaction was to embrace Him (John 20:1). Jesus responded in a way that, on the surface, may appear to be rather distant and uncaring. He said, "Do not cling to Me, for I have not yet ascended to My Father" (John 20:17). Actually, His warning was loaded with love. When Christ met Mary that morning, the payment for sin had previously been *made* at Calvary, but had not yet been *presented* at the heavenly mercy seat. Until that took place, Mary, along with all believers, remained in their sins (1 Corinthians 15:14, 17). Had she touched Jesus while in her sinful state, Calvary's blood offering would have been defiled before it was ever properly presented. Had that happened, the accomplishment of Calvary would have been nullified, and every believer would still be in his sins, unfit to proceed to heaven. Christ's first appointment on that resurrection morn was to do just that—present His shed blood at the heavenly mercy seat (Hebrews 9:12).

Once that was accomplished, Jesus went on to His second appointment. He visited Abraham's bosom, where He led captivity captive (Ephesians 4:8). Abraham's bosom can best be described as a temporal holding area that housed all the Old Testament saints who had placed faith in the true Lamb portrayed at the yearly celebration of the Passover Feast. The term "Abraham's bosom" simply means being of the same spiritual family as Abraham (Galatians 3:28-29). Old Testament saints such as Adam, Eve, Abraham, Moses, Isaiah, and David had been

camped in this holding area for a very long time, anxiously awaiting the arrival of the promised Lamb of God (I sort of picture it
like planes circling in a holding pattern over Atlanta waiting for
clearance to land). How excited they must have been when Jesus
appeared and proclaimed His payment for sin had been both
made and presented, and found acceptable! Now, free of their
sins, they could be escorted on to heaven, thus enabling Jesus to
cross off his second appointment of the day.

His final appointment was back here on earth. Once His
blood had been presented, it could no longer be defiled, and He
was now able to mingle freely with friends and loved ones and
even invite Thomas to touch Him (John 20:27). Finally, Mary
Magdalene was able to give her Lord a big hug!

Resurrection Proofs

Have you ever wondered why Jesus didn't proceed to heaven
immediately after He was crucified? Why wait three days before
heading home? Until His blood was presented, the sins He bore
separated Him from the other members of the Trinity. One
would think He would have been anxious to return home, yet He
remained in the tomb for three long days. He chose to make one
last statement before departing. He wanted to make it 100 percent clear that He was indeed God in the flesh. The Jews of that
day believed once a person died, he began to decompose after
the second day. In addition, they believed that only God had the
power to resurrect a body. By remaining in the tomb three days,
Jesus proved, once and for all, He was God in the flesh. For the
same reason, just a week earlier, Jesus left his friend Lazarus in
the tomb three full days, proving He had power over death—that
He was indeed God!

Most critics do not dispute the fact that Jesus was crucified. What they do challenge is His resurrection. If you were asked why you believe in the resurrection of Christ, what would be your reply? To say you believe because the Bible says so would not cut it with most nonbelievers. As believers, we should have plausible answers at our fingertips. Following are several logical reasons that prove something unique took place three days after the crucifixion of Christ. Proofs that would be viewed as valid confirmation in any of today's courts:

1. *Silence of Christ's Critics* - Had there been no resurrection, Christ's critics in the Jerusalem area would have gone to the tomb, taken a photo of the decaying corpse and printed it on the front page of the Jerusalem Herald—above the fold. Well, not really, but they would have certainly produced the corpse and ended any further talk about a resurrection. Shortly before His death, Jesus proclaimed publicly who would be His executioners (the religious leaders); the place of His execution (Jerusalem); the method of execution (crucifixion), and that three days later, He would rise from the grave (Matthew 20:19). An astounding announcement! Had these events not happened, He would have been labeled a false prophet and viewed by God as an unacceptable offering for sin. The Christian movement would have come to a screeching halt, for it could not have been built upon a lie!

    The Jerusalem critics challenged every one of Paul's doctrines, with the exception of the resurrection. The reason being, Christ was seen wandering around the Jerusalem area for fifty days after His resurrection. To reject the resurrection would have made them appear to be fools. The silence of the Jerusalem critics made a profound statement. Something unique definitely took place three days after the crucifixion of Christ!

2. *The Changed Lives of the Disciples* - After Christ's death, the disciples were defeated, discouraged, and in fear of perse-

cution from the Jewish religious leadership. Their leader was dead, and it appeared the Christian movement would soon fizzle out. After the resurrection, however, the lives of the disciples were suddenly transformed. Instead of fearing persecution, they constantly put themselves in harm's way by boldly preaching the gospel. Throughout history, people have died for a cause they believe in, but only a fool would die for a lie. The transformed lives of the disciples also made a significant statement that something profound took place three days after the crucifixion of Christ!

3. *Jewish Worship Was Abolished* - To understand the significance of the changes in Hebrew worship, we must place ourselves in the shoes of the Jewish population of Christ's day. A Jew would never abolish a religious ritual that had been ordained by God unless they believed God approved the change. Following are some of the age-old Jewish religious rituals that were abolished by converted Jews:

a) Passover Feast - The number one Jewish feast was the annual Passover. It was the foundation for all other religious rituals. When believing Jews abolished this ritual, it would have been on a par with today's Christians refusing to honor Christmas and Easter. Can you imagine the flak the converted Jews received from their families and neighbors when they no longer participated in the Passover? Once Christ became their Passover Lamb, it would have been a slap in His face to continue worshiping a ritual—a shadow.

Christ our Passover was sacrificed for us.

1 Corinthians 5:7B

b) Feast of Unleavened Bread - This feast followed the Passover ritual and was also abolished by believing Jews. This feast spoke of one's status after placing faith in what the Passover Feast symbolized. In the Bible, leaven always speaks of sin. In turn, unleavened pictures the absence of sin. Once Christ's blood was sprinkled on the heavenly mercy seat, believers were no longer in their sins. From God's perspective they were as pure as unleavened bread—possessing the righteousness of Christ. For Jewish believers to continue celebrating this feast would have also been an insult to the accomplishments of Christ, for now they truly were unleavened in the eyes of God!

> Purge out the old leaven, that you may be a new lump, since you truly are unleavened.
>
> 1 Corinthians 5:7A

c) Feast of the Firstfruits - This Old Testament feast spoke of the resurrection of the slain Lamb. Since the resurrection was now a fact of life, this feast was also discontinued. To continue celebrating this shadow would also have been an insult to Christ.

> Christ is risen from the dead, and has become the firstfruits of those who have fallen asleep.
>
> 1 Corinthians 15:20

(d) The Sabbath - Saturday was Israel's holy day—their day of worship. The Sabbath was the core of Hebrew life, and no self-respecting Jew would abolish this day of worship unless he was totally convinced God ordained the change. After the resurrection, the Sabbath was abolished and resurrection day, Sunday, became the new day of celebration for believers. Imagine the controversy this change alone would have created in Jewish communities!

(e) Priesthood - For believing Jews, the Old Testament priesthood was no longer significant for Christ was now their High Priest. There was no longer a need for an earthly mediator, for Christians could now go directly to the throne of grace in prayer. Neither did they have to rely on a priest to interpret the Word, for they now had the Author residing within.

The abolishment of these Old Testament religious rituals definitely confirmed something quite unique took place after the death of Christ—the resurrection of the slain Lamb.

It must have taken enormous courage for converted Jews to walk away from those religious rituals and feasts. In their communities, their names would have been mud. Have you discovered that lining up with the Word of God invites flak? Whenever we decide it is necessary to go against the religious flow, we can expect opposition. Jesus constantly went against the established religious beliefs of His day, and we know where that got Him. For example, He healed on the wrong day of the week. He broke the oral laws of the religious hierarchy (not the law of Moses). One has to admit He was anything but complementary to the clergy of His day, and He really rattled their chains when He proclaimed Himself to be God. Jesus certainly didn't fit the image the religious Jewish leaders had of the promised Messiah.

As mentioned in a previous chapter, the Old Testament rituals and feasts were simply shadows of what Christ would fulfill through His death and resurrection (Hebrews 8:5). They were inferior to the real, as the rituals did not have the power to change a life. Once Jesus arrived, the inferior shadows were to be set aside by Christians.

These were only temporary rules that ended when Christ came. They were only shadows of the real thing—of Christ himself.

Colossians 2:17 (LL)

Why No Graver Marker?

Have you ever wondered why there never has been a grave marker or shrine at the tomb of Christ? Most who die have some means of identification placed at their grave site, so why was there nothing at Christ's tomb? The reason is obvious. Only a fool would place a marker at an empty tomb!

After the crucifixion of Christ, Joseph of Arimathea and his friend Nicodemus went to Pilate to obtain permission to bury Christ in Joseph's family tomb.

Chuck Missler tells a cute story of how he thinks the conversation might have gone between Joseph and Pilate.

> Pilate: Why would you waste your expensive family tomb on this Jesus?
>
> Joseph: Well, it's only for the *weekend!*

Significance of the Resurrection

On Easter weekend it is common to hear Christians wishing each other Happy Easter. Why is there so much expressed happiness over an event that took place over two thousand years ago in a graveyard? Why the joy and excitement? We have been set free from our sin status and are no longer under the old law based covenant! We are joyful, because the resurrection struck a fatal blow to Satan, the deceiver, and he no longer has any legal authority over our lives. We are joyful because we are no longer concerned about our destiny once we pass through death's door. As Christians we believe death is simply a door that leads to a superior way of life. At Easter, and every day, we celebrate an *empty cross*, an *empty tomb*, and an *occupied throne!*

As believers, we tend to focus on Calvary, as that is where Jesus *died* for our sins. We must also be resurrection focused, as that is when Christ *rose* for our sins. It was vital that the Lamb of God not only be crucified for our sins, but that He also rose and presented His shed blood on the heavenly mercy seat.

When Peter looked into the empty tomb that long ago Easter morn, he saw something that should have thrilled his heart. Not only did he see an empty tomb, but Jesus left a message saying He would be returning to earth shortly. The Bible says the burial napkin was "folded together in a place by itself" (John 20:7). The key word here is folded! I don't know if Peter picked up on the significance of the folded napkin, but as a Jew, he should have understood the message Jesus left behind. The Jews of Peter's day had a dining custom that involved their napkin. When the master of the home finished eating, before leaving the table, he would wad his napkin and leave it beside his plate. The wadded napkin was a signal to the servants that he wasn't planning to return, and they could begin clearing the table. If the master were planning to return to the table momentarily, he would fold his napkin neatly beside his plate—a signal to the servants not to remove his plate. The folded napkin in the tomb was a clear message saying He was planning to return shortly! Did Peter and the others get it? I don't know. But if he did, I can just hear Peter saying when he next met Christ, "That folded napkin message sure was cool!"

Three Arks

The Bible speaks of three arks and each is a type of Christ. The first ark was Noah's. God pronounced judgment upon sin, and the ark was God's provision for escaping pending judgment. In order to ensure a safe voyage to the new world, the ark was lined with pitch. The second ark was used to preserve baby Moses from Pharaoh's judgment. To ensure their child's safe voyage, his parents sealed the ark with pitch. The third ark, as we know, was located in the tabernacle—the ark of the covenant. As long as the law was exposed, Israel remained under judgment. Once the blood of the innocent lamb covered the mercy seat, Israel was no longer under pending judgment, but under the pitch (blood) of the slain lamb. Yes, they went to their graves in their sins, but because of their faith in what the Old Testament Passover ritual pictured, from God's perspective, they were justified.

The word "pitch" originates from the Hebrew word *kaphar*, which is where such words as atonement, cleansing, pardon, mercy seat, and purge also originated. Just as the pitch preserved Noah and Moses, the blood of Christ preserves believers in the Lamb's Book of Life.

> Having believed, you were sealed with the Holy Spirit of promise.
>
> Ephesians 1:13B

> You were sealed for the day of redemption.
>
> Ephesians 4:30B

As believers, we remain sealed in the Lamb's Book of Life until Jesus Christ, our Kinsman Redeemer, steps forward to break the seals. This event will take place in the future when Revelation chapter five comes into play. At that time, the seals on the Lamb's Book will be broken, and the names of the redeemed will be confirmed. Once this transaction takes place, the wedding feast will commence, and following that event, the saints, along with Christ, will return to redeemed earth for the Millennium Reign.

> Let us be glad and rejoice, and give honor to him; for the marriage of the Lamb has come, and his wife hath made herself ready. And to her was granted that she should be arrayed in fine linen, clean and white: for the fine linen is the righteousness of the saints.
>
> Revelation 19:7-8 (KJV)

Questions

- What are your anchors in life? Is your anchor currently seated behind the veil? Or have you been trusting in the temporal things of this world?

- Are you still under the judgmental law? Or have you found refuge in the true ark?

- Are you still abiding in Adam, spiritually dead? Or are you like Aaron's rod in the ark—alive and displaying fruit?

PART III: SECOND GENERATION

GRASSHOPPERS
OR BREAD

Once the assembling of their transportable tabernacle was complete, Israel resumed their journey to the Promised Land. After wandering aimlessly in the wilderness for two years, we find them camped close to the Canaan border at a place called Kadesh-Barnea. For twenty-three of those twenty-four months, they should have been enjoying life in Canaan, residing in mortgage-free homes and dining on the abundant fruit of the land. Instead, their ever-wavering faith restricted them to a substandard life in the desert, living in sand-infested tents and eating a boring diet of manna, manna, and more manna. Instead of claiming their inheritance in Canaan, they were living like paupers in the barren desert. Cheese and cracker believers!

Until they came to the understanding that God does not lie and began placing faith in His promises, it was impossible for the Lord to lead them into the land of rest. Once in the land, they would be exposed to major faith challenges. Worry, fear, and anxiety would have quickly surfaced at the sight of such cities as Jericho, causing them to look like wimps in the eyes of the armed squatters, not to mention what a negative testimony, to the power of their Lord, they would have been. How sad to have robbed themselves of God's blessings. Every day spent in the wilderness was a day Israel missed enjoying their inheritance in Canaan. Let me repeat, from day one, God's purpose had always been to get Israel *out of* Egypt so He could lead them *into* the land of milk and honey—the land of freedom and blessing. No matter how you cut it, living in the stressful barren desert was far from that.

> He brought us out from there (Egypt), that He might bring us in, to give us the land of which He swore to our fathers.
>
> Deuteronomy 6:23

Is God's desire any different today? Of course not! God's purpose for His people remains the same yesterday, today, and forever. His desire is to motivate each of us to defect from Egypt (the world) and begin to enjoy our citizenship in His kingdom. Then, once in the kingdom, He so wants to lead each of us to a place of rest. Only then can we begin to enjoy a life free from stress, anger, and worry. Once in that place, hopefully, we will learn to further trust the Lord to manage our daily lives, putting an end to continual manipulation by this fallen world, its residents, and most cunning of all, our own flesh.

If that is God's desire, why do so many believers seem to miss the mark so miserably? Why do they so often allow others to be the dominating forces in their lives? First of all, they are not responding to the constant challenge of the Word to seek a different quality of life. As a result, along their Christian pilgrimages, they frequently get bogged down, contented to more or less stew in the pew.

Another reason for missing out is plain old stubbornness. They refuse to let go of the reins, still believing they are the most qualified person in the universe to manage their lives. Instead of experiencing peace in the midst of the storm, they constantly struggle with fear and worry, eventually becoming convinced the quality of life outlined in the Bible is just for spiritual giants like the apostle Paul and perhaps Billy Graham. As a result, everything they experience is substandard. Yes, because of salvation, they defect *out of* the world, but never appropriate the faith to enter *into* the land of rest.

> There remains therefore a rest for the people of God. For he who has entered His rest has himself also ceased from his works as God did from His. Let us therefore be diligent to enter that rest.
>
> Hebrews 4:9-10

Many think the "rest" mentioned in the above verse is only to be experienced in heaven. Of course, our ultimate and eternal rest is in heaven, however, the rest spoken of in the above verse is to be enjoyed right here on planet earth—in the midst of our tribulations. The writer of Hebrews clearly states that some believers will enter the land of rest (v. 4:6). All believers will eventually reside in heaven, not just some! It should be our earnest desire to enter into that rest and begin enjoying the normal Christian life. Worry, fear, anger, and depression are not what God has in mind for His children!

The above verse talks about ceasing from our efforts. What does that actually mean? Does it mean no longer having to work? Obviously not! It means giving up the struggle of trying to live the Christian life under our own steam. It means, by faith, placing the reins of our lives in Christ's most capable hands. Nothing in the spiritual realm works as it should until this decision is made. Turning the reins over to Christ often requires more commitment and fortitude than receiving Him as Savior. Ceasing from our efforts means no longer walking by sight and having every bump in the road controlling our emotions. It means viewing our battles as rigged fights. It means no longer attempting to gain the Lord's approval abiding by certain laws, but getting our lives in the right spiritual shape, so we naturally begin fulfilling the law of Moses. It means giving up the struggle to educate and polish our flesh. Certainly a fruitless effort! Ceasing from our works means no longer struggling to eliminate our negative fleshly symptoms—snipping the smoke, but dealing with the char in our lives. The byproduct of ceasing from our efforts is summed up in three wonderful words—freedom, rest, and fruitfulness!

Just as many Christians are reluctant to turn the reins of their lives over to Christ, Israel was hesitant to cross the border into Canaan. It required a huge leap of faith! Observing their fear, God asked Moses to select a representative from each of the twelve tribes. Those twelve men were instructed to cross into Canaan as an advance scouting party (Numbers 13:1-20). After spending forty days in the land, the twelve spies returned and reported their findings.

Just as God had promised, they found an abundance of food. They also found well-fortified cities filled with illegal squatters. The spies were so impressed with the fruit that they returned with huge clusters, borne on long poles, as evidence. A month after they left Egypt, Israel had exhausted their food supply and for the next twenty-three months they existed on a boring diet of manna. Is it any wonder they told Moses, "Our soul loathes this worthless bread"? (Numbers 21:5B). One of my favorite types of food is Italian, but if I had no choice but to eat Italian food three times a day for two years, I'd never again darken the door of an Italian restaurant. When Israel saw the fruit from Canaan, one would think they would have immediately packed up their tents and headed for the border. Not the case!

> Nevertheless the people who dwell in the land are strong; the cities are fortified and very large.
>
> Numbers 13:28

"Nevertheless" is almost always followed by a negative. The majority of the spies (ten) were *yes, but*...believers. "Yes, the fruit was impressive, but what about the fortified cities?" Having heard the full report, the congregation came to the conclusion that Jericho and the other cities were well beyond their ability to conquer. Rather than being promise-focused, they became problem-focused. Just as on the western shore of the Red Sea, again at the bitter waters of Marah, later still when they ran out of water, Israel continued to walk by sight. Instead of visualizing the battles ahead as rigged fights, they saw themselves squashed like grasshoppers (Numbers 13:33). Spiritual blindness caused them to leave the most important person out of the equation—the Lord!

> We are not able to go up against the people, for they are stronger than we.
>
> Numbers 13:31B

> Do not rebel against the Lord, nor fear the people of the land, for they are our bread; their protection has departed from them, and the Lord is with us. Do not fear them.
>
> Numbers 14:9

Joshua and Caleb were part of the scouting party. While in Canaan, they tasted the same fruit and saw the same fortified cities as the other ten. Rather than seeing themselves as grasshoppers waiting to be squashed, they saw the squatters as their *bread*. Just as Moses visualized Israel camped safely on the eastern shore of the Red Sea, under the power of God, these two men saw Israel victoriously camped across the border. Joshua and Caleb were not fools who had their heads buried in the desert sand. They had previously seen God's power demonstrated in Egypt. They saw His power displayed at the Red Sea, and in eliminating Pharaoh's army. They saw how He faithfully supplied food and water for two million people in the barren desert for two full years. They were aware that during their years in the desert, neither their shoes nor clothing wore out (Deuteronomy 29:5). They believed that same power would continue to prevail in the land of rest. Apparently Moses had a positive influence on Joshua and Caleb. When they saw Moses was not influenced by the whining majority at the Red Sea, I expect his unwavering faith spoke to their hearts.

Joshua and Caleb were now faced with a similar challenge. Instead of being swayed by the majority, they made a decision to stand upon the promises of God, deciding to view the battles they would face in Canaan as rigged fights. Joshua and Caleb were cut from a different cloth. They lived 2 Corinthians 5:7 before the verse was recorded—"We walk by faith, not by sight." Instead of seeing themselves as defeated grasshoppers, they visualized their enemies as good old sourdough bread, readily consumable! They *saw* themselves residing in Canaan, living in homes they had not built and dining on the fruit of the land! Instead of uttering the word "nevertheless," and being "yes, but" believers, Joshua and Caleb said, "Let's go get 'em!" Notice the two different ways of thinking in the following verses.

> Let us go up at once and take possession, for we are well able to overcome it. If the Lord delights in us, then He will bring us into this land and give it to us, a land which flows with milk and honey. Only do not rebel against the Lord, nor fear the people of the land, for they are our bread; their protection has departed from them, and the Lord is with us. Do not fear them.
>
> Number 13:30, 14:8-9

> Why has the Lord brought us to this land to fall by the sword, that our wives and children should become victims? Would it not be better for us to return to Egypt?
>
> Numbers 14:3

The wimpy ten spies had to come up with logical reasons for their fear and disobedience. Similar to Adam's behavior in the Garden, they found a scapegoat, in fact the same scapegoat. First they blamed the Lord, then they used their wives and children as excuses for their disobedience.

Let's get to where the rubber meets the road! Had we been in Israel's shoes, which group would we have lined up with—the wimpy ten, or the faithful two? Would we have focused on the positive fruit, and said, "Lets go," or would we have said, "Yes, the fruit looks inviting, but..."? Would we have viewed the squatters as our bread? Or would we have viewed ourselves as grasshoppers? Our answer to this question determines the quality of Christian life we experience during our remaining years on earth!

> Whatever is not from faith is sin.
>
> Romans 14:23B

Peace is not an automatic byproduct of Christianity. Peace in the midst of negatives can only be experienced by believers who are walking by faith and holding tightly to the promises of Christ. Only then can we be more than conquerors when confronted with the pressures of life.

> In all these things we are more than conquerors through Him who loved us.
>
> Romans 8:37

Today, there are many Christians who hear, or read about God's promises, but view their particular problem as too big a challenge for the God of the universe. Can you believe it? They think the victory verses recorded in the Bible sound wonderful, *but*...! For example, many believe their marriage problems are beyond God's ability to mend. They believe such addictions as fear, worry, and anger are too deeply imbedded in their lives for God to flush them out. Christians find themselves hooked on various other kinds of addictions and believe they have to learn to live with such bondage. When trying to encourage a troubled Christian to begin walking on victory turf, how often we have heard them say, "God's promises sound inviting, nevertheless…"

As the saying goes, Kadesh-Barnea was that generation's last kick at the cat! Having rejected God's invitation to enter the Promised Land, He ceased striving with that generation. Sadly, they would spend their remaining years struggling, as second-class citizens, in the barren wilderness—thirty-eight long years. How sad to think they were within a stone's throw of the land of rest and their inheritance, yet, because of fear, disobedience, and stubbornness, they missed the boat! They began their journey as cheese and cracker believers, and forty years later they died in the wilderness in the same sad spiritual condition.

> With whom was He grieved forty years? Was it not with them that had sinned, whose carcasses fell in the wilderness? And to whom swear he that they should not enter into His rest, but to them that believed not? So we see that they could not enter in because of unbelief.
>
> Hebrews 3:17-19 (KJV)

> How often they (Israel) provoked Him in the wilderness, and grieved Him in the desert!
>
> Psalm 78:40

"Grieve" is a love word. You cannot grieve the loss of someone unless there has been a love relationship established. Despite Israel's disobedience, for the next thirty-eight years, God continued to love them and provide their basic needs—water, manna, and an occasional quail as a change of diet.

After a night's sleep, out of guilt, Israel had a change of heart, and under their own power, crossed the border into Canaan. Moses had previously warned them about moving ahead of the Lord, and they soon returned to Kadesh soundly defeated (Numbers 14:40-45).

For their remaining years, the first generation, once again, found themselves boxed in. There was no going back to Egypt, and they were not able to enter the Promised Land. Bogged down in the wilderness, they enjoyed neither the leeks and garlic of Egypt, nor the abundant life in Canaan. Perhaps that is where the expression "going around in circles" originated, for they made no progress during all those years. Many of today's Christians find themselves stuck in a barren wilderness of their own making, their minds like concrete—mixed up and permanently set! As believers, we simply must be open to God's purpose for our lives and committed to continually moving forward, *under the cloud.*

God's goal for a believer has not changed over the years. It is still His desire to get us *out,* so He can get us *in.* Anything short of entering the land of rest means short-changing ourselves and living a substandard brand of Christianity. Remember, the key to entering the land of rest is ceasing from our own works. I believe at some stage of every Christian's life, the Holy Spirit nudges him to do just that—trust the Lord to be the reigning authority in his life. If he rejects that invitation, there may come a time when the Lord ceases to strive with him and leaves him sitting on the fence, in a spiritually barren wilderness of his own making, enjoying little benefit from either the world or the kingdom of Christ. Oh, he may be involved in a church, but his relationship with Christ will be seriously lacking—a mechanical brand of Christianity. In that condition, he will most likely turn to the world to satisfy his inner cravings, and any joy and peace he experiences from those endeavors will be short lived. Regardless of his position in the community, and the assets he may have accumulated, stress, anxiety, and a lack of peace will prevail.

Ten Spies

Ten men who failed to see God,
Saw cities impregnably high,
Two men, "looking off" unto God,
Saw doom for those cities draw nigh.

Ten men who failed to see God,
Saw giants affrightingly tall,
Two men, "looking off" unto God,
Saw giants as grasshoppers small.

Ten men who failed to see God,
Reported, "We're certain to fail",
Two men, "looking off" unto God,
Cried, "Up! For with God we prevail"

Ten men who failed to see God,
Discouraged their brother men,
Two men perceived God everywhere,
Are you of the two—or the ten?

Author Unknown

Majority Versus Minority

When it came to trusting in God's promises, Joshua and Caleb were certainly in the minority. As Christians, we must always be cautious about lining up with the majority, as often their thinking will lead us down blind alleys. Throughout the history of the Bible, it is amazing how often the thinking and actions of the majority were wrong. The flood was certainly an example of the majority being wrong. Millions made a conscious decision to reject God's provision for avoiding pending judgment, while a minority of eight took refuge in the ark. When boxed in at the Red Sea, the majority failed to place faith in God's promises, while a minority of one visualized Israel camped safely on the eastern shore. The majority at Kadesh heard about the fortified cities and viewed themselves as grasshoppers, while a minority of two saw the squatters as their bread. A ratio of 2:2,000,000! The entire army of Israel cowered in fear when Goliath appeared on the battlefield, while a minority of one placed faith in God's promise, viewing the battle as a rigged fight. Jesus warned that at any particular time in history, the majority would reject His free gift of salvation, while only a few would depart from this world in the right spiritual condition. Today, it appears as if the majority of Christians live a self-managed life, while a rather small minority have made the decision to live a Christ-managed life. Which group do you find yourself lined up with?

> Narrow is the gate and difficult is the way which leads to life, and there are few who find it.
>
> Matthew 7:14

World history has often proven the majority to be wrong. For example, the majority said the horseless carriage would never replace the horse, while a minority of one proved them wrong—a guy by the name of Henry. The minority in the medical profession claimed unsterilized surgical instruments were causing unnecessary deaths, yet for many years the majority had their heels dug in, causing those very same deaths. The majority said if man was meant to fly, God would have given him wings, and a minority of two shot holes in that theory.

Standing against the majority almost always invites opposition, flak, and ridicule. When Joshua and Caleb opposed the view of the majority, the Israelite leaders held an emergency board meeting and decided to execute them (Numbers 14:10). Fortunately for Israel, that recommendation never became a reality. When Jesus opposed the religious hierarchy, they not only attempted to discredit Him, they eventually had Him crucified. The final nail in Christ's coffin was driven when He raised His friend Lazarus from the dead. Because of that miracle, many Jews began defecting from the local temples to follow Jesus. The scribes and Pharisees held a board meeting and came to the conclusion that unless drastic action was taken, they were in danger of losing their entire flock to Christ (John 12:19). "From that day on, they plotted to put Him to death" (John 11:53). It is interesting that the opposition Jesus experienced did not come from the Romans, but from the very religious community he came to rescue! Under Roman domination, the Jews were forbidden to execute, so the Jewish religious hierarchy reported a false charge to the Roman authorities concerning Jesus. The Romans were simply the legal tool the Jewish religious leaders used to eliminate the Messiah.

He who walks with God will be out of step with the world!

When we line up with the Word of God, and refuse to go along with the religious majority, we can expect opposition and flak. Just as with Jesus, the majority of criticism we receive will not come from the world, but from religious people.

Beware lest anyone cheat you through philosophy and empty deceit, according to the tradition of men; according to the basic principles of the world, and not according to Christ.

Colossians 2:8

Israel's Bread

Since this chapter is about faith, allow me to jump ahead thirty-eight years in time and share an astounding story of faith.

After the first generation of Israelites perished in the wilderness, the new generation found themselves on the eastern shore of the Jordan River. Across the river was Canaan, with Jericho located just five miles down the road. While they sat on the eastern shore waiting for God's green light to cross the river, two spies were sent across to check out Jericho (Joshua 2:1). In the city, they met a woman by the name of Rahab who recounted the most amazing story.

She told of how the residents of Jericho had heard how the God of Israel had parted the Red Sea and destroyed Egypt's army. The citizens would have heard of the devastating plagues God showered upon Egypt, and how He had miraculously provided food and water for two million people for forty years in the desert. Rahab said the residents of Jericho had been living with *melted* hearts for the past forty years—dreading the day Israel's God would lead them to Jericho's doorstep (Joshua 2:11). The residents must have been puzzled as to why Israel took forty years to actually enter Canaan and reclaim their land. Knowing Israel was camped across the Jordan, they knew they were number one on Israel's hit list and feared their days were numbered. They didn't view Israel as *grasshoppers*, but because of Israel's God, saw themselves as Israel's *bread!* The idol-worshiping pagans of Jericho had more faith in God's power than the first generation of Israelites! Amazing!

Questions

- In the midst of life's dark clouds, do you find yourself displaying peace and rest? Or do tension, stress, and worry prevail?

- In your Christian journey, who do you find yourself lining up with the majority or minority?

- Do you view your enemies as bread? Or do you view yourself as a grasshopper waiting to be squashed?

- Is the phrase "We are well able to overcome" becoming a part of your vocabulary? I sincerely hope so!

ELIMINATING DEBT

Company Store

Years ago Tennessee Ernie had a huge hit with a song called "Sixteen Tons." There was a line in the chorus that said, "I owe my soul to the company store!" The term company store originated in the Kentucky coal mining shantytowns that housed the miners and their families. The heart of these towns was the company store, where the miners could purchase food and clothing at exorbitant prices. Inevitably, the miners would end up owing the company store more money than they could ever expect to earn. The bondage of the company store still exists. It has just taken on a different form. Credit card companies have replaced the company store of old. The average household credit card debt in 1990 was $2,966. Today it is $14,500. Do you find it amazing that there is over 400 percent more credit card debt today than in 1990? Who knows what tomorrow's figures will be? Like the company store debt of old, this too has to be viewed as a form of bondage. A credit card company was recently advertising their product on TV and the background music for the ad was, if you can believe it, "Born Free." What a contradiction! A newborn child today begins life $161,000 in debt. That is his share of the national debt! According to the Federal Reserve, over 40 percent of American families spend more than they earn.

Currently, the U.S. national debt is 12 trillion dollars! The daily interest of the debt is 500 million dollars! The alarming national debt is just the tip of the U.S. financial problem. For every dollar in circulation, there used to be an equal amount set aside in gold reserves. Sadly, this is no longer the case. The national mint continues to print new paper dollars with no gold backing, and today, for every dollar we have in our pocket, there is just a few cents in gold backing the currency. Can you believe that Congress has allowed the national debt to reach such a level that the government can no longer pay the interest, let alone reduce the principal? When a person finds himself in such a financial mess, he is well on the way to declaring bankruptcy. Perhaps our politicians should alert the citizens of the existing financial crisis by hanging out a bankruptcy sign on the steps of congress! Despite the efforts of many liberal minded people, the words "In God We Trust" should definitely remain on U.S. bills as a reminder of the only place our faith can be directed. Throughout history, any nation that reached such a financial crisis eventually collapsed and never fully recovered. Are our current financial woes an indication we are headed in that direction? There are those who think so!

To add to the nation's financial dilemma, the savings in U.S. households has plummeted since the early 1990s.

I place economy among the first and most important virtues and debt as the greatest of damages to be feared.

Thomas Jefferson

Growing domestic and international debt has created the condition for a global economic and financial crisis.

Bank for International Settlements, June 2005

No generation has a right to contract debts greater than can be paid off during the course of its own existence.

George Washington, 1789

God has always been concerned about His people incurring debt they are unable to pay. It is another form of bondage and points us to a far greater bondage which I think it is worth taking time out to discuss in this chapter. "You shall not borrow" (Deuteronomy 28:12B). If an Israelite in the Old Testament found himself in debt, he became a slave to his debtor until the debt was totally paid off. In the Old Testament days there were three ways an Israelite could have his debt eliminated.

One way was to personally pay it off. Because a slave received no salary, this method of eliminating debt simply wasn't an option. Another was to wait until the next Jubilee Year. Every fiftieth year, all debt in Israel was automatically cancelled. If this ruling was in force today, it is doubtful credit card companies would be handing out their cards so freely. On the surface, this method of eliminating debt has its appeal, but it also had a built in problem. What if the Israelite in debt died before the next Jubilee Year? He would go to his grave in financial bondage and disgrace. The third method of eliminating debt proved to be the most satisfactory. Out of compassion, a family member could step forward and redeem the debt of a brother, uncle, father, etc. This person became known as the *kinsman redeemer.*

When an Israelite incurred debt, the details of the debt were recorded on a papyrus scroll; the scroll was then sealed and stored in the local temple (Leviticus 25:47-54). On the inside of the scroll the name of the person in debt was recorded. On the outside, the amount of the debt was recorded, along with the three conditions the kinsman redeemer had to satisfy in order to redeem his relative's debt. When a near kin agreed to eliminate the debt, he would go to the temple and ask the high priest to locate the scroll. Once the scroll was located, the kinsman redeemer then had to prove he was able to satisfy the three conditions, which were:

1. *Near kin*: He had to prove he was related to the debtor. There had to be a blood relationship.

2. *Able to pay*: He had to prove he was able to pay the debt in full. Installment payments were unacceptable. It was an all or nothing deal!

3. *Willing to pay*: Out of love and compassion for his near kin, he was willing to have the debt credited to his account. Once the debt was transferred to his account, he would settle the debt.

Once the kinsman redeemer satisfied the three conditions, the seals on the scroll were broken, in the presence of witnesses, and the scroll was opened. The name of the debtor was confirmed, and the high priest would declare him debt free. Just as with today's court system, there was no double jeopardy. The person could never again be charged with that particular debt.

Christ Our Kinsman Redeemer

All have sinned and fall short of the glory of God.

Romans 3:23

The law of Moses confirms that we have all broken God's Commandments to some degree. It really doesn't matter if we committed murder, lied, stole, coveted, or broke every law in the book. With God, the degree of sin is not the issue. From God's perspective, both the murderer and liar are viewed as sinners, and both have incurred a sin debt with God. The Scripture says, "A little leaven spoils the whole loaf." In that condition, both are under the same condemnation and in the wrong condition to spend eternity with God. James makes this truth abundantly clear in the following verse.

Whoever shall keep the whole law, and yet stumble in one point, he is guilty of all.

James 2:10

For the past six thousand years a major question has prevailed with each generation. The question is, "How do we have our sin debt eliminated, and how do we become justified and set right in God's eyes?" After the Fall, Adam and Eve attempted to cover their sin condition by clothing themselves with leaves—the world's first religious act. That act was similar to sweeping sin under the rug! Since then, the majority of mankind has attempted to find God's approval by sewing on various types of religious leaves. Some attempt to find God's approval abiding by a list of rules, hoping their good deeds outweigh their bad. Others believe they find God's favor when they join a church or when they were sprinkled with water as an infant or baptized as an adult. All noble efforts, but, like Adam and Eve's leaves, all of man's efforts fall drastically short of God's requirement for being set right (Titus 3:5).

> Though you wash yourself with lye, and use much soap, the stain of your guilt is still before me, says the Lord God.
>
> Jeremiah 2:22 (RSV)

Sometime in the future, when Revelation chapter five becomes a reality, one of the most important events in the history of the world will unfold! The apostle John was given a vision of this future event and recorded it for the encouragement of believers. "Come up here, and I will show you things which must take place after this" (Revelation 4:1).

> I saw in the right hand of Him who sat on the throne a scroll written inside and on the back, sealed with seven seals.
>
> Revelation 5:1

John, a Jew, saw a scene in heaven that he recognized and fully understood. The sealed scroll would have brought to mind the Old Testament redemption scroll, and that an important transaction was about to take place at the throne of God. John gave the scroll an appropriate name—the Lamb's Book of Life. I mentioned the Lamb's Book in a previous chapter, but because of its importance, allow me to quickly review the highlights of the Lamb's Book. Many believe their name is recorded in the heavenly scroll when they become a Christian. That is clearly not the case. Before the foundation of the world, the name of every person that would be born into this world was recorded in the Lamb's Book. God keeps a detailed record of each individual, just as He knows our every hair.

At some future time, those who rejected God's provision for sin will have their names permanently blotted out of the Book. Only the names of believers will remain. Throughout eternity, the Lamb's Book will serve as God's census, listing the names of those who are citizens of His kingdom. If a person arrives at heaven's gate with any degree of sin credited to his account, he will be informed he is in the wrong spiritual condition to spend eternity in heaven and will be ushered to the kingdom that will honor his citizenship—Satan's camp. His name will have been permanently blotted out of God's census ledger!

> In Him you also trusted after you heard the word of truth, the gospel of your salvation; in whom also, having believed, you were sealed with the Holy Spirit of promise, who is the guarantee of our inheritance until the redemption of the purchased possession.
>
> Ephesians 1:13-14

In the above verse, "until" is a time word! Once we become a Christian, our name remains sealed in the Lamb's Book of Life until Revelation chapter five takes place. The word "until" is another way of confirming the eternal security of a believer. The only one who has the authority to break the seals of the Lamb's Book and open it is our heavenly High Priest—Christ Jesus. Contrary to the false thinking of some, so-called big sins do not have the power to break the seals and remove the names of those who committed such sins.

When John saw Jesus approaching, he saw Him as "a Lamb as though it had been slain" (Revelation 5:6B). John remembered Calvary's scars and was aware the slain Lamb of God was about to fulfill the role of kinsman redeemer. With his Hebrew background, John knew the drill. He knew Jesus was about to prove He met the three redemption conditions recorded on the outside of the heavenly scroll. Once the conditions were met, the seals on the scroll would be broken, and the names of the redeemed confirmed. Christ was about to take the heavenly roll call. Let's quickly examine why Jesus is qualified to be our Kinsman Redeemer and how He more than satisfied the three conditions:

Near kin: The instant we become a Christian, a permanent blood bond exists between ourselves and Christ. We become kin to Him—family. The Bible says Jesus is not ashamed to call us brethren (Hebrews 2:11B). At birth, I entered this world with my earthly father's blood flowing through my veins, and nothing can ever change that blood relationship. When I placed faith in what Christ accomplished at Calvary, I became born-again. Through the royal blood of my Kinsman Redeemer, I am forever related to Christ.

> Abide in Me, and I in you…If anyone does not abide in Me, he is cast out as a branch and is withered (no spiritual life).
>
> John 15:4

Able to pay: The shed blood of Christ is the only currency God views as legal tender for dealing with sin. God announced, "In Him I am well pleased." Jesus is the Just One. He, and He alone is qualified to "justify" (Romans 3:26). In the following verse, the apostle Peter makes it clear that we are not redeemed as a result of our conduct, but by our placing faith in Christ's conduct on our behalf.

You were not redeemed with corruptible things, like silver or gold, from your aimless conduct received by tradition from your fathers (law), but with the precious blood of Christ, as of a lamb without blemish and without spot (sinless).

1 Peter 1:18-19

Willing to pay: Despite the shame of having the sins of the world imputed to His account, Jesus counted it joy to make the redemption payment for sin.

Looking unto Jesus, the author and finisher of our faith, who for the joy that was set before Him endured the cross, despising the shame, and has sat down at the right hand of the throne of God.

Hebrews 12:2

Did you notice the above verse does not say the pain of the cross, but the shame? Crucifixion is an excruciating way to die, but the physical pain Jesus endured at Calvary paled in comparison to the spiritual agony He experienced. Because of the collective sin Christ bore at Calvary, until His blood was sprinkled on the heavenly mercy seat, He remained separated from the other two members of the Trinity. Contaminated with the sins of the world, the Father was forced to turn His back on His beloved Son. With our limited understanding, it is impossible for us to identify with the agony our Lord experienced. The three days in the tomb must have seemed like an eternity to Him. We sense a tiny indication of the agony He experienced when we read of His lonely cry from Golgotha—"My God, My God, why have you forsaken Me?" (Mark 15:34B).

Do you not find it humbling to think our sins actually caused a temporal division in the Trinity? Had you been the only person in the world, Jesus would still have experienced the shame of

Calvary in order to redeem you. The cross is eternal proof that there is no limit to His love!

> You are worthy to take the scroll, and to open its seals; for you were slain, and have redeemed us to God by Your blood out of every tribe and tongue and people and nation, and have made us kings and priests to our God; and we shall reign on the earth.
>
> Revelation 5:9-10

Once our Kinsman Redeemer proves He satisfies the three conditions recorded on the outside of the heavenly scroll, the seals will be broken in the presence of witnesses, and the Lamb's Book will be opened. That time word "until" will finally have arrived! When the Book is opened, the names of the redeemed will be confirmed, which will enable the wedding feast of the Lamb to commence and the Millennium Reign to begin. When the seals are broken, there will not be a handful of witness to confirm the transaction, but 100,000,000 angels (Revelation 5:11)! This will be a major event! As the musicians say, "You won't want to miss this gig!"

Earth's Redemption

> The whole creation groans and labors with birth pangs together until now. Not only that, but we also who have the firstfruits of the Spirit, even we ourselves groan within ourselves, eagerly waiting for the adoption, the redemption of our body.
>
> Romans 8:22-23

Not only are believers anxiously awaiting confirmation of their redemption, but our planet is also groaning and travailing waiting for legal confirmation of its redemption. Before Christ can return to earth for the Millennium Reign, another legal transaction must take place. Earth's redemption must be verified. We hear teaching about the redemption of man, but little about the redemption of our planet.

When Adam was placed on earth, he became the legal tenant, and in that position, he was given dominion (Genesis 1:28). When he stumbled he relinquished his position, and guess who picked up the reins? Satan became the prince of this world and legally retains that position until Revelation five becomes a reality. When Jesus died on the cross, He not only became our Kinsman Redeemer, He also made payment to redeem our planet. When earth's redemption is confirmed then, and only then, can Christ legally return to earth for the Millennium Reign and rule from the throne of David—in Jerusalem. At that time, Satan's princely rule will be over. He will be removed as tenant of this world and escorted to the big house. The planet will no longer be groaning, waiting for its rebirth. Jesus referred to this transfer of authority when He announced, "The ruler of this world will be cast out" (John 12:31B). All these things will begin to occur when the last *living stone* is ushered into the kingdom of Christ.

> The devil has come down to you (booted out of heaven), having great wrath, because he knows that he has a short time.
>
> Revelation 12:12

Satan is on a short leash fully aware that, with each passing day, he is nearing the end of his rope. As we get closer to the reality of Revelation five, the war that exists between the kingdom of Satan and the kingdom of Christ will intensify. In the final days of any battle, all the heavy guns come out. That is exactly what we are seeing today. The Bible tells us that as we approach the end of this church age, there will be an increase in wars, famines, and earthquakes. The attack upon Christianity will become more open and more severe. People will become more distant, cold, and less compassionate. The deterioration of families will escalate. More and more prisons will be required to house criminals. Despite the efforts of such organizations as the Drug Enforcement Agency, the usage of drugs, prescription and otherwise, will continue to accelerate in every level of society. Unless a person has their head stuck in the sand, one surely has to admit Satan is nearing the end of his rope, and the church age is quickly winding down!

The question is, are you ready for the sound of the trumpet?

Imperfection in Heaven

The Bible clearly teaches that, throughout eternity, believers will have perfect bodies. Our blemishes, tattoos, scars, and corrupt flesh will be history. A woman once asked me if her excess weight would also be left behind. When I told her I expected we would all be an ideal size, a smile slowly came to her lips. Throughout eternity, there will only be one heavenly resident with imperfections—Christ! "In the midst of the elders, stood a Lamb as though it had been slain" (Revelation 5:6B). Throughout all eternity, Jesus will bear Calvary's scars as a reminder of what it cost to fulfill His role as our Kinsman Redeemer. Humbling isn't it? If that does not bring a tear to your eye, nothing will!

Questions

- If Revelation chapter five were to take place today, would you arrive at heaven's gate knowing your name was preserved in the Lamb's Book of Life? Or would there be a blank space where your name was once recorded?

- To ensure a place in heaven, are you still placing faith in your accomplishments rather than in the accomplishments of our Kinsman Redeemer?

SUCCESSFUL FARMING

The land which you go to possess is not like the land of
Egypt from which you have come, where you sowed your seed
and watered it by foot, as a vegetable garden; but the land
which you cross over to possess drinks water from the rain of
heaven…I will give you the rain for your land in its season.

Deuteronomy 11:10-11, 14

Inferior Irrigation System

In an earlier chapter entitled "Holy of Holies," we saw the first
generation of Israelites placed on a shelf because of their lack of
faith in God's promises. For the remainder of this book, we will
focus on the next generation.

In Canaan, farming would be a way of life. The system for
growing crops and fruit, however, would be much different than
methods employed by their forefathers in Egypt. Due to the lack
of rain, an ingenious irrigation system had been developed. Water
was moved from the Nile River to the land through a system of
channels and sub-channels. Moving the water in these channels
was the job of the Israelite slaves who turned water wheels by
foot. Picture it somewhat like peddling a bicycle all day long, for
days on end.

Despite their laborious efforts, the fruit produced in Egypt would never have been labeled Blue Ribbon. The winds constantly blew sand into the Nile, turning the river into a flowing mud puddle. As a result, the land produced a poor quality of fruit—yucky, in fact.

Superior Irrigation System

In Canaan the irrigation system would be far superior. The polluted Nile was left behind forever, and the Lord promised to supply fresh rain from above. There would be no need for trenches or water wheels; the Lord promised just the right amount of rain when needed. There would be no need for prayer meetings pleading for rain. The only effort required would be to harvest the crops and pick fruit, which promised to be Blue Ribbon quality!

> Take heed to yourselves, lest your heart be deceived, and you turn aside and serve other gods and worship them, lest the Lord's anger be aroused against you, and He shut up the heavens so that there be no rain, and the land yield no produce.
>
> Deuteronomy 11:16-17

Even though God's system was superior to any method devised by man, it contained a potential negative. The heavenly rain was conditional! Israel's conduct would determine the amount of rain released. If Israel fell in with the ways of the pagan squatters and began drifting from the Lord, the heavenly spigot would be turned off. Bottom line—no fruit! In Egypt, this was not the case. The Israelites could adopt the ways of the Egyptians and worship their idols, and through their hard work peddling day after day, they would have water, a rather poor quality of water to be sure, but water, and therefore fruit. Yucky perhaps, but fruit!

In Canaan, if God stopped the rain, there would be no backup system and consequently no fruit!

Today, through our own efforts, we can produce various degrees of success. We can build beautiful homes, buy the latest new toys, take exotic vacations, even successfully manage our stock portfolios, however, I think you will agree, the enjoyment experienced from these efforts is usually short-lived and never brings the lasting satisfaction hoped for. Certainly not the results we expect from the money and effort put forth. Just as Israel could not produce heavenly rain without the indwelling Holy Spirit, it is impossible to display spiritual fruit. The best we can do on our own is imitate or counterfeit. "It is the Spirit who gives life; the flesh profits nothing" (John 6:63).

> I am the vine, you are the branches. He who abides in Me, and I in him, bears much fruit; for without Me you can do nothing.
>
> John 15:5

> I set before you today a blessing and a curse: the blessing if you obey the commandments of the Lord your God which I command you today; and the curse if you do not obey the commandments of the Lord.
>
> Deuteronomy 11:26-28

Once the second generation crossed into Canaan, life would be a whole new ball game. No longer were they to sight walk as did their parents. Instead, they were to begin walking by faith in the Word of God. Their daily conduct would determine the amount of rain the land received and the quality of crops and fruit they enjoyed. As long as they stayed on track, God promised to shower them with heavenly blessings. The life they would experience, in the land of rest, would be vastly superior to their former life. Once they set up camp in Canaan, the ball would be in their court! They were solely responsible for the quality of life they would experience.

> He will cause the rain to come down for you—the former rain, and the latter rain in the first month.
>
> Joel 2:23B

> I have come that they may have life, and that they may have it more abundantly.
>
> John 10:10

God's formula for showers of blessing remains the same today. If we remain shackled to the world, and adopt its carnal ways, we will find ourselves reaping what we sow. The fruit of our labor will be worry, fear, anxiety, anger, depression, and above all else, stress and more stress. Certainly an unappealing quality of life!

The *may* in the above verse is one of those conditional words. Our salvation experience is the foundation to our Christian life. It keeps us safe from the pending judgment and makes us a legal citizen of God's kingdom. The abundant life Jesus promised, however, is not a natural byproduct of our salvation. If that were the case, today's Christian community would be displaying a much different quality of life. The life Christ has in mind for His people is a natural result of our having a healthy relationship with Him. It means coming to the conclusion that He cannot lie and that we can place 100 percent faith in His promises. It is a result of our acknowledging Him as the one most capable to manage our lives. *May* comes as a result of solid Bible teaching followed by faith in and obedience to that teaching. Without obedience, the teaching is in vain. If we find ourselves constantly in turmoil and experiencing little peace, it is certain that changes need to be made. Just as with Israel, we call the shot. We determine the quality of life we experience. The abundant life Jesus promised is there for the taking! Why then are we so foolish, robbing ourselves, so much of the time, by making wrong decisions? Over and over again, we see that with our free will comes much responsibility.

Watch the Pride

> Beware that you do not forget the Lord... when you have eaten and are full, and have built beautiful houses and dwell in them; and when your herds and your flocks multiply, and your silver and your gold are multiplied, and all that you have is multiplied; when your heart is lifted up, and you forget the Lord your God who brought you out of the land of Egypt... then you say in your heart; My power and the might of my hand have gained me this wealth.
>
> Deuteronomy 8:11-17

There was another way in which Israel could cause the heavenly rains to be turned off. That reason is summed up in one word— pride! If Israel attempted to take credit for the Lord's blessings, the heavenly spigot would definitely become clogged. Once pride reared its ugly head, the fruit they once enjoyed would begin to diminish or disappear altogether.

> Pride goes before destruction, and a haughty spirit before a fall.
>
> Proverbs 16:18

Have you noticed that when things are going badly the Lord often catches the blame, *but* when blessings are rolling our way, so often God receives little recognition? There is a long trail of Christian organizations that were once fruitful, but pride seeping into the hearts of the leadership resulted in God's turning off the heavenly blessings. There may still be an abundance of self-generated activity within the organization, but the spiritual fruit will be of poor quality—leaving a sour taste. Instead of being a lighthouse in the community, that organization will eventually evolve into a spiritually dead religious club. Lots of flurry and action, but little spiritual substance! The members will have a more intimate relationship with the workings of the club than with Christ.

Once pride surfaces, and God begins removing His blessings, a downward spiral begins. Usually the first evidence of decline is solid Bible truths that were once preached are rather quickly replaced by a watered down version. When that happens, the spiritual decline continues. Those in the congregation who have a hunger for solid spiritual food will begin leaving in search of more nourishing teaching. The congregation will then consist mostly of non-believers and carnal Christians. When there is a need to fill a position, unqualified people will step up eager to fill the slot, further contributing to the decline. Unless drastic action is taken, all the spiritual life will eventually be drained from the group. That congregation may know *about* God, but the majority in the pews will sit with darkened hearts—their lives having never been illuminated by the Holy Spirit (Romans 1:21). In times past, it was usually the lost or carnal Christians who left a church in search of more liberal teaching. Today, this is no longer the case. Because there is so little solid Bible teaching in way too many of our churches, it is now the spiritual Christians who are checking out in search of solid food. I firmly believe this is one of the main reasons home Bible studies are flourishing in our day.

Remaining Word-Focused

> Lay up these words of mine in your heart and in your soul, and bind them as a sign on your hand, and they shall be as frontlets between your eyes.
>
> Deuteronomy 11:18

Israel's response to the Word of God would determine the quality of life they were to experience in Canaan. If they were to enjoy the abundant life to the fullest, and not be led astray by the idol worshiping nations around them, it was imperative they remain Word-focused. God advised them to do three things with His Word, and those instructions still hold true. If we want to experience the normal Christian life, and find freedom from fleshly bondage, we must give weight to God's advice. Hopefully we are beginning to get it into our thick skulls that His Word is not for His benefit, but for ours!

Rather than storing God's Word in their minds (head knowledge), or tucked away in some rarely opened drawer, Israel was instructed to store His Word in their hearts. What does it mean to store the Word in our hearts? Simply put, it means believing the promises contained in the Bible and making them a living reality, daily. Those same truths stored in our head will be of little value when dark clouds appear. If our only exposure to the Word is twenty minutes on a Sunday morning, I guarantee you our lives will be no different than those in the world around us.

While in the safety of a harbor (our homes), we should be storing the Word in our hearts, as it will only be a matter of time before we find our faith tested on the high seas. When we see the enemy on the horizon, it is too late to flip open our Bibles and begin preparing ammo. When someone takes a verbal shot at us, there is no time to search the Scriptures for an appropriate response. With an abundance of God's Word stored deep in our hearts, when the negatives come, and they will, we will be well-equipped to respond appropriately.

> This Book of the law shall not depart from your mouth...For then you will make your way prosperous and then you will have good success.
>
> Joshua 1:8

Mouth certainly suggests chewing it over and digesting. When the Word of God abides in our hearts, we will be successful and prosperous in every area of our lives whether it be at work, in our homes, or among our friends and neighbors.

> Let the word of Christ dwell in you richly in all wisdom...
>
> Colossians 3:16

God also instructed Israel to bind His promises to their *hands*. To me that says the Word of God was to be constantly at their fingertips—within reach. They were to be as familiar with the Word as they were with the palms of their hands. I'm sure you will agree that in this stress-filled world, we too need to have the Word at our fingertips. As we approach end times, we are going to have our faith challenged more and more often with false doctrines. If we are to remain on track, we must know the Truth.

God also told Israel to place the Word like frontlets between their *eyes*. Simply put, they were to keep their eyes focused on the Word rather than on whatever problem might arise. Had Israel been promise-focused at the Red Sea, instead of whining and grumbling, they would have thrown a victory party while boxed in on the western shore. Had the disciples remained promise-focused in the boat, they would not have displayed fear even when a fierce storm overtook them.

Can you believe the legalistic Pharisees actually took this instruction and made it into a religious ritual? In an attempt to demonstrate how holy they were, they placed a portion of Scripture in a frontlet (a small box) and tied it to their foreheads. Simply amazing to what lengths religious people will go in order to impress!

If Israel was to experience a life of rest in Canaan, it was imperative they have God's promises stored in their hearts, at their fingertips, and foremost on their minds. Once in the land, their faith was going to be constantly challenged, and if they were to remain victorious, it was vital they follow the Lord's instructions. Only then would they be able to deal effectively with walled cities and heavily armed squatters.

This advice remains valid today. On a regular basis, our faith is going to be challenged. If we are to stand victorious, no matter what comes our way, we must commit ourselves to being Word-focused instead of problem-focused. The Word truly must be as familiar to us as the palms of our hands. If God's Word is stored only in our minds or on some dusty shelf, we have no one to blame but ourselves when the world and its inhabitants continually manipulate our emotions and time.

The Bible says there are two ways to walk the Christian life. Either by sight or by faith (2 Corinthians 5:7). Stress, anger, and fear are indications of sight-walking—responding to what we see! Walking by faith, on the other hand, is responding to what we believe—Standing on the Promises of God! A major difference exists between the two camps!

> As you therefore have received Christ Jesus the Lord, so walk in Him, rooted and built up in Him and established in the faith.
>
> Colossians 2:6

In the Bible, there are many examples of believers who had God's Word stored in their hearts, at their fingertips, and on their minds. Despite being faced with enormous challenges, they clung to the promises. Noah comes to mind. Prior to the Flood, he had never seen rain. The earth was watered by dew and subterranean wells, which meant there were no vast bodies of water or large boats (Genesis 2:5-6). When God told Noah that judgment was coming in the form of a devastating flood, Noah was asked to believe in something unseen. Human logic would have said, "No way," yet Noah believed and therefore experienced 2 Corinthians 4:18 before it was ever recorded. "We do not look at the things which are seen, but at the things which are not seen." Despite never having seen a large ship, Noah was told to begin building a sizable vessel. A 450-foot long, 75 feet wide boat would have been too large to erect secretly in his basement. Can you imagine the ridicule heaped on Noah by friends and neighbors when he began building such an apparent monstrosity? By faith, Noah *saw* the promised flood before the first drop of rain fell, and faithfully made provision to avoid the coming judgment (Hebrews 11:7).

Despite several hard knocks, and ending up in an Egyptian prison on a bad rap, Joseph believed God's promise that he would one day rule over Israel. Despite his circumstances, he *saw* himself reigning over the nation of Israel.

Before reaching for his sling, because God had previously promised he would one day be king, David *saw* Goliath defeated. A rigged fight!

The young Virgin Mary believed in God's promise of a supernatural event and *saw* herself bearing the Messiah (Luke 1:35).

These believers didn't walk on water, or have a halo over their heads. They were ordinary people who experienced extraordinary challenges. With God's Word hidden deep in their hearts, they saw what God promised well before the event.

God who cannot lie.

Titus 1:2

When we fail to place faith in God's promises, am I being too bold to say we call Him a liar? When we think our problems are too deeply entrenched in our lives for God to flush them out, seems to me we are inferring His promises sound great, but they don't seem to actually hold water in the real world. The truth is, the degree of freedom, dominion, and peace we experience in our daily journey is directly related to the degree of faith we place in His promises. The Christian life is that simple. One of the recent Bible translations is called the Living Bible. An appropriate name, as the promises of God should be a living reality in our hearts.

> Faith comes by hearing, and hearing by the word of God.
>
> Romans 10:17

Win-Win Situation

> You [parents] shall teach them [the Word] to your children, speaking of them [the Word] when you sit in your house.
>
> Deuteronomy 11:19

Before receiving God's green light to enter Canaan, God gave Israel one final instruction. A warning that is generally ignored by today's Christian community.

God told Israel they were to teach the Word to their children. The old fashioned phrase for that is the family altar. In many homes these days, it seems the television altar is the only place families gather.

Parents would be the first to benefit from a family Bible study. In order to find solid teaching material, they would be forced to find a church or Bible study that taught quality spiritual food. They would have to sit in that meeting with pen and notebook in hand. When they returned home, they would then have to rework their notes, tailoring them to the needs of their children. Producing these lessons would be a hat trick for the parents. First, they would have heard the Word taught. Second, by taking notes, the Word would penetrate deeper. Third, by using their notes to prepare lessons, the retention rate would be greatly increased. You can see that, in time, the parents would have the Word imbedded in their hearts as well as at their fingertips.

Child and parent relations would naturally improve. Statistics tell us the average quality time parents spend with their children is approximately half an hour a day! In this pressurized world, with both parents often working, family members find it difficult to even eat together, let alone a weekly gathering, centered around the Word. A home study would call for discipline from both parents and children. Initially, it is unlikely the children would be overjoyed with a weekly study, but once they began to feel comfortable and understand that they were learning important life skills, in time they would look forward to the gatherings. Children have many concerns, and what better place to air their concerns than in the safety of their own home? It is impossible to create this atmosphere and family relationship when the parent-child interaction consists of a few minutes each day.

A regular family study would force dad and mom to live the Christian life in the home. For example, it would be difficult for dad to teach about anger being bondage and sin, and then regularly behave that way himself. It would be difficult for mom to teach that gossip is sin and then rake friends and neighbors over the coals at the dinner table. Dad might have to deal with his pride. Mom might have to deal with her worry and depression. In other words, they would be compelled to walk the talk.

Without a doubt, these family gatherings would decrease the currently high level of Christian divorce. Instead of dad and mom constantly bickering over issues and allowing problems to create conflict in their marriage, they would eventually find themselves on the same side of the fence—facing the problems as one solid unit. Certainly a better way of dealing with problems than facing each other from opposite sides in divorce court. When their children marry, having seen a positive Christian marriage at home, the odds of their own marriages working out would be greatly increased. Launched from a Bible-based home life, these young adults would leave for college or the work force with a solid Christian foundation to build upon. Proverbs 22:6 would be in motion! Over time, a home study would create a deep bond between parent and child which, in far too many cases, is sadly lacking in today's world.

In his book, "The Last Christian Generation," Josh McDowell claims 78 percent of children view their parents as the greatest influence in their lives. The question is, "What type of influence?" If the parents are freewheeling about sex before marriage, addicted to harmful substances, prescription or otherwise, and constantly struggling with anger, worry, and a critical spirit, there is a good chance their children will begin their adult lives enmeshed in these same behavior patterns. Children are natural mimics. They act like their parents even though we make an effort to tell them to act differently. It seems to me the best way to teach our children is for our lives to be an example. If children see their parents living the Christian life as it is defined in the Bible, not only in church, but in the home, the odds of them leaving home in good spiritual shape will be greatly increased.

I firmly believe reinstating the old fashioned family altar would be a win-win situation for all members of the household. Apparently, so does God!

No society has ever survived after its family life deteriorated.

Dr. Paul Popenoe, founder and president the
American Institute of Family Relationships

Questions

- Where do you store the Word of God—in your mind, on a shelf, or in your heart?

- Is your Christian life (fruit) self-generated or Holy Spirit-generated? In other words, who is in control?

- What about pride? When you are being blessed, do you find pride surfacing, or do you acknowledge the Source of your blessings?

- Do you find that you are manipulated by the world, or are you are motivated and directed by the Word?

- Do you find yourself walking by sight, allowing negatives to dictate your mood and emotions, or by faith—beginning to *see* what you believe?

PART IV:
HOME AT LAST

JUMP IN AND GET YOUR FEET WET

After forty years of wandering in the wilderness, we now find the new generation camped on the eastern shore of the Jordan River, awaiting God's green light before returning to their homeland. It has now been thirty-eight years since unbelief in God's promises prevented their parents from crossing into Canaan at Kadesh-Barnea. How would this new generation react to the negative obstacles facing them across the river? When faced with fortified Jericho, would they view themselves as defeated *grasshoppers* as did their parents, or would they believe God's promise to defeat their enemies?

The land of Canaan contained both positives and negatives. The positives were their inheritance and freedom from the stressful and monotonous lifestyle experienced in the wilderness. The negatives were the armed squatters and mightily fortified Jericho five miles across the river. During the past thirty-eight years, little had changed in Canaan. The abundant fruit still prevailed, as did the illegal squatters, all those *ites*—the Moabites, Jebusites, Amorites, and so on. Most of the foreign nations who occupied the land had been living in Canaan for the better part of four hundred years and would not willingly surrender without a fight. Squatters' rights definitely would have been their thinking.

The Jordan River has always held an important place in Biblical history. For Israel it was a line in the desert that separated a life of hardship and struggle from a life of freedom. A line that separated an unproductive piece of real estate from a land of abundance. It separated a life of walking by sight from a life where they would be required to walk by faith. Across the line Israel would no longer be confined to a boring diet of manna, but would dine on the abundant fruit of the land. Once in the land of rest, they would no longer have to live in sand-infested tents, but would live in mortgage-free homes they had not built.

The Jordan was the river of decision. Would this generation take a step of faith by crossing the river, believing God was capable of dealing with whatever awaited them in the land? Or would they react as their parents did at Kadesh?

At some stage of our Christian journey, I believe every Christian is confronted with their very own Jordan River. A time of decision. A time when we are urged by the Holy Spirit to invite Christ to reign in our lives (Romans 12:1). A time when we begin to realize a life filled with various forms of stress, anger, and worry is not normal Christianity. A time when we wonder what life would be like if we began placing total faith in the promises of our God. Over the years I have met Christians who said they have entertained such thoughts, but in the end, decided to play it safe and stay put on the eastern shore! During the revival movement that took place in Western Canada over forty years ago, we saw many Christians make the decision to get off the fence, enter the land of rest, and begin to claim their inheritance. "Seeing therefore it remaineth that some must enter therein, and they to whom it was first preached entered not in because of unbelief" (Hebrews 4:6, KJV). The peace those Christians experienced was written all over their faces, often followed by tears of joy. Incidentally, that is what true revival really means. You cannot revive someone unless they have previously experienced new life.

Ultimately, true revival will produce new believers as a result of the testimony of the revived ones. Ruth and I personally know this to be true as that is exactly how we came to know the Lord in that very revival in Western Canada. Most of today's churches even have that backwards as they promote revivals as a means of reaching the lost, instead of a much-needed revival of worn out broken down Christians.

Had we been standing on the eastern bank of the Jordan, how would we have responded to God's invitation to enter Canaan? Would we have reacted as the first generation of Israelites—playing it safe by sitting on the fence with their heels dug in? Would we have thought freedom from the substandard desert life sounded wonderful, *but...*? Would we have been content to continue living a substandard life in the desert? Or, would we have stepped across the line and claimed our inheritance in the face of serious obstacles? I wonder.

Today, when confronted with the Lordship of Christ, most Christians are still reluctant to take that step of faith. The sad result is that they neither enjoy their life in the world nor the life of peace and abundance available to all, in the kingdom of Christ. Fence sitters never really enjoy much of anything.

When we become a Christian, legally speaking, Christ becomes both our Lord and Savior. However, we only begin to experience His Lordship when we personally offer Him His rightful position in our lives. Otherwise we settle for paid up fire insurance when so very much more is readily available to us, as we journey through this old world. Acknowledging Christ as Savior is wonderful, as it settles where we spend eternity. However, that experience does little to enable us to enjoy the abundant life Jesus promised. Making a conscious decision to invite Christ to take over the management of our lives opens the door to our enjoying the Christian life as it is defined in the Bible.

Therefore let all the house of Israel know assuredly that God
has made this Jesus, whom you crucified, both Lord and
Christ.

Acts 2:36

Irritants and Thorns

If you do not drive out the inhabitants of the land from before
you, then it shall be that those whom you let remain shall be
irritants in your eyes and thorns in your sides, and they shall
harass you in the land where you dwell.

Numbers 33:55

Having spent their entire lives in the desert, this generation of
Israelites would have been very familiar with annoying sand
specks in their eyes and irritating thorns in their flesh. Whenever
I get a speck in my eye, my entire focus is suddenly consumed by
that annoying particle. There have been times, while driving, that
my focus became so impaired by a speck in my eye, that I had
to pull over and remove the irritant before proceeding. Thorns
can also be a problem. Our home in Mexico was surrounded by
walls of bougainvillea, which seems to be able to grow profusely
even in drought conditions and with the longest, well-hidden,
thorns you can imagine. When trimming the branches, unless
I was extremely careful, I inevitably ended up with several of
those pesky thorns in my hands. Experience taught me to remove
them as soon as they were detected as, left unattended, infection
soon followed. Those irritating thorns have taught me a valuable lesson about living the Christian life. How easily the thorns
became lodged in my flesh. All it took was one act of careless-
ness. Removing them was another story. It can be a painful and
difficult process!

If they were to experience freedom and rest in Canaan, it was imperative Israel deal with the squatters as they appeared in their path. If their enemies were allowed to remain in the land, there was the potential for Israel to be influenced by their worldly ways, not to mention intrigued by their pagan gods. Should they be enticed by the pagans and their lifestyle, they would eventually become irritants and thorns to Israel.

Why would this speck and thorn illustration be recorded in the Bible? Is it possible that God intends for us to learn from the advice He gave Israel? Certainly! When a so-called insignificant speck from the world becomes imbedded in our lives, it suddenly becomes our focal point and will cause our spiritual vision to become blurred. For instance, Christians can have their spiritual eyesight blurred by struggling to keep up with the Joneses. Our spiritual vision can also become blurred when we look to the world's toys, vacations, and religion to quench our inner thirst. When a thorn from the world becomes imbedded in our lives, we will soon find our lives infected, and unless quickly removed, the infection will eventually spread to other areas and unchecked often on to others close to us.

How easily the thorns of the world become imbedded in our lives! Removing them can be a different story. For example, in order to be popular with friends, a teenager can begin playing around with nicotine, booze, and/or drugs. One day he awakens to find himself hooked! Getting addicted is one thing. Getting free of that same bondage is an entirely different story. After what appeared to be an innocent fling with her boyfriend, the teenage girl wakes up one day and finds herself pregnant. Now she has a serious problem on her hands that could affect her entire life. The husband who makes a decision to have an affair suddenly faces a major problem once his sin is exposed. Plus the consequences always infect other innocent family members.

Any person who is addicted, or ever has been, to harmful sub-stances knows how hard it is to get free. There are also Christians addicted to and consumed by fear, worry, and anger. Getting free can be a struggle. If you find yourself hooked on some irritant of the world, I have good news for you. With God anything is possible! If He can part the Red Sea, surely He can flush out our specks and thorns!

There is nothing wrong with many of the things in this world, but once they begin to control our emotions, and how we think, it is time to eliminate the annoyances. The question that constantly needs to be asked is "Who (or what) controls whom?" One of the many benefits of attending a solid Bible study is that it helps to keep us properly focused on what is important in life. "Set your mind on things above, not on things on the earth" (Colossians 3:2). As Christians, we are pilgrims passing through, and instead of being world focused and dominated, we are challenged to soar like eagles well above the negative irritants of this fallen world. No bird can soar as high as an eagle. Pilots have spotted them at 30,000 feet! Jesus never allowed the carnal ways of the world to touch His life. He soared constantly. He wasted little time responding to criticism, but simply allowed His life to speak for itself.

> Those who wait on the Lord shall renew their strength; they shall mount up with wings like eagles, they shall run and not be weary, they shall walk and not faint.
>
> Isaiah 40:31

A Nobody Becomes a Somebody

When Moses died, Joshua inherited his leadership position (Joshua 1:1-2). Their backgrounds were quite different. Moses was raised as Pharaoh's son in the Egyptian palace where he was educated and taught leadership skills. I guess you could say he was raised with a silver spoon in his mouth. From the world's perspective—a somebody! This was not the case with Joshua. He was born in slavery—on the wrong side of the tracks, one might say. As a slave, he would have received little education, and his leadership skills were nonexistent. By those same standards, he would have been perceived as a nobody.

When Israel left Egypt, Joshua must have walked close by the side of Moses hanging onto his every word. Along the way, he somehow became educated to the point that he was later able to write the book that bears his name. Observing Moses daily, Joshua obviously developed leadership skills, as during those forty years in the desert, he rose to the rank of general in Israel's army. Watching Moses in action, he learned another trait that is a vital requirement for a successful leader. He learned not to be swayed by the desires of others. He never became a people pleaser! We saw Joshua demonstrating this attribute at Kadesh-Barnea when he refused to be swayed by the opinions of the majority. Joshua chose instead to be a God pleaser! Joshua did not check the opinion polls to see which way the wind blew. His yardstick was God's Word!

Strong leadership qualities are sadly lacking among the majority of today's leaders, especially in the political arena. Instead of a commitment to serving the people who placed them in office, the number one concern of most politicians is fund raising for reelection. To accomplish this, they devour the polls, and then tell people exactly what they want to hear. This same kind of behavior prevails in too many of today's church leaders, as well. Instead of boldly proclaiming the Word of God, and possibly offending members of their congregation, they preach ear-tickling sermons—safe topics that won't offend. A former pastor of ours, who appeared to have no solid stand on eternal security, comes to mind. When I met with him to discuss his position, for nearly an hour, he tap-danced around my question. Finally, he told me what he thought I wanted to hear. He then went on to say he would, however, continue to preach both beliefs from the pulpit (one of them obviously wrong). I was dumbfounded to hear that he would preach a lie rather than risk the possibility of offending members of his congregation, and perhaps face replacement. It probably didn't happen overnight, but he had become a people pleaser. Keeping his paycheck rolling in was more important than preaching the Word of God with conviction. Is it any wonder that pastor has a pablum ministry and a spiritually weak congregation? Joshua and Caleb were quick to discover that standing upon the Word at all times invited flak. One also has to agree that Jesus was anything but a people pleaser. He constantly stepped on toes in the religious community of His day—especially the hierarchy. Did He receive flak? Certainly!

Joshua not only watched Moses in action, and learned from his example, more importantly, he saw his God in action. Having seen the Lord's power demonstrated time and again during the plagues in Egypt, at the Red Sea, and His meeting the needs of two million people for forty years in the desert, Joshua learned a valuable lesson. He learned the promises of God were like gold—bankable! Because of his faith, Joshua became a somebody, and when it came time for Moses to pass on the mantle of leadership, Joshua was number one on the short list.

We all entered this world in the same spiritual condition as Joshua, inheriting Adam's fallen genes—spiritually dead and graceless—born set wrong! From God's perspective, certainly born on the wrong side of the tracks. Because of His great love, He provided a way for us to be set right—made righteous. The instant we become a believer, God no longer views us as a nobody but as a somebody. In fact we are called, "The apple of His eye" (Psalm 17:8). As a Christian, a child of the King, I think it is an insult to Jesus for us to walk around displaying a long sad face and feelings of unworthiness. Clothed in His righteousness makes us a "somebody" for all eternity.

> He made Him who knew no sin to be sin for us, that we might become the righteousness of God in Him.
>
> 2 Corinthians 5:21

As Christians, we need to occasionally remind ourselves of our spiritual status. The apostle John wrote that we possess a "crown of life" (Revelation 2:10B). A crown speaks of authority and position. Several chapters back I wrote at length about our occupation as Christians—kings and priests (Revelation 5:10). As kings, we are to exercise dominion in this world and no longer view ourselves as unworthy nobodies. This does not mean walking around with a cocky arrogant attitude, but with a quiet authoritative demeanor. We inherit the crown of life when we become Christians, and regardless of our conduct, we retain that position forever! The question is, do we walk our position?

Knowing Jericho was only five miles away, Joshua must have wondered how God was planning to defeat the city. Realizing his concern, God comforted Joshua with the following encouraging words:

> Every place the sole of your foot will tread upon I have given you... No man shall be able to stand before you all the days of your life; as I was with Moses, so I will be with you. I will not leave you nor forsake you.
>
> Joshua 1:3, 5

In so many words, God told Joshua the battle would be a rigged fight. It should be comforting to know that for a Christian this encouraging promise remains valid today. No matter the size of the battle before us, by faith we can stand on victory turf, and all our battles should be rigged fights.

Never Put the Lord in a Box

Israel arrived at the Jordan River at the worst possible time of year—the height of the rainy season (Joshua 3:15). With the riverbanks overflowing, it would have been impossible for two million people to make the crossing safely. Since there were no lakes or rivers in the desert, this generation of Israelites had never learned to swim either. Did God make a mistake by leading them to the river at this time of year, or did He have a purpose in mind?

Have you discovered God always has a reason for when and how He does what he does? Many years had passed since God demonstrated His power to Israel, and now the Jordan gave Him that opportunity once again. Watching God deal with the Jordan would be a final shot of faith for Israel before their confrontation with Jericho.

Can you picture the Israelites sitting around their camp-fires discussing how God was going to get them across the river? Knowing human nature, I imagine they came to the conclusion God will perform another Red Sea miracle and part the waters. Instead, God shifted gears and damned up the river (Joshua 3:13, 16). Have you discovered that it is difficult to put the Lord in a box?

We live in Florida, and it is common to hear many of the northern transplants say, "We used to do it this way up north." The phrase became such a turn off that someone finally came up with a bumper sticker that said, "We Don't Care How You Did It Up North!" When we lived in Mexico, it was no different. We constantly heard new arrivals saying the very same thing. It was common to hear them say, "We used to do it this way up north." We could probably have made a small fortune importing a pile of those old Florida bumper stickers.

As Christians, we are constantly trying to put the Lord in a box. For example, the leadership of a church installs a program that has had successful results elsewhere, but are deeply puzzled when the program does not produce the same positive results in their church. It is vital for church leaders to have spiritual discernment and be open to change. Before launching any new program, the leadership must understand the needs of their particular congregation and then devise a program that meets those needs. The spiritual requirements of one church will differ from those of another. Many years ago, Robert Girard wrote a book with the wonderful title, *Brethren Hang Loose*, which addresses the need for spiritual discernment in the leadership of today's churches. If you do not have the book in your personal library, I suggest ordering it.

> Everyone who partakes only of milk is unskilled in the word of righteousness, for he is a babe. But solid food belongs to those who are of full age, that is, those who by reason of use have their senses exercised to discern both good and evil.
>
> Hebrews 5:13-14

Get Your Feet Wet

> You are to cross over the Jordan today, and go in to dispossess nations greater and mightier than yourself, cities great and fortified up to heaven.
>
> Deuteronomy 9:1

At the Jordan River, the priests found their faith placed on public view. They were told to step into the Jordan and *get their feet wet*. When God saw their trusting obedience instead of parting the waters, He damned up the river, and led them safely across— once again on a dry riverbed (Joshua 3:13-17).

What a great lesson on faith! That is how faith actually works. We demonstrate faith in Christ's promises, then when the time is right, He responds to our display of faith. Too often we want to reverse the proceedings. First, we want to *see* evidence of His power. Then we are willing to express faith in that power. That's baby Christianity! That's exactly what Israel did at the Red Sea. Once they saw God's power demonstrated, they threw a victory party—after the fact. As we have seen in the lives of the first generation, sight walking and displaying faith, after the fact, does not mature a believer one iota. Too often we react exactly as Israel. Once we see the problem solved, we talk about faith, and remain faithful—until the next test surfaces.

We must instead emulate those obedient Levite priests, always ready to get our feet wet. "My brethren, count it all joy when you fall into various trials, knowing that the testing of your faith produces patience" (James 1:2-3).

Had you been a Levite priest at the Jordan, would you have put your faith on the line by getting your feet wet, fully expecting God to perform a miracle? I believe this is how Jesus hopes today's Christian leaders will function. As parents, we must demonstrate this faith to our children. By far the biggest challenge to our faith is taking the plunge of inviting Christ to manage our lives. We can view Him as Lord in our minds, but that is no indication He is actually Lord in our hearts. Head knowledge is basically a waste of time and gets us nowhere in our life of faith.

Jumping in and getting our feet wet can mean many things. It can mean walking away from a pablum ministry and waiting upon the Lord to lead us to a solid Bible study. It may mean being more than conquerors when faced with a negative and trusting Christ to deal with our Jerichos. Getting our feet wet may mean making a decision to stop sight walking and begin placing faith in the Lord's promises. Let's get to where the rubber meets the road. It may mean no longer running up charge cards, waiting instead, until the money is in the bank, before purchasing that new whatever or taking that vacation to some far away spot. Living within our means is a concept few seem to have a handle on these days. Still it is the kind of lifestyle that produces peace, while being up to one's ears in debt is pure bondage, I think you will agree!

Without faith it is impossible to please Him.

Hebrews 11:6

Faith is like radar that sees through the fog—the reality of things at a distance that the human eye cannot see.

Corrie Ten Boom

On occasion, we all fail to trust Christ and His promises—even the disciples. One sunny day Jesus invited the disciples to join Him on a boat ride; His invitation was, "Let us cross over to the other side" (Mark 4:35B). Had you been one of the disciples would you have climbed into the boat? Of course! Who wouldn't want to spend time sailing with the Lord? As they left the peaceful shore behind, they were suddenly overtaken by a severe storm. Several in the boat were experienced fishermen and knew a bad storm when they saw one. Suddenly their peace and joy flew out the window only to be replaced by fear and worry. In the midst of the storm, Jesus asked them a question which they must have thought was off the wall. He said, "Why are you so fearful? How is it that you have no faith?" (Mark 4:40). Self-preservation surfaced and fear overwhelmed them. They forgot what Jesus said before they departed. He never promised clear sailing, only that they were going to the *other side*. The key word in Christ's invitation was the tiny word *us*.

When we become Christians, we have in fact, climbed in the boat with Christ—citizens of the same kingdom. We abide in Him. In our journey to the other side (heaven), Jesus actually promised there would be an occasional storm en route, but that in the midst of the storms, we *may* experience peace (John 16:33).

May only becomes a reality when we have jumped in and gotten our feet wet—fully trusting the Lord with every aspect of our lives. We must remember Jesus will never perish, and as long as we are in the boat with Him, despite the storms of life, we will one day arrive safely on the other side! En route, we are meant to enjoy our pilgrimage with peace in our hearts.

While the Israelites were crossing the Jordan, the priests were instructed to remain stationary with the ark in the middle of the river. When the congregation passed by the ark, surely it reminded them whose power and might dammed up the water. After four hundred years enslaved in a foreign land, God's promise to Abraham was now a reality. Israel was finally home!

Two Memorials

Take for yourselves twelve stones from here, out of the midst of the Jordan, from the place where the priests feet stood firm. You shall carry them over with you and leave them in the lodging place where you lodge tonight.

Joshua 4:3

The first memorial was a pillar of twelve stones which Israel erected on the Canaan side of the river. Each stone represented one of the twelve tribes and was to be a memorial to the faithfulness of their God. Whenever their children asked what the stones meant, it gave their parents an opportunity to tell them how God, ever true to his promises, led them from bondage in Egypt to freedom in their homeland (Joshua 4:6-7).

As Christians, we have a similar story to tell. When the opportunity arises, we should be prepared tell our personal story of how Christ set us free from bondage in the old kingdom, and we should be able to give examples of how much better life is in the new kingdom. That, my friend, is called witnessing!

> Then Joshua set up twelve stones in the midst of the Jordan, in the place where the feet of the priests who bore the ark of the covenant stood; and they are there to this day.
>
> Joshua 4:9

A second twelve stone memorial was also erected. Those stones were placed in the middle of the Jordan, and once the river returned to its normal level, they were never seen again. They were buried in the waters of the Jordan. This memorial also made a statement. It spoke of the substandard quality of life Israel left behind on the other shore. Walking by sight and leaning unto their own understanding was left on the other side of the river. The memorial spoke of their leaving behind a life of stress, worry, and fear. It was as if their old lifestyle was left behind forever, and they now could look forward to a life of abundance as they trusted God to lead and direct in every area of their new life in Canaan.

If we have a desire to experience the Christian life as it is outlined in the Bible, it is imperative we get our feet wet, cross our Jordan, and leave the old carnal lifestyle behind—in a sense buried at the bottom of the sea. Crossing the Jordan speaks of saying goodbye to a self-managed life, ceasing to walk by sight, and no longer viewing ourselves as the center of the universe. It means leaving behind a life of stress and entering into a life of rest! Why anyone would choose not to go forward is a great puzzle to me.

> There remains therefore a rest for the people of God. For he who has entered His rest has himself also ceased from his works as God did from His. Let us therefore be diligent to enter that rest.
>
> Hebrews 4:9-11

Peace I leave with you. My peace I give to you; not as the world gives do I give to you. Let not your heart be troubled, neither let it be afraid.

John 14:27

Questions

- Are irritants and thorns imbedded in your life, causing you grief?

- Do you still see yourself as a nobody? If you are a Christian, hopefully you are beginning to accept the fact that you are a somebody in the kingdom of Christ!

- Do you occasional attempt to put the Lord in a box—expecting Him to function today as He did yesterday, last month, or last year? Or do you find yourself learning discernment—knowing how he wants you to operate in the now?

- Was there ever a time in your Christian life when you jumped in and got your feet wet? Or are you still playing it safe? If so, why not jump in and discover the life of faith and abundance the Lord has in store for you?

- Have you put a stake in the ground in the land of rest to forever remind you that you have chosen to walk away from a substandard brand of Christianity?

GOD HUFFED
AND PUFFED

Now that Israel was home, it was time to begin flushing out the illegal squatters. First on the hit list was Jericho. Jericho is believed to be the oldest city in the world, which may or may not be true, but one thing is certain, it was the most fortified city of its day. The outer city wall was twelve feet thick, enabling horse-driven chariots to travel around the rim. Whenever the city was under siege, well-armed soldiers would line the outer wall prepared to eliminate any and all on-comers. As a backup, there was also a six-foot thick inner wall. How could unarmed Israel be expected to defeat such a foe? Under their own strength and ingenuity, they never would. However, under God's power the city was facing a rigged fight.

Our Commander-in-Chief

After the two spies reported their findings to Joshua, he must have wondered how God planned to defeat Jericho. Would He rain fire and brimstone upon the city as He did at Sodom and Gomorrah? No. God was about to do a new thing. The Lord appeared on the scene announcing that He was taking over as Israel's commander in chief. Music to Joshua's ears!

When Joshua was by Jericho, he lifted his eyes and looked, and behold, a Man stood opposite him with His sword drawn in His hand. And Joshua went to Him and said to Him, "Are You for us or for our adversaries?" So He said, "No, but as Commander of the army of the Lord I have now come."

Joshua 5:13-14

The Lord has never lost a battle. An accomplishment no other military leader can claim. Let's briefly review some of His victories. The first recorded battle took place not on earth but in heaven. On behalf of the Godhead, Michael and his angels warred with Lucifer (Satan) when he rebelled.

War broke out in heaven: Michael and his angels fought with the dragon; and the dragon and his angels fought, but they did not prevail, nor was a place found for them in heaven any longer. So the great dragon was cast out, that serpent of old, called the Devil and Satan, who deceives the whole world; he was cast to the earth, and his angels were cast out with him.

Revelation 12:7-9

Initially, Satan was the top angel in heaven, but there came a time when he aspired to be equal with his Creator. This act of rebellious pride introduced sin in heaven, and since God cannot dwell in the presence of sin, Satan, along with the angels who lined up with him, was banished. Earth became their temporal residence.

When Adam and Eve arrived on the scene, Satan saw an opportunity to strike back at God. If Adam could be encouraged to sin, the negative consequences of that decision would be far-reaching, as Adam's fallen nature would contaminate all future generations. Each generation would bear Adam's contaminated DNA and would be born a citizen in Satan's empire.

Immediately after Adam stumbled, God made a declaration of war between Satan's empire and the Seed of a woman—Christ.

At that time God proclaimed the victor approximately four thousand years in advance, "He shall bruise your head, and you shall bruise His heel" (Genesis 3:15). The bruising to Christ's heel took place at Calvary, which was painful, but not fatal. The bruising to Satan's head would be fatal, and that blow took place at the resurrection of the bruised Lamb of God.

Having heard the announcement of his defeat, Satan set out to eliminate the promised Seed. He attempted to eliminate anyone who appeared spiritual. The first person to be targeted was Adam's son Abel. When Abel's offering was deemed acceptable by God, while refusing Cain's contaminated offering, Satan motivated Cain to kill his brother (Genesis 4:4, 8). Later, when Satan heard that God was raising up a deliverer who would lead Israel out of bondage in Egypt, Satan thought perhaps this could be the Messiah. Pharaoh was prompted to kill all the newborn Israelite sons in hopes of catching the Messiah in the net. Always staying one step ahead, God found a most unique way to spare Moses.

Satan knew several things about the promised Seed, which enabled him to narrow down his search. For example, he knew the sex of the Seed—male—thus reducing his search for the Seed by 50 percent (Genesis 3:15). He also knew the Seed would be the result of an unusual birth—a miraculous conception—born of a virgin (Isaiah 7:14). Knowing about such an unusual birth certainly narrowed his search immensely. Satan was aware of the prophecy that the Seed would stem from the tribe of Judah (Isaiah 11:1, Micah 5:2, Psalm 76:1). He also was aware of the location of the prophesied birth—Bethlehem. When Satan heard the announcement of a young virgin from the tribe of Judah giving birth to a male in Bethlehem he thought, "That's Him!"

Satan was quick to take action to eliminate the Seed. Knowing King Herod's concern about the Messiah arriving and overthrowing his throne, Satan motivated Herod to execute all male babies in the Bethlehem area under the age of two. Again, one step ahead, God moved Christ out of harm's way by relocating His parents to Egypt until the death of Herod.

> The devil took Him up on an exceedingly high mountain, and showed Him all the kingdoms of the world and their glory. And he said to Him, all these things I will give You if You will fall down and worship me.
>
> Matthew 4:8-9

Shortly after Christ began His earthly ministry, the deceiver took a different approach in his attempt to defeat Christ. Satan told Jesus he would give Him this world if He would bow down and worship him. Had Christ given into that temptation, Satan would have won the earthly war that began in the Garden. By acknowledging Satan as His king, Jesus would have sinned and become a citizen in Satan's sinful empire, and in that condition, would not have been an acceptable sin offering. God, the Father, would never have been able to declare, "In Him I am well pleased." This temptation of Christ raises an obvious question. Could Jesus have sinned? Satan was convinced He could, otherwise, why would he have wasted time in the wilderness tempting Christ? Did you pick up on the fact that Jesus never said to the deceiver, "What do you mean, your world? Don't you realize this planet belongs to Me, its Creator?" Jesus was aware that Satan is the temporary prince of this cursed world and will remain the prince until Revelation five becomes a reality.

Having failed in his attempt to tempt Christ, Satan's next plan of attack was to motivate the Jewish religious leaders to have Him eliminated. The Romans were simply the tool to make His crucifixion legal. Just as Jesus foretold, the Jewish clergy of that day would be His executioners (Matthew 20:18-19). Motivating the hierarchy to eliminate Christ was not a problem, for they were anxious to have Him out of their hair.

Satan made several blunders. First, he failed to understand what the Jewish Feast of Firstfruits symbolized—the resurrection of Christ. Satan thought by having Jesus executed, He would be removed from the scene once and for all. Then, Satan could continue as the legal tenant of this world throughout eternity. Satan failed to realize Jesus had no intention of establishing His earthly kingdom until the Millennium Reign took place. Neither did Satan understand the law of the harvest—death must precede life. Jesus had to die and then be resurrected, so He could present His innocently shed blood on the heavenly mercy seat in order to set believers free from their sin status. Only then would Christ have a legal kingdom to reign over. Then, and only then, could He eventually fulfill the role of kinsman redeemer and officially set up His kingdom during the Millennium. After the resurrection, Satan realized he had blown it big time! The resurrection was the ultimate victory over Satan. The fatal blow to his head that was announced in the Garden approximately four thousand years earlier was now a reality. Don't you know if Satan had understood the power in Christ's resurrection, he would never have plotted His execution?

> We speak the wisdom of God in a mystery, the hidden wisdom which God ordained before the ages for our glory, which none of the rulers of this age knew; for had they known, they would not have crucified the Lord of glory.
>
> 1 Corinthians 2:7-8

It was imperative that Jesus die a Roman execution rather than a Jewish execution.

> As Moses lifted up the serpent in the wilderness, even so must the Son of Man be lifted up.
>
> John 3:14

If I am lifted up from the earth, will draw all peoples to Myself.

John 12:32

In the above verses, reference is made to the way Jesus would be executed—raised up. Had the religious Jews executed Christ, they would have reverted to their Old Testament law and stoned Him, just as they did with Stephen (Leviticus 24:16). Had He been stoned, His death would not have fulfilled either Old Testament prophecy or Christ's own statements concerning his method of execution (Matthew 20:19). Consequently, He would have been labeled a false prophet and deemed an unworthy offering for sin. It was imperative He die a Roman execution rather than a Jewish one.

Since defeating Satan in heaven, Jesus has had an impeccable track record as commander in chief. Throughout history, there have been many impressive military leaders—Napoleon being one of the most successful. Yet Napoleon experienced an overwhelming defeat. Remember his famous quote, "If it hadn't been for that one spot [Waterloo], I'd have conquered the world." Waterloo was his downfall! Throughout eternity, Satan will be thinking, "If it hadn't been for that one spot [Calvary], I'd have remained ruler of this planet forever." The resurrection of God's slain Lamb surely was Satan's downfall!

Despite the fatal blow he was dealt as a result of the resurrection, Satan continues to battle against the kingdom of Christ. After Satan was cast out of heaven, he knew he was on a short leash (Revelation 12:12). With every passing day, Satan is aware his leash is becoming shorter and shorter. As with any ongoing battle, the final days are the most intense. That's when the heavy guns come out. In these latter days, Satan's attacks on the kingdom of Christ are becoming more and more intensified. We see evidence of this all around us. Satan's main thrust is to prevent people from defecting from his kingdom by promoting the law of

Moses as a means of being justified. With few exceptions, Satan has watered down the teaching that stems from many of today's pulpits, causing the sheep to live substandard lives in their communities. Satan has successfully eliminated the teaching of the tabernacle almost to the point of extinction. Satan constantly attacks individual believers by tossing bait in their path, hoping they will succumb and be forced to live with the negative consequences of that decision.

As Christians, we must understand we are involved in spiritual warfare. The question is, who is winning the battle? Are we constantly striking blows to the enemy? Or, is the enemy, all to often, the victor? Stress, anger, fear, and worry are indicators we are succumbing. An unopened Bible in way too many of our homes is another proof Satan is winning.

> The God of peace will crush Satan under your feet shortly.
>
> Romans 16:20

As soldiers in Christ's army, we must understand we are at war with an enemy, who in actual fact, has already been defeated. The roaring lion has been de-fanged! On a daily basis, we have the power and authority to strike victory blows at Satan. We do that whenever we ignore the tempting bait he tosses into our path. When we display peace and joy in the midst of our daily trials, we are striking a blow to the enemy. When we encourage one of Satan's citizens to defect to the kingdom of Christ, or encourage a troubled Christian to begin walking in victory, we strike a severe blow to Satan. We also strike a blow to the enemy when we make the promises of Christ a reality in our daily lives.

Becoming a well-trained soldier in Christ's kingdom is not an automatic byproduct of salvation. If we are to be victorious on the battlefield, just as with Joshua, we must acknowledge Christ as our commander in chief—the one most capable in the universe to manage our lives. We need to flee from pablum ministries and find a place where solid spiritual food is being served. We must begin to walk by faith, trusting in every Bible promise. We must put on the whole armor of God. The enemy does not attack our strengths. All he needs to find is one weakness, one chink in the armor (Ephesians 6:11-18). Once the armor is in place, we will be able to sing with confidence, "Onward Christian Soldiers!"

Unusual Battle Strategy

When Israel first saw Jericho, they must have been blown away. The massive secured gates and the intimidating soldiers lining the outer wall must have seemed overwhelming (Joshua 6:1). Any ordinary army considering attacking such a city would have assessed the situation and quickly come to the conclusion—no way! Before going to battle, God gave Joshua a rather encouraging promise. He said, "I have given Jericho into your hand, its king, and the mighty men of valor" (Joshua 6:2). This is the kind of commander in chief I want to serve under—one who promises victory before the first blow is struck! Yet another rigged fight!

God's battle instructions, however, were most unusual. Israel's entire army of forty thousand were told to walk clear around the walls of Jericho once a day for six days and then seven times on the seventh day (Joshua 6:3-4). A total of thirteen times. A number which turned out to be altogether unlucky for the residents of Jericho. Perhaps even the origin of unlucky number thirteen! The Levite priests joined the soldiers and carried the ark before them as a reminder of God's presence and whose power would defeat Jericho.

Israel's army put into motion the Three Step Program. First, they did what they could do to defeat the problem, which in this situation was remaining ark and promise focused. Secondly, they placed the problem in the Lord's hands, trusting Him to defeat this fortified city. Thirdly, they marched around the city, not with fear and worry in their hearts, but with peace and anticipation of victory prevailing. Instead of viewing themselves as grasshoppers, under God's power, they viewed Jericho as their bread—a rigged fight! Isn't that exactly how Christ expects Christians to function? We do what we can to rectify the problem, then, having exhausted our resources, we turn the problem over to Christ and walk on in peace—viewing each battle before us as a rigged fight. If repeated often enough, perhaps each and every one of us will get these truths down deep in our hearts.

The soldiers on Jericho's outer wall must have been puzzled by Israel's unorthodox battle strategy. Israel carried no battering rams, nor did they have ladders to scale the walls. What they observed was a group of poorly armed Israelites following an elevated box around the city for six days. Then, on the seventh there was much shouting and blowing of trumpets by Israel's army—acting as if they were already the victors! Puzzling behavior for sure! Jericho's army failed to understand that Israel possessed the best possible weapon of mass destruction—God's promise of victory.

Shout, for the Lord has given you the city.

Joshua 6:16B

Deadlier than anything contained in the military arsenals of the world, the Word of God is by far the most powerful and destructive force against evil. Today, most homes in North America have this weapon at their disposal, yet rarely call upon it for spiritual strength. They plod along doing what seems right in their own eyes, going down in defeat every time the enemy attacks. Lives filled with anger, worry, fear, and depression bear constant evidence of such defeats.

Have you ever wondered why God instructed Israel to march around Jericho so many times? After all their exhaustive trekking in the desert, wouldn't once have been sufficient? The reason certainly was not to check the outer wall for weak points or to intimidate Jericho's army. The purpose of the thirteen trips I suspect was to impress upon Israel that defeating Jericho was well beyond *their* ability. Just as God responded to the priest's faith when they willingly got their feet wet in the Jordan, God responded to Israel's faith, huffed and puffed, and down came the mighty walls.

Remember the two spies sent to check out Jericho? Rahab protected them, and at that time, they assured her she and her family would be spared from God's pending judgment upon the city. The Lord honored that promise, and of the many residents of Jericho, Rahab and her family were the only ones spared (Joshua 6:23). Certainly a minority! In much the same way, out of the vast majority who have lived on this planet, because of placing faith in God's provision for being justified, Jesus said only a *few* will avoid God's pending judgment against sin (Matthew 7:14).

> By faith the harlot Rahab did not perish with those who did not believe.
>
> Hebrews 11:31

Because of her shady past, Rahab would have been viewed as a nobody by the residents of Jericho. At one stage of her life, she became a believer and became a somebody in God's eyes. Just as the Gentile Ruth was grafted into the tree of Israel when she married Boaz, as a believer, Rahab was also grafted into the Royal Line. She is one of only four women listed in the genealogy of Christ. She eventually became the mother of Boaz and the great-grandmother of King David (Matthew 1:5). Because of her faith, Rahab became a somebody in the eyes of the only One who counts!

Conquering Our Jerichos

We all face seemingly insurmountable circumstances from time to time in our own spiritual journey. If we are to be more than conquerors, it is vital that we acknowledge Christ as our commander in chief. In addition we must remain *under the cloud* and ark-focused. Then, and only then, will we be able to view the negatives of life as opportunities to display faith in the promises of Christ.

> My brethren, count it joy when you fall into various trials, knowing that the testing of your faith produces patience.
>
> James 1:2-3

Questions

- Who is your commander in chief? Do you still hold the reins tightly in your own little fist or have you willingly relinquished them to the Lord Jesus Christ?

- When you are faced with a battle, where is your focus? Do you trust in your own strength to defeat your enemies? Or are you ark-focused, holding tightly to the promises of God?

NEVER RUN RED LIGHTS

So the Lord was with Joshua, and his fame spread throughout all the country.

Joshua 6:27

After the defeat of Jericho, Joshua's fame spread throughout the land which, in the life of a believer, can sometimes create problems. We discussed in an earlier chapter how taking credit for what the Lord has accomplished has caused many Christian organizations to lose their anointing and begin a downhill spiral. After the victory at Jericho, would Joshua heed the Lord's warning and not touch the glory (Deuteronomy 8:11-17)?

Ai was the next town in Israel's path. Compared to Jericho, Ai was a seemingly insignificant little town, with a population of twelve thousand. With Jericho's defeat fresh in his mind, Joshua made the mistake of viewing Ai as a stroll in the park. However, when Israel attacked Ai, the outcome was anything but a rigged fight. They were miserably defeated and retreated with melting hearts, their tails tucked between their legs. How was that possible? What went wrong? As human nature goes, we usually learn more from our defeats than we do from our victories. So let's examine closely the cause of Israel's downfall so we won't make the same mistakes.

No Green Light

Joshua sent men from Jericho to Ai...

Joshua 7:2

The first problem we see is that Joshua ran ahead of the Lord! At Jericho, the Lord gave Israel the green light to go to battle. This was clearly not the case with Ai. When Joshua decided to attack Ai, the light was still red. Because of Ai's small size, Joshua made the mistake of thinking he could handle this little problem on his own. No need to bother the Lord with this one. With the recent victory at Jericho under his belt, surely he could handle little Ai all on his own. Ever been there? Will we ever get it through our thick skulls that running ahead of the Lord almost always invites negative consequences?

There is another clear example of this truth in the lives of Abraham and Sarah. After waiting ten years for the Lord to honor His promise to provide a legal heir, they decided to help the Lord out, if you remember. They too ran a red light. Through Hagar, their Egyptian handmaiden, Abraham produced a son (Ishmael), and today we still live with the consequences of that decision.

God revealed to Paul that his ministry would be among the Gentiles. In his eagerness to reach his fellow countrymen with the gospel, he galloped ahead of the Lord and began preaching to the Jews. In the process, he very nearly got himself killed by the people he was trying to reach with the gospel. Beyond that, had he been successful, we would have missed out on the entire ministry of Paul the apostle to the Gentiles. Never mind the wealth of books he penned that we hold so dear to our hearts today.

Today we live in a fast-paced world, a throwaway society. It is instant this and instant that. In our impatience, we often find ourselves running ahead of the Lord, and later we are left to wonder why our decision created such a mess. Seems pretty clear to me it is necessary to remain stationary until we receive the green light from above. Another word for recognizing a green light is discernment, which is a byproduct of exposure to solid Bible teaching (Hebrews 5:14).

> Your word is a lamp to my feet and a light to my path.
>
> Psalm 119:105

Overconfidence

> So about three thousand men went up there from the people, but they fled before the men of Ai.
>
> Joshua 7:4

The second reason for Israel's defeat can be summed up in one word—overconfidence. At Jericho, Israel's entire army of forty thousand men went to battle, but, because of the insignificant size of Ai, Joshua dispatched only three thousand men. Have you discovered that it isn't always the Jerichos in life that defeat us, often it is the little Ais? When a big problem surfaces, we are usually quick to put on the whole armor of God. We run to the Lord in prayer, ask others to pray for us, open our Bibles in search of direction and seek advice from Christians we respect. When minor problems surface, however, there is a danger of going to battle spiritually unprepared. Regardless of the size of the problem, we are instructed to "Put on the whole armor of God" (Ephesians 6:11). Remember, all Satan needs is one small chink in the armor to defeat us!

Stealing from the Lord

All the silver and gold, and vessels of bronze and iron, are consecrated to the Lord, they shall come into the treasury of the Lord.

Joshua 6:19

Now we come to the third reason—stealing from the Lord. God clearly told Israel not to take treasure from Jericho after their defeat. All treasure was to be consecrated to Him. One among them, a man named Achan, took gold and silver worth about ten thousand dollars, and buried it in his tent—thinking, "Who will discover my well-hidden disobedience?" Achan thought he had covered his tracks, but forgot about the One who knows all—the Lord.

Isn't it interesting that when we are doing something that we know is wrong, we are compelled to hide it? A person who is into porn doesn't usually leave a porn magazine laying on the coffee table for all to see. An employee doesn't usually tell his boss he is low on pens at home as he secretly slips a few in his pocket. A person doesn't notify the IRS when he has padded his expense account. A man doesn't tell his wife that he is considering having an affair.

Scapegoat

Joshua was grieved and humiliated over Israel's defeat at Ai. The fame and accolades showered upon him from the Jericho victory were short-lived. In his frustration and self-pity, Joshua looked for a scapegoat. Guess who he came up with? God! Not very original, was he? He blamed God for bringing Israel into Canaan and for allowing him to be placed in such an embarrassing situation. He told the Lord it would have been better if Israel had remained on the other side of the Jordan River rather than experiencing this humiliation. Do you sense a bit of self-pity? He feared Israel's defeat would soon reach the ears of the squatters, building their confidence to such a point they would begin to believe they actually could defeat Israel. Joshua envisioned Israel's name being wiped off the map (Joshua 7:7-9).

As Christians, we are quick to find a scapegoat for our stumbles. We think, "If it weren't for that obnoxious person taking a shot at me, I'd never have retaliated in anger." "If it weren't for that negative situation bombarding my life, worry and fear would never would have surfaced." "If my spouse hadn't been so critical, I never would have responded in such a harsh cutting tone." "If people would just line up with my thinking and my do and don't list, I wouldn't be so critical and judgmental." "If..." These responses are both immature and carnal. As long as we react in this manner, any peace we experience will be temporal. When we stumble, instead of searching for a scapegoat, we must begin to point the finger in the right direction—at ourselves!

After Israel's defeat at Ai, we find Joshua on his face in the dirt filled with self-pity and whining to the Lord. I love what God said to him. "Get up! Why do you lie thus on your face?" (Joshua 7:10). In so many words, He told Joshua to pack in his self-pity, get his thumb out of his mouth, set right the problems that caused the defeat, and move on.

A righteous man (believer) may fall seven times and rise again.

Proverbs 24:16

In our stupidity, we all stumble from time to time. When we do, God's instruction is to get up, deal with our mistakes and move on, hopefully learning from our stupidity. Over the years, I have asked many groups if anyone had stumbled to some degree in the past week. In my forty years of teaching only once did anyone say,

"No." That person was a full-time worker in a megachurch, and was either attempting to impress the group with his spirituality, or he was a total fool. I believe he was both! Within an unbelievably short time, that pious Christian was publicly accused of dipping into the church funds and subsequently fired! To top that off, he was having an affair with a choir member, not even very original in his sin.

> Do not be afraid, nor dismayed; take all the people of war with you, and arise, go up to Ai. See, I have given into your hand the king of Ai, his people, his city, and his land.
>
> Joshua 8:1

After dealing with Achan's buried sin, the Lord gave Joshua the green light to attack Ai. This time Joshua went to war, fully prepared, and Ai became just another rigged fight (Joshua 8:3, 25). The defeat at Ai was a valuable lesson well learned by Joshua. After he picked himself up, and got back on track, there was no looking back. The remainder of his life was a credit to the Lord, and of all the men mentioned in the Bible, I believe the life of Joshua to be the most Christ-like.

Questions

- Do you ignore red lights, or do you wait for a green light before moving forward. In other words, do you ever find yourself running ahead of the Lord?
- Do you tend to become overconfident when facing your seemingly insignificant Ais?

PART V:
THE CHALLENGE

JOSHUA'S CHALLENGE

Be very courageous to keep and to do all that is written in the
Book of the Law of Moses, lest you turn aside from it to the
right hand or to the left, and lest you go among these nations,
these who remain among you?

Joshua 23:6-7

At this point in the Scripture, Israel had been living in Canaan
for fifteen years and enjoying the abundant life God promised.
When we examine the lifestyle Israel experienced in Canaan, I
believe their years under Joshua's leadership to be perhaps their
most productive.

In the final chapter of the book of Joshua, as he approaches
the end of his earthly life, Joshua gives several challenges that
apply not only to Israel, but also to today's Christian community. If they were to continue enjoying rest in the Promised Land,
as well as future victories over their enemies, it was imperative
Israel heed Joshua's advice. These truths still prevail today. His
first instruction was to remain obedient to the Word of God.
In today's free-wheeling society, obedience is often viewed as
an unpopular word—especially when it comes to lining up with
Biblical advice. We must constantly remind ourselves that being
obedient to God's Word is not for His benefit, but for *our benefit*!

At Ai, Joshua learned there could be serious consequences for
disobedience and running ahead of the Lord. Joshua knew that,

upon his death, there was the potential for Israel to drift from the Word and begin taking on the ways of the pagan nations surrounding them. Once that happened, the peace, freedom, and rest they had been experiencing would once again be replaced by envy, anger, fear, worry, anxiety, and stress.

> If indeed you do go back, and cling to the remnant of these nations—these that remain among you—and make marriages with them, and go in to them and they to you, know for certain that the Lord your God will no longer drive out these nations from before you. But they shall be snares and traps to you, and scourges on your sides and thorns in your eyes.
>
> Joshua 23:12-13

Joshua reminded Israel that if they became enticed by the ways of the world around them, they would soon find themselves trapped like a caged animal. In today's Christian circles, there are many who have done just that. They may sit in a pew for an hour each week looking presentable, but during the other one hundred and sixty-seven hours of the week, they function much like the residents of the world. Despite the fact that they refer to themselves as Christians, they have made a conscious decision to basically ignore God's Word and look to the world for their fulfillment. In that backslidden condition, they are no different than a caged animal, experiencing little freedom, yet with a distinct disinterest in and little or no desire for spiritual things. In time they will surely ask themselves:

HOW IN THE WORLD DID I GET IN THIS MESS AND HOW WILL I EVER GET OUT OF IT?

Had past generations of Christians heeded Joshua's advice of old, today's Christian community would be experiencing a much different quality of life! There wouldn't be the lukewarm brand of

Christianity that is so prevalent today. Instead of living with various degrees of bondage, believers would be enjoying an exciting life of rest and freedom. Rather than having the world manipulating and controlling their emotions, they would be enjoying their God-given position as kings—displaying dominion. They would also be fulfilling their roles as priests, bridge-builders working in unison with the Holy Spirit encouraging a deeply troubled world to come to Christ, in addition to motivating troubled believers to rise to higher spiritual levels. Christian families would be more unified, and the current Christian divorce rate would certainly be much lower. Christians would no longer be content to play church and sit under pablum ministries. They would not rest until they found a place that taught nourishing spiritual food. In almost every community, there are solid Bible teaching churches and Bible study groups that can effectively meet the spiritual needs of believers. If we find ourselves in much the same spiritual condition as we were a year ago, perhaps that is an indication that we should take Joshua's advice and find a new place to worship. Obedience to the Word being taught will always result in a life of freedom, dominion, and fruitfulness. Always! What more could we ask as we journey through this life?

He who heeds the word wisely will find good.

Proverbs 16:20

Yoked to Christ

You shall hold fast to the Lord your God, as you have done to this day.

Joshua 23:8

Come to Me, all you who labor and are heavy laden, and I will
give you rest. Take My yoke upon you and learn from Me, for
I am gentle and lowly in heart, and you will find rest for your
souls. For My yoke is easy and My burden is light.

Matthew 11:28-30

Holding fast and being yoked to the Lord are one and the same.
That word *yoke* reminds me of our time in Southeast Asia. When
it was time for a rice farmer to train a young ox, he would yoke
junior to an experienced ox. If junior was to mature and become
of value to the farmer, it was important that he learn obedience
and follow in step with the more experienced ox. If junior decided
to deviate from the set path, the senior ox would snap his head,
and junior would be quickly brought back in line. If junior per-
sisted in going his own way, he would not only frustrate the work,
but would soon find himself with a chafed neck. After a few hard
knocks, the younger ox would begin to realize obedience was the
only way to go. Obedience was for his benefit and made life a
whole lot easier.

Once we step out from *under the cloud* and attempt to go our
own way, we remain yoked to Jesus, but life suddenly becomes
strained and frustrating. Once we go the way of the world, we
may find ourselves suffering from a chafed neck for a long time.

Oh, that we would believe the above verse in Matthew! Read
it again! Being yoked to Christ can be the most wonderful experience imaginable. He promises that he will carry the bulk of the
load at *all* times. I am completely convinced that following Him
is definitely the way to go in this old world! He knows the way,
He knows the pitfalls, and He has *my* best interests in mind every
single step of the way. I believe that from the bottom of my heart.
I wrote briefly in an earlier chapter about this old world being a
veritable minefield. I believe God knew there was the potential
for this to happen if man fell into disobedience through the trick-

ery of Satan. A foolproof plan had to be devised to rescue mankind should that happen which, of course, it did. If it hadn't been Adam, it would have been me! If we could see that obedience is our *only* means of protection in this minefield through which we travel, I believe we would finally see the wisdom in following Him. He truly is the only One who knows the way.

> We know that all things work together for good to those who love God, to those who are called according to His purpose.
>
> Romans 8:28

When we become a Christian, we not only become permanently yoked to Christ, but He also has a purpose for our earthly lives, as well as for our eternal lives. We will discover our purpose as we are exposed to solid spiritual teaching and begin to obey that Word. As the verse implies, the majority of the load will be on His shoulders. We are promised that our load will be light— allowing lots of time to enjoy the rest promised.

> Let us therefore fear, lest, a promise being left us of entering into his *rest*, any of you should seem to come short of it. Seeing therefore it remaineth that some must enter therein, and they to whom it was first preached entered not in because of unbelief. [Emphasis mine.]
>
> Hebrews 4:1, 6 (KJV)

Straddling the Fence

> Choose for yourselves this day whom you will serve...
>
> Joshua 24:15

Joshua challenged Israel not only to remain obedient to the Word of God, but also to avoid straddling the fence. For forty long years the first generation of Israelites did exactly that. They longed for the quality of life God promised in Canaan, yet there were other times when they longed for the life they left behind (Numbers 11:5-6). So, there they were, left straddling the fence for many years—not enjoying life in either camp, settling for cheese and crackers, when the world could have been their oyster.

Today many Christians exist in those same conditions, not really enjoying either the world or the kingdom of Christ. Despite a lot of effort, the satisfaction they receive from the world is fleeting and often short-lived. They keep coming up empty and feeling somehow discontent. On the other hand, a constant lack of obedience to the Word keeps them from enjoying most of the benefits that should be theirs in the kingdom of Christ.

While Israel was bogged down in the desert, Moses pleaded with them not to miss out on their inheritance in Canaan. He constantly encouraged Israel to stay *under the cloud* as it moved on methodically toward Canaan. He begged them not to settle for less. He promised, again and again, there would be rest and everything they hoped for, and more, once they reached their homeland.

> You shall not at all do as we are doing here today—every man doing whatever is right in his own eyes—for as yet you have not come to the rest and the inheritance which the Lord your God is giving you. But when you cross over the Jordan and dwell in the land which the Lord your God is giving you to inherit, and He gives you rest from all your enemies round about, so that you dwell in safety.
>
> Deuteronomy 12:8-10

The parable of the Prodigal Son finds the son in the pigpen at one point. I guess you could say he too was straddling the fence.

The ways of the world had let him down, so there he sat, enjoying little of either the world or his father's blessings. Eventually he did come to his senses, returning to his father's loving arms. While in the world, his relationship with his father had become distant, but not severed. He still had a blood connection, and despite his wayward lifestyle, he remained a part of the family. Upon his return, his father confirmed his position by placing a robe on his back and a ring on his finger. The robe identified him as a family member, while the ring spoke of his restored authority. While in the pigpen, I think you will agree, his authority was limited. He found himself swallowed up by the world he had chosen. We shouldn't necessarily visualize the Prodigal Son as getting involved with drugs, booze, and satisfying every desire of his flesh. Perhaps he did, but the major error he made was walking away from the relationship he once enjoyed at his father's side, choosing instead to look to the world to satisfy his needs. Would you agree that a Christian can sit in a pew each Sunday looking entirely presentable but actually experiencing somewhat of a pigpen life style? Perhaps not wallowing in the gutter, addicted to drugs or alcohol, or having an affair, nevertheless, in much the same spiritual condition as the Prodigal Son, trying to find peace and satisfaction in the world. He may still have a prominent position in some company or own his own business. He may even be an elder or teach a Sunday school class, but when everything is stripped aside, his spiritual authority is limited. Proof of his wayward lifestyle will be a life plagued by disappointment, worry, anger, anxiety, and stress, just to name a few.

And the people said to Joshua, "The Lord our God we will serve, and His voice we will obey."

Joshua 24:24

Don't you just love Israel's response to Joshua's challenges? A response that should resound throughout today's Christian community. That generation of Israelites did remain obedient to God's Word, and as a result, experienced one of the most productive and restful times in Israel's entire history.

Walking away, once and for all, from a straddling the fence lifestyle, requires decisive action. It may mean taking an honest look in the mirror and admitting the brand of Christianity we have been living falls short of the life described in the Bible. It may mean admitting the things of this world provide little permanent satisfaction and are certainly not worth striving and struggling a lifetime for. Getting off the fence may mean realizing we have become trapped like a caged animal by the ways of the world and making a decision to seek freedom. It may mean admitting, for the first time, that worry, fear, anger, and stress should not be a part of normal Christianity and are, in fact, sin. Getting off the fence may mean taking that huge step of faith (getting our feet wet) where we decide in the depths of our being to trust Christ to manage our lives. Getting off the fence may mean finding a place where solid Bible truths are taught, and reacting in obedience to the taught Word. Getting off the fence may mean choosing to no longer blame family and friends for our bad behavior, instead taking personal responsibility for our bad conduct. It may mean altering our prayer life by beginning to pray *show me* prayers. Only when we make the decision to get off the fence and claim our inheritance in Canaan will we begin to experience the more than a conqueror mentality—viewing our battles as rigged fights. Studying the Word will be exciting, instead of drudgery. Each new day will be joy filled as we continue our journey *under the cloud!*

> Show me Your ways, O Lord; Teach me Your paths. Lead me in Your truth and teach me, for you are the God of my salvation; On You I wait all the day.
>
> Psalm 25:4-5

Minefields

Since the first chapter of this book, we have covered a lot of territory and perhaps passed a few challenges your way. It is my hope that you clearly understand your position in the kingdom of Christ. It is also my hope that you have discovered the freedom and dominion Jesus promised and are willing, no matter where He leads, to continue your journey.

I want to leave you with a few thoughts which I hope will dispel, once and for all, any mistaken ideas concerning the word *obedience*. I think Satan has very cleverly put his spin on this word *obedience*. In our minds, it conjures up someone with a big stick just waiting for an act of disobedience. "Do good and I'll bless you—do bad and I'll punish you" thinking. Simply not true. God is constantly trying to protect us from the slick and deceiving lies of the enemy. Everything that comes from his mouth is cursed, sometimes sugar-coated, but still cursed. God pronounced His judgment on sin and Satan a long time ago—the wages of sin is death (Romans 6:23). All our God is attempting to do is point out to us the only safe path on this earthly journey is where He leads us. Disobedience places us in grave danger. Oh, it may not manifest itself for a period of time, but eventually it will get the better of us. That is why Jesus so many times in the New Testament said in one form or another, "Follow Me (I can get you safely through to the other side of this minefield)."

Satan constantly tries to make us believe that obedience takes all the fun out of life. Just the opposite is true! Obedience puts all the real fun in life! Obedience brings blessing; that is a Scriptural promise. On the other hand, disobedience introduces us to cursed behavior. If we choose sinful behavior and choose to follow the *cursed one*, we open ourselves up to the judgment that has been placed on him and his kingdom. Oh, if only we would believe, once and for all, that God has devised this path of obedience for *our* benefit! How much better our lives here on earth would be.

Picture yourself following an experienced soldier navigating through a minefield. I guarantee you will walk exactly where he is walking! No questions asked! That is exactly the way we should think about Christ's instruction to follow Him. This cursed earth is a veritable minefield, and if we simply wander around on our own, it will get us sooner or later.

I can tell you that God hates sin in all its forms, every hour of every day. Why? Because it robs us, whom He loves, of a good and productive life while we are here on earth. He punishes sin, not us. And so the curse that is pronounced in the verse quoted earlier found in Deuteronomy is on disobedience and what it produces—sin, and not on the disobedient one.

Let's briefly retrace Israel's steps. The Exodus was not supposed to have been a difficult journey. God led them on their way with plenty of supplies to last the entire journey. He made a dry path through the Red Sea for them. He protected them in the hot desert by hovering over them in the form of a cloud. He provided water which, by the way, followed them. If they had obediently crossed over at Kadesh-Barnea, as God had planned, Jericho would have been quickly dealt with and they would have been home free, as the saying goes.

I repeat, the journey from Egypt to Canaan was supposed to have taken approximately one month. However, when they were camped at Kadesh, already two years into the journey, the Bible says God was *grieved* with that generation, and they would not be able to continue. Satan has been successful in making this, too, look like punishment. Not so. First off, you cannot grieve someone unless there is love involved. God did everything He could to build their faith, and they failed at every turn. He could not allow them to proceed into Canaan in their fearful and faithless condition, as they surely would have been annihilated at Jericho, if not before. Where would that leave us today? The Royal Line had to be preserved at all costs or we would be still in our sins.

Now let's focus more fully on this word *grieved*. It is my considered belief that the God of the universe was grieved because he could also see what could have been. He looked down, with heartbreak, on Israel mucking around in the hot unproductive desert, and he could see where they should have been. At the end of a month's journey, He planned to take the entire group into the land flowing with milk and honey, their homeland, and that generation would never see it. No wonder He was sad!

You know we cannot do anything about what we have already missed, but we can do something about the future. Learn from Israel's mistakes; don't repeat them! That has to be why the Holy Spirit saw fit to include, in such detail, this entire journey. You know the Scripture makes it clear that the only difference between a believer and a nonbeliever is that a believer picks himself up time after time and continues his journey. So come along with me and let's continue our journey *under the cloud* together. It is bound to be exciting and filled with abundance. What more could we ask?

This is the way, walk ye in it...!

Isaiah 30:21 (KJV)

CONTACT

Jack and Ruth McDonald are currently living in
Ormond Beach, Florida, and still conduct
a weekly Bible study.

The McDonalds are both available for
teaching seminars, retreats, conferences,
book signings, and readings and may be
contacted at:

uniquebiblestudyresources@yahoo.com